THE ULTIMATE
HARRY POTTER
AND
PHILOSOPHY

The Blackwell Philosophy and Pop Culture Series

Series Editor: William Irwin

South Park and Philosophy
Edited by Robert Arp

Metallica and Philosophy
Edited by William Irwin

Family Guy and Philosophy
Edited by J. Jeremy Wisnewski

The Daily Show and Philosophy
Edited by Jason Holt

Lost and Philosophy
Edited by Sharon Kaye

24 and Philosophy
*Edited by Richard Davis,
Jennifer Hart Weed, and
Ronald Weed*

Battlestar Galactica and
Philosophy
Edited by Jason T. Eberl

The Office and Philosophy
Edited by J. Jeremy Wisnewski

Batman and Philosophy
*Edited by Mark D. White and
Robert Arp*

House and Philosophy
Edited by Henry Jacoby

Watchmen and Philosophy
Edited by Mark D. White

X-Men and Philosophy
*Edited by Rebecca Housel and
J. Jeremy Wisnewski*

Terminator and Philosophy
*Edited by Richard Brown and
Kevin Decker*

Heroes and Philosophy
Edited by David Kyle Johnson

Twilight and Philosophy
*Edited by Rebecca Housel and
J. Jeremy Wisnewski*

Final Fantasy and Philosophy
*Edited by Jason P. Blahuta and
Michel S. Beaulieu*

Iron Man and Philosophy
Edited by Mark D. White

Alice in Wonderland and
Philosophy
Edited by Richard Brian Davis

True Blood and Philosophy
*Edited by George A. Dunn and
Rebecca Housel*

Mad Men and Philosophy
*Edited by Rod Carveth and
James South*

30 Rock and Philosophy
Edited by J. Jeremy Wisnewski

THE ULTIMATE HARRY POTTER

AND

PHILOSOPHY

HOGWARTS FOR MUGGLES

Edited by
Gregory Bassham

WILEY

John Wiley & Sons, Inc.

Copyright © 2010 by John Wiley & Sons. All rights reserved

Published by John Wiley & Sons, Inc., Hoboken, New Jersey
Published simultaneously in Canada

Chapter opener design by Forty-five Degree Design LLC

For general information about our other products and services, please contact our Customer Care Department within the United States at (800) 762–2974, outside the United States at (317) 572–3993 or fax (317) 572–4002.

Wiley also publishes its books in a variety of electronic formats. Some content that appears in print may not be available in electronic books. For more information about Wiley products, visit our web site at www.wiley.com.

Library of Congress Cataloging-in-Publication Data:

The ultimate Harry Potter and philosophy : Hogwarts for Muggles / edited by Gregory Bassham.
     p. cm. — (The Blackwell philosophy and pop culture series)
   Includes bibliographical references and index.
  ISBN 978-0-470-39825-8 (paper: alk. paper); ISBN 978-0-470-62708-2 (ebk);
  ISBN 978-0-470-62734-1 (ebk); ISBN 978-0-470-62735-8 (ebk)
   1. Rowling, J. K.—Philosophy. 2. Rowling, J. K.—Themes, motives. 3. Rowling, J. K.—Characters. 4. Potter, Harry (Fictitious character) 5. Hogwarts School of Witchcraft and Wizardry (Imaginary organization) 6. Philosophy in literature. 7. Children's stories, English—History and criticism. 8. Fantasy fiction, English—History and criticism. I. Bassham, Gregory, 1959–
  PR6068.093Z8888 2010
  823'.914—dc22

                                              2010016880

Printed in the United States of America

10 9 8 7 6 5 4 3 2 1

For David Baggett

CONTENTS

PART FIVE

BEYOND THE VEIL: DEATH, HOPE, AND MEANING

FOREWORD

Tom Morris

In 2004, there was an important literary event involving Harry Potter that didn't require sleepy parents to show up before midnight at bookstores around the world with hyperactive, well-costumed children trembling in anticipation of a new adventure and completely unable to sleep. It didn't involve J. K. Rowling writing something new or even leaving her home for a special appearance, and it never sparked front-page newspaper headlines or special television news bulletins. It was the surprising publication of an unexpected book: *Harry Potter and Philosophy: If Aristotle Ran Hogwarts*, edited by the philosophers David Baggett and Shawn Klein.

What made this a remarkable occurrence for Harry and his fans and the broader world of readers is that it demonstrated the range and depth of attention this ongoing story was receiving, not only among kids, teens, and imaginative young adults, but also throughout the professorial ranks of the academic world. The wizards of wisdom in our colleges and universities were taking note of Harry's remarkable story and were finding in it great ideas and lessons for life. Courage, duplicity, friendship, happiness, justice, love, and ambition joined issues of good, evil, death, and freedom, among many other topics, in this remarkable examination of themes to be found in the adventures of Harry Potter as they unfolded before us, book after book.

When I was initially asked to write an essay for that first collective philosophical look at the deeper themes in the Potter tales, I must admit that I was simply perplexed. At the time, I wasn't a Potter reader. I thought these were just books for kids. But after one of the editors of the project vigorously assured me that the Harry Potter stories were for everyone and were enthralling people of all ages around the globe, I cracked open the first volume mainly out of curiosity and then, like many adults before me, was instantly hooked. In no time at all, whenever I prepared to sit down to read, I felt a strange urge to dress up in black robes and a tall, pointed hat. I breezed through the first four volumes, which were then the only ones in print, and subsequently began to read each one again, slowly, while awaiting the new books, savoring the intricacies of the story and the sparks of wisdom I started to see everywhere.

By the time the series was complete, I had read most of the seven large volumes six times through, and with deeper insights as my reward each time. There was much more going on in Harry's world than met the casual glance, and far beyond the hidden skullduggery and secret machinations of the many characters. Ideas were percolating under the surface. Real wisdom was suffused throughout the pages. The former classics major Joanne Rowling was not merely a masterful storyteller, but was also a talented weaver of profound perspectives on some of the things that matter most in our lives.

I was inspired. I quickly wrote an essay on what I saw as one of Harry Potter's central attributes, his courage, and then could not stop writing. In no time at all, I had written an entire book of my own, examining the philosophical insights to be found in these incredible stories that were linking the generations like perhaps nothing else in our time. I had to wrap up my book and send it in for publication right after Rowling's sixth volume of her planned seven installments came out. So I ended up holding my philosophical breath for a good while in anticipation of the concluding storyline and what it would say about my take on the earlier books. I'm happy to report that I was able to breathe a great sigh of relief when the series ended and all of my major interpretations had held up. But I had not had the last word, as a philosopher, on Harry and his friends.

This exciting new book that you now have before you, *The Ultimate Harry Potter and Philosophy: Hogwarts for Muggles*, is a fresh and distinctive report on the great ideas in the series. All of the authors of the chapters have had the advantage of thinking through their chosen issues and writing up their conclusions after the entire Potter storyline was complete and Rowling had even had her say in public about things that never made it into the pages of the official texts. The philosophers and other top Harry Potter experts who are gathered together here offer new voices and new perspectives on many of the most important ideas that come up in the books—some of which can be genuinely life changing. Reading this book will be like putting on a Philosophical De-coder Ring. It will show you vital aspects of the deepest story that lies behind these famous novels.

The dust has settled and the air has cleared. The great battle is over, and the surviving characters have gone on with their lives. It's time to take stock and cast a long view over the most remarkable literary phenomenon of our time and to see what it says about some of the ultimate issues we face in our lives. As you read these pages and personally grapple with their important issues, you will experience anew the real magic that will forever animate J. K. Rowling's immortal tales.

ACKNOWLEDGMENTS

Some House Points I'd Like to Award

Someone must have spiked my Chocolate Cauldrons with Felix Felicis, because this book has been a pure pleasure to work on from beginning to end. House points are due to the long-suffering contributors for their efforts, patience, and good humor through the long gestation of this book. I am grateful to Potter scholars John Granger and Travis Prinzi for answering my queries and providing helpful feedback at various stages of the project. Drafts of several chapters were helpfully discussed by my students in Honors Philosophy II class at King's College. Thanks are due to all of the good Muggles at Wiley, particularly Connie Santisteban, Lisa Burstiner, and Eric Nelson, for believing in this project and seeing it through to completion. I am deeply indebted to Tom Morris, public philosopher extraordinaire, for agreeing to write the foreword. Kudos, also, to the biggest Mugwump of all, series editor Bill Irwin, whose editorial skill and passion for using insights from popular culture to teach philosophy continue to be second to none. A special word of thanks is due to Dave Baggett, who was exceptionally generous with his advice, criticism, and time. Finally, I must thank those who share Bassham Burrow with me and make it a place of love, laughter, and warmth: Mia and Dylan. Love is truly the most powerful magic of all!

INTRODUCTION

Harry Potter and the Enchantment of Philosophy

Let's play a little word-association game. What comes to mind when you hear the word *philosophy*? Deep. Dense. Complex. In short, *heavy stuff*, right?

So, what's the connection between philosophy and the Potter books and films? How can there be any real philosophy—or any *good* philosophy—in fantasy works aimed primarily at kids? Easy!

Philosophy, as Plato said, begins in wonder. And kids wonder about everything. They're naturally curious, questioning, and eager to learn. Often they understand a lot more than adults give them credit for.

That's why J. K. Rowling—like J. R. R. Tolkien, C. S. Lewis, and other great children's writers—doesn't hesitate to raise complex issues and pose challenging questions. Of course, Rowling realizes that most of her readers won't grasp all of the subtleties and complexities of the issues she raises. But she also knows that young readers—like Fang gnawing on a large, meaty dragon bone—can get a great deal of nourishment from foods they can't completely digest.

This book is for Rowling fans who want to explore some of the deeper issues posed in the Potter books and films. What is love? Is it, as Rowling says, the most powerful magic of all? Is there an afterlife? If so, what might it be like? Is death something to be feared—or "mastered," as Harry ultimately was able to do? Do people have souls? If so, how are they related to their bodies? Can souls, if they exist, be divided, as Voldemort fragmented his by means of the Horcruxes? What can shape-shifters like Animagi and boggarts teach us about personal identity and the self? Does power inevitably corrupt? Is Hogwarts a model school, or are there real shortcomings with the education students receive there? Is it true, as Albus Dumbledore says, that our choices reveal far more about us than our abilities do? What can the complex and intriguing character of Severus Snape teach us about moral conflict, character judgment, and the possibility of redemption? Would it ever be ethical to use a love potion? Is it true, as Kingsley Shacklebolt proclaims, that "[e]very human life is worth the same"? Is it true, as Dumbledore says, that something can be real even if it exists only inside a person's head?

This is a book written *for* Potter fans *by* Potter fans, most of whom happen to be professional philosophers in their nine-to-five lives. Like other volumes in the Blackwell Philosophy and Pop Culture Series, it uses popular culture—in this case, the Potter books and films—as a hook to teach and popularize the ideas of the great thinkers. Some of the chapters explore the philosophy of the Potter books—the basic values and the big-picture assumptions that underlie the series—while others use themes from the books as a way to discuss various philosophical ideas and perspectives. Like others involved in the popular culture and philosophy movement, our hope is to bring philosophy out of the ivied halls of academia and make its methods, resources, and critical spirit available to all.

Several of the philosophers who contributed to this book also contributed to *Harry Potter and Philosophy* (Chicago: Open

Court, 2004; coedited by David Baggett and Shawn E. Klein). In some ways, this book is a follow-up to that earlier volume. The earlier book covered only the first five volumes in the Potter series. Some of it, therefore, was guesswork, because many of the important revelations and plot developments occur only in the last two books of the series. This volume covers the entire seven-book saga and focuses particularly on developments in the climactic final two books.

So, the wait is over. The faculty has assembled for one last time; the Great Hall, ablaze with light, is buzzing with excitement, and the long wooden tables groan with delectable things to eat. Once more, it's time to don your robes, take a generous nip of Baruffio's Brain Elixir, and prepare for a philosophical feast. It's going to be a great year.

All references to the Harry Potter novels are taken from the following American editions, published by Scholastic, Inc., in New York: *Sorcerer's Stone* (1998); *Chamber of Secrets* (1999); *Prisoner of Azkaban* (1999); *Goblet of Fire* (2000); *Order of the Phoenix* (2003); *Half-Blood Prince* (2005); *Deathly Hallows* (2007).

PART ONE

THE HORCRUX OF THE MATTER:
DESTINY, IDENTITY, AND THE SOUL

THE SOUL IN HARRY POTTER

Scott Sehon

Souls play a huge part in the Harry Potter saga. At different points in the books, Harry, Sirius Black, and Dudley Dursley narrowly avoid having their souls sucked out by dementors; Barty Crouch Jr. does not escape this fate. And notoriously, Lord Voldemort intentionally creates six Horcruxes, and unintentionally creates a seventh in Harry, thereby dividing his own soul into eight parts, all of which must be destroyed before Voldemort can die.

So, what is the soul? In Harry's world, people have souls that generally survive bodily death. But it is not entirely obvious how souls work and what their nature is. Over the centuries, philosophers and theologians have proposed and debated various accounts of the soul. In this chapter, we'll survey some of those accounts before turning to the questions of how souls work in J. K. Rowling's books and whether her picture of the soul is plausible.

Philosophical Conceptions of the Soul

While competing conceptions of the soul are legion, we'll focus here on five different philosophical views.

The Life-Source View

According to some ancient Greek philosophers, the soul accounts for life itself. In this view, the essential difference between living and nonliving things is that living things have a soul and nonliving things do not. Yet because the lowest animals and even plants are alive, this means that all plants and animals have souls. Blast-Ended Skrewts and even gillyweed would have souls, according to this view. These days, not too many people think that this conception of the soul is correct.

The Sentience View

According to a second conception, the soul is responsible for *sentience*, the ability some organisms have to feel pleasure and pain and sense the world around them. If an organism is consciously aware of its surroundings, then the organism *feels*, it has experiences. According to the sentience view, the soul is responsible for sentience, along with all higher-level thought. Plants, one assumes, do not have sentient awareness and so, in this conception, would not have souls. (Of course, in the universe of Harry Potter some magical plants, like the Whomping Willow, do have some direct sensation of the world and would thus have souls.)

The Cartesian View

A third view of the soul further narrows the scope of ensouled organisms. According to a view associated with the philosopher René Descartes (1596–1650), the soul is not responsible for sensation and awareness. Descartes thought that those features of mental life could be accounted for by purely material causes; however, he believed that mere material causes would never be able to explain our ability to use language and formulate complex beliefs. For this, we need souls. So Descartes said that our immaterial soul is responsible only for higher-level cognitive functions, including beliefs, desires, and, especially, our ability to use language.

One consequence of the Cartesian view is that nonhuman animals do not have souls—at least, if those animals lack linguistic ability and higher-level thought. Descartes was willing to accept this and thought that nonhuman animals were entirely soulless. Some of the magical creatures in the Harry Potter stories might blur this distinction within the Cartesian view. For instance, owls seem to understand human speech, although they don't speak in return, and magical pets like Crookshanks seem much more intelligent than your average cat.

According to the life-source, sentience, and Cartesian views, the soul is usually thought to be some sort of immaterial substance, something not made of matter but still associated with, or connected to, a person's material body. If souls are in fact like that, then there is a possibility that the soul could survive a person's bodily death. On the other hand, there are many philosophers and scientists who would deny the existence of a soul, if what we mean by a soul is some sort of entity independent of the brain and the body. This leads to a fourth view of the soul: materialism.

Materialism

Materialists hold that ultimately there is nothing but matter and physical forces. All mental functioning, including language and emotions, is due to physical processes in the brain, and there simply is no extra entity above and beyond this. Needless to say, according to a materialist view, there is no life after death; with bodily death, the processes that underlie our mental and emotional life simply cease, and that's all there is to it.

The Sentimental View

In everyday talk, the word *soul* is often used in a way that does not clearly correspond with any of the more abstract conceptions just discussed. From the Hoagy Carmichael tune, we have: "Heart and soul, I fell in love with you./Heart and soul, the way a fool would do, madly."

Or we might speak of a person seeking his or her soul mate. We talk of people having good souls. We might describe music or art as soulful or as soulless.

These sorts of everyday sentimentalist uses of the word *soul* need not be taken to imply any particular metaphysical view. That is, they don't commit one to any view on which the soul is an actual substance existing independently of the body. If we say, "Unlike her later work, the artist's early paintings were soulless," clearly we are not suggesting that the artist literally lacked and then later somehow obtained an immaterial soul. Rather, we are suggesting that the artist's early work was uninspired or somehow lacked genuine emotional depth. Or if I say that I love her, heart and soul, or that we are soul mates, I am commenting about the emotional depth of my attachment and the deep connection we feel for each other.[1] If we say that someone has bared her soul, we mean she has let us see through the superficial trappings and down to what is most deeply important to her. These uses of the word *soul* are essentially metaphorical ways of talking about that which makes us most human and makes life most full: our deepest emotions, our ability to love, our moral conscience. Materialist philosophers don't need to renounce any of these ways of talking and certainly don't need to go back and translate Hoagy Carmichael's lyrics into some sort of thesis about brain states ("C-fibers firing, I fell in love with you . . . ").

With these sundry options on the table, we are now ready to turn to Harry Potter and try to place the conception of the soul as developed in the story. To foreshadow, we'll see that

Rowling's picture of the soul is an interesting mix of views. In many ways, it seems that her conception of the soul is closest to the sentimental view, but she combines it with a metaphysics that incorporates parts of the Cartesian and sentience views.

Ghosts and "Going On"

Materialism is the dominant view among philosophers and scientists in our world today. But materialism is false in the world of Harry Potter, where souls typically survive bodily death. Here is Hermione Granger's explanation of souls:

> "Look, if I picked up a sword right now, Ron, and ran you through with it, I wouldn't damage your soul at all."
>
> "Which would be a real comfort to me, I'm sure," said Ron. Harry laughed.
>
> "It should be, actually! But my point is that whatever happens to your body, your soul will survive, untouched," said Hermione.[2]

So we know that in Rowling's world, the soul survives destruction of the body. Beyond the fact of survival, it's not entirely clear what happens to the soul of a deceased person. In *Order of the Phoenix*, in the room at the Ministry of Magic where Sirius dies, there is a mysterious archway with a veil, and both Harry and Luna Lovegood hear voices from beyond the veil. Luna's interpretation is that dead people exist just beyond and that we will see them again. Later, Nearly Headless Nick tells Harry that the recently killed Sirius will have "gone on," but he has no further light to shed on what happens in the ordinary case. Nick, of course, is a ghost, and he explains to Harry that a wizard is able to avoid "going on" by remaining behind as a ghostly imprint of his former self. He says that few wizards choose this path, and perhaps it is not too hard to see why. Nick lives on, sort of, in a ghostly imitation of a body, one that can see and be seen, hear and be heard, but that otherwise walks through walls and has few physical effects. Rowling's ghosts apparently induce an icy sensation when a person has contact with them, and Moaning Myrtle is somehow able to make splashes in toilets, but beyond this, they seem to mostly lack bodily effects. Voldemort presumably could have had this sort of immortality all along, but it is a form of immortality devoid of real physical contact and, more important for Voldemort, devoid of power.

Besides being a ghost, there are several other ways in which souls can appear on earth after their bodies have died. First, there is the case of Voldemort himself, who, because of his Horcruxes, survives bodily death when his killing curse aimed at baby Harry backfires. We'll talk more about Horcruxes later, but at this point it is worth noting that when Voldemort's soul continues, it is in an incredibly weak form; he later describes his condition at the time as "less than spirit, less than the meanest ghost."[3] In that state, Voldemort needs to attach himself to a living body to have any physical effects at all.

Second, there is the semi-ghostly condition in which Harry twice sees his departed loved ones. In the graveyard scene in *Goblet of Fire*, Cedric Diggory, Bertha Jorkins, Frank Bryce, and Harry's parents appear out of Voldemort's wand. These ghostly figures look to Harry much more solid than ordinary ghosts, and they have enough of a physical presence that James Potter tells Harry that they will give him some time to escape once the wand connection is broken. Similarly, when Harry uses the Resurrection Stone in *Deathly Hallows* he sees Sirius, Remus Lupin, and his parents, and it seems that they are again, at least in some sense, real. Less substantial than living bodies and here only temporarily, they are nonetheless not mere ghosts; they are described as "neither ghost nor truly flesh."[4]

So, it seems that although souls normally "go on" in some undescribed way, disembodied souls can stay or return to earth in certain circumstances, and when they do, they take one of a variety of forms, ranging from Voldemort's almost entirely nonphysical state to Nick's ghostly state, to the temporary but slightly more substantial physical states of the souls brought back by the Resurrection Stone.[5] All of this would be impossible if materialism were true. So, materialism is false within the Potter universe. But to learn more about the nature of souls, we need to consider dementors and Horcruxes.

The Dementor's Kiss

Dementors suck good feelings and happy memories out of people. Worse than that, they can destroy your soul. As Lupin explains to Harry:

> "You see, the dementor lowers its hood only to use its last and worst weapon."
> "What's that?"
> "They call it the Dementor's Kiss," said Lupin, with a slightly twisted smile. "It's what dementors do to those they wish to destroy utterly. I suppose there must be some kind of mouth under there, because they clamp their jaws upon the mouth of the victim and—and suck out his soul."
> [. . .]
> "What—they kill—?"
> "Oh no," said Lupin. "Much worse than that. You can exist without your soul, you know, as long as your brain and heart are still working. But you'll have no sense of self anymore, no memory, no . . . anything. There's no chance at all of recovery. You'll just—exist. As an empty shell. And your soul is gone forever . . . lost."[6]

This is very interesting. A wizard's soul normally survives bodily death, and the natural further assumption would be that souls are immortal. But with dementors around, not all souls achieve this happy state, for dementors can apparently destroy souls completely. *You* can still exist even without your soul, however. Lupin's words here are open to more than one interpretation. He might merely mean your *body* can still exist and keep functioning biologically as long as your organs are still intact. According to this reading, the Dementor's Kiss would leave the victim in something like a permanent vegetative state, in which basic metabolic functions continue but in which there is no substantial mental life at all. Yet if this is what Lupin means, it's odd that he portrays it as the continued existence of the person but in a state worse than death. If the soul is the source of all conscious mental life, and if *all* of that disappears after the Dementor's Kiss, then it would seem more appropriate to say that the person truly is no more, that the empty shell of a body is just that—a body but not a person.

Because Lupin is insistent that a person can continue to exist without a soul, a different picture seems to be suggested. This is speculative, but here's my guess. A soulless person still has sensations and even thoughts about the passing show. After the Kiss was applied, Barty Crouch Jr. may have still recognized that there were people in the room, but he had no idea who they were or who *he* was, for he had no substantial memory or sense of self. Accordingly, perhaps we should think of existence after the Dementor's Kiss as akin to a severe case of dementia or Alzheimer's disease—perhaps similar to the condition Lockhart found himself in after one of his memory charms backfired.

The Dementor's Kiss would appear to rule out at least two, if not three, of the remaining conceptions of the soul. If one can be alive without one's soul, then the soul cannot be the source of life itself, and so the life-source view cannot be correct. And if a victim of the Dementor's Kiss still has sensations, and even a body in a vegetative state may be somewhat respon-sive to sensory stimuli, then the sentience view also seems ruled out. Moreover, if the Dementor's Kiss does allow some-one to think, feel, and notice the passing show, albeit lacking memories or a sense of self, then even the Cartesian view seems unlikely. According to the Cartesian view, the soul is that which is responsible for our higher-level functions, our ability to have beliefs and, especially, to understand language. In the interpretation I have suggested, the Kiss might leave those abilities at least partially intact, despite the soul itself being utterly destroyed.

Horcruxes

A central plot element for the Harry Potter story as a whole is Tom Riddle's quest to defeat death using Horcruxes. Professor Horace Slughorn explains to a young Riddle what happens when a wizard creates a Horcrux: "'Well, you split your soul, you see,' said Slughorn, 'and hide part of it in an object outside the body. Then, even if one's body is attacked or destroyed, one cannot die, for part of the soul remains earthbound and undamaged.'"[7]

Indeed, later, when Voldemort attacks the infant Harry using the Avada Kedavra curse that rebounds then destroys Voldemort's body, Voldemort himself remains alive, albeit as "less than spirit, less than the meanest ghost."[8]

The young Riddle presses Slughorn further and asks how one splits one's soul. Slughorn answers, "By an act of evil—the supreme act of evil. By committing murder. Killing rips the soul apart. The wizard intent upon creating a Horcrux would use the damage to his advantage: He would encase the torn portion—."[9] Slughorn does not answer Riddle's further ques-tion about exactly how one encases the soul, other than say-ing that there is a spell. Riddle then asks, "Can you only split your soul once? Wouldn't it be better, make you stronger, to have your soul in more pieces, I mean, for instance, isn't seven the most powerfully magic number, wouldn't seven—?"[10] Slughorn is horrified that Riddle would apparently think of killing repeatedly to do this, but he also warns against it for another reason. He has already told Riddle that "the soul is supposed to remain intact and whole" and that splitting "it is an act of violation, it is against nature."[11]

Two points from Slughorn's words are worth emphasizing. First, that it requires a supreme act of evil to make the soul such that it can be ripped, and, second, that the soul is thereby damaged or made unstable, and that ripping it more than once presumably increases the damage. This is a point that Hermione makes as well, after she read *Secrets of the Darkest Art*, which, along with other dark magic books, she summoned from Dumbledore's office after his death: " 'And the more I've read about [Horcruxes],' said Hermione, 'the more horrible they seem, and the less I can believe that he actually made six. It warns in this book how unstable you make the rest of your soul by ripping it, and that's just by making one Horcrux!' "[12]

Although both Slughorn and *Secrets of the Darkest Art* are clear that ripping the soul damages it, it is not immediately obvious how the damage to the soul translates into harm to the living human being. There is, after all, no indication that Voldemort's mental faculties or magical abilities are in any way diminished. Indeed, Dumbledore warns Harry, "Never forget, though, that while his soul may be damaged beyond repair, his brain and his magical powers remain intact. It will take uncommon skill and power to kill a wizard like Voldemort even without his Horcruxes."[13]

This seems quite clearly to rule out the Cartesian view, according to which the soul is responsible for all higher-level thought. If a Cartesian soul were horribly damaged, then one's thoughts, skills, and, presumably, magical abilities would be damaged as well, but all of this is left intact in Voldemort. Because Voldemort's sensory abilities seem unharmed, too, despite his damaged soul, it seems that the sentience view is also excluded.

Rather than applying the Cartesian or sentience views, Rowling adopts the *sentimental view* of the soul, according to which the soul is associated with that which makes us most human, with our capacity to love and our moral conscience. This was already suggested by the fact that one rips and damages the soul by committing the supremely evil act of murder. If the soul is associated with what makes us deeply human and good, then it at least makes poetic sense that the soul would be damaged by committing the ultimate evil. The key evidence lies in what seemed different about Voldemort after he damaged his soul so badly: not his higher cognitive functions, but his *humanity*. Dumbledore tells Harry, "Lord Voldemort has seemed to grow less human with the passing years, and the transformation he has undergone seemed to me to be only explicable if his soul was mutilated beyond the realms of what we might call 'usual evil.'"[14] Specifically, after ripping his soul and creating Horcruxes, the handsome young Tom Riddle undergoes a significant physical transformation. Few of us look better as we age, but with Riddle/Voldemort, the change is extreme. In *Goblet of Fire*, when he has completely regained his body in the graveyard, he is described as "whiter than a skull, with wide, livid scarlet eyes and a nose that was flat as a snake's with slits for nostrils."[15]

Voldemort's change in appearance is Rowling's metaphor for what was happening to Voldemort on a deep emotional and moral level. Of course, the child Riddle in the orphanage already had a significantly sinister side to him, and there is no evidence that he ever truly loved anyone, but in his early days at Hogwarts he at least had the ability to charm people. He was a leader among his peers, even among older students, and he accomplished this through personality rather than fear. He charmed Professor Slughorn, who predicted that Riddle would become Minister of Magic, and managed to get him to discuss

Horcruxes, which was a banned topic at Hogwarts. By the time Riddle begins his reign of terror as Lord Voldemort, however, all indications are that Death Eaters continue to follow him out of fear, rather than because of anything remotely approximating devotion. Even Bellatrix Lestrange, his most devoted follower near the end, seems worshipful of his power but hardly *charmed*. That capacity, Riddle's most human attribute, seems to have utterly disappeared after his soul was ripped into seven pieces (eight, if you count Harry as the seventh Horcrux).

Voldemort might have been able to repair his damaged soul, but not by use of a potion or an appropriate incantation (not even with the Elder Wand). Rather, according to *Secrets of the Darkest Art*, a ripped soul can perhaps be repaired through *remorse*; as Hermione puts it, "You've got to really feel what you've done."[16] In none of the other views of the soul would there be any reason for the particular emotion of remorse to have a special effect on the immaterial soul. But according to the sentimental view, the soul is most closely connected with our deepest emotions and our moral conscience. Our goodness and humanity are damaged by evil actions, but we can go some ways toward restoring that goodness and humanity if we feel genuine remorse. In the climactic scene, Harry in fact suggests to Voldemort that he "be a man" and try to feel some remorse.[17] Voldemort, of course, having gone so far beyond even the "usual evil," feels no inclination toward remorse, and Voldemort is finally killed when his own killing curse, shot from the Elder Wand of which Harry is the master, rebounds off Harry's Expelliarmus.

A Plausible View?

If Rowling indeed adopts the sentimental conception of the soul, she does so with an interesting twist. The sentimental view is not a philosophical theory developed by theologians or philosophers but rather a distillation of various ways we use the word *soul*. These ordinary uses of the word could easily be taken as metaphorical and do not necessarily imply that there really is some sort of independent and immaterial entity that explains our deepest emotional commitments and moral conscience. Even materialists can and do use the word *soul* as a perfectly good metaphor. But within the Harry Potter universe, Rowling clearly also presupposes a metaphysical view: that the soul is independent of the body, is not harmed by normal physical events, and can even survive the destruction of the body. In other words, Rowling takes the metaphysical picture normally associated with the more philosophical views of the soul (especially the sentience view and the Cartesian view) and combines it with the metaphorical picture suggested by the sentimental view.

So, does Rowling offer a theory of the soul that is likely to be true? Probably not, but the issues are contentious. First, many philosophers and scientists plausibly argue that there is no good evidence for the existence of an immaterial substance that is causally responsible for anything above and beyond what the human body does. It would be possible to have such evidence someday: if neuroscientists saw that there were events that happened in brains with no observable physical cause, then this would at least be an indication that the events had an immaterial cause. But we have not seen any such brain events up to now.

Moreover, philosophers have pointed out for centuries that it is difficult to see how an immaterial soul would even be *able* to interact with a purely material body. If the soul is not made of matter and does not have physical properties, then it is mysterious how it could cause the human body to move or how anything in the material world would have any effect on it. This kind of dualism of mind and body would be outside anything of which we have experience. Dualism is not incoherent, and it is possible that it is correct, but it faces substantial obstacles.[18]

Finally, Rowling's combination of an implausible metaphysics with the sentimental view of the soul probably makes the problems worse, rather than better. It is especially implausible that there would be an immaterial part of us that is specifically responsible for only our deepest emotions and moral traits but not for other psychological capacities. These traits may seem linked to us because they are arguably what makes us most human, but from the standpoint of scientific psychology, there is nothing that is so different in kind here. So there seems to be no need to postulate something altogether different from the brain to explain these traits. In addition, as mentioned earlier, within the story the immaterial soul can sometimes remain on earth with a variety of different physical powers or presences, depending on whether the soul is here as a ghost, as something conjured by the Resurrection Stone, or as a bare soul saved from destruction by a Horcrux. If, as we've seen, it would be difficult to explain how an immaterial soul could interact at all with the physical world, then it would be even more difficult to explain why the soul would have different physical abilities depending on what magic spell is at work.

Of course, the implausibility of Rowling's metaphysics is not a strike against her work of fiction. After all, it is also extremely unlikely that there are witches, wizards, and magic in the real world. And Rowling's picture of the soul does have a way of making vivid what we care about, or what we hope we care about. Besides, talk of souls, Horcruxes, dementors, and magic makes for a terrific story, and that's reason enough.[19]

NOTES

1. Originally, the idea may have been different: according to some myths, our souls were split in two, and finding one's soul mate literally meant finding one's other half. But such an overtly metaphysical picture is clearly not presupposed in our colloquial uses of the phrase.

2. *Deathly Hallows*, p. 104.

3. *Goblet of Fire*, p. 653.

4. *Deathly Hallows*, p. 698.

5. When Harry "dies" in the Forbidden Forest toward the end of *Deathly Hallows*, he finds himself with Dumbledore in a place that appears to him as King's Cross Station. One interpretation is that he is in a way station between death and the afterlife. Even so, Harry learns nothing about what will happen if he decides to die by, say, taking a train. Dumbledore merely says that the train would take him "on." Moreover, Rowling is deliberately ambiguous about whether this is some real sequence of events in which Harry actually encounters Dumbledore's postmortem self or whether it's simply a vision or a dream in Harry's mind.

6. *Prisoner of Azkaban*, p. 247.

7. *Half-Blood Prince*, p. 497.

8. *Goblet of Fire*, p. 653.

9. *Half-Blood Prince*, p. 498.

10. Ibid., p. 498.

11. Ibid.

12. *Deathly Hallows*, p. 103.

13. *Half-Blood Prince*, p. 509.

14. Ibid., p. 502.

15. *Goblet of Fire*, p. 643.

16. *Deathly Hallows*, p. 103.

17. Ibid., p. 741.

18. For more detailed recent arguments of this sort, see Scott Sehon, *Teleological Realism: Mind, Agency, and Explanation* (Cambridge, MA: MIT Press, 2005), chap. 2; and Jaegwon Kim, *Philosophy of Mind* (Boulder, CO: Westview Press, 2005), chap. 2.

19. Special thanks to Josephine Sehon and Hayden Sartoris for years of reading and discussing Harry Potter and for useful comments on earlier drafts of this chapter.

SIRIUS BLACK

Man or Dog?

Eric Saidel

Imagine yourself virtually imprisoned, cooped up inside, unable to go outdoors for several months. Now, finally, you get to go outside. You're free to do anything you want—you can run around, enjoy the fresh air, go to a movie, do whatever you wish. What would you do?

Now suppose you had a tail. Would you do anything different? Would you run around in circles, trying to bite your tail? Neither would I. Oddly enough, this is exactly what Sirius Black does in *Order of the Phoenix* when he transforms into a dog in order to escort Harry to the Hogwarts Express at the beginning of the school year. And he does it because he's excited to be outside. Or so J. K. Rowling tells us. This behavior strikes me as so strange that I'd ask Sirius about it if I could. Unfortunately, I can't, as Sirius is no longer alive.[1] So we'll have to try to answer this question using the tools of philosophy. Fortunately, even though most philosophers are Muggles, we can use the same skills of rational analysis that enabled Albus Dumbledore to discover the twelve uses of dragon's blood. So, let's push on.

Chasing his tail wouldn't be so strange if Sirius were a dog. But he's not a dog. He's a man in a dog's body. Or is he? How can we best describe Sirius: as a man who is sometimes in a dog's body (and sometimes in a man's body), as a dog who is sometimes in a man's body (and sometimes in a dog's body), or as someone who is sometimes a dog and sometimes a man? If the answer is the last, then what is that "someone" who stays the same while Sirius changes between being a dog and being a man?

Sirius is not the only one who transforms in the Potter series. During the course of the seven books, we come into contact with other Animagi (Peter Pettigrew, Rita Skeeter, Professor McGonagall), as well as werewolves (Remus Lupin and Fenrir Greyback), boggarts, and the frequent use of Polyjuice Potion.[2] Several transformers behave in odd and sometimes illuminating ways.[3] For example, a transformed Lupin would attack Harry, Ron Weasley, and Hermione Granger, and as Mad-Eye Moody, Barty Crouch Jr. is the one of the best Defense Against the Dark Arts teachers Harry ever has, even going beyond the call of duty to teach Harry to resist the Imperius Curse.[4] Why do they do these odd things?

This is a question about their identities, about what makes them who they are. It is also a question about the relationship between one's mind and one's body. It seems obvious that Padfoot's body is a dog's body, but is his mind a dog's mind or a man's mind? Let's see whether we can answer these questions. The path we follow will be full of twists and turns, like a Snitch trying to avoid a Seeker, but if we keep our eye on the gold, we should be able to catch it.

Mind-Body Distinctions

When Sirius transforms into a dog, sometimes he acts as if he's a man, and other times he acts as if he's a dog. Why does the transformed person sometimes act as if he is his normal self and other times act as if he is the person or the animal he has transformed into? Answering this question requires us to understand just what a transformed person is. Put simply, when Sirius transforms, does he become a dog, or is he still a man?

Both of these options are too crude. Sirius transformed is not merely a dog: a dog would not do many of the things that Padfoot does (for example, standing on his hind legs, putting his forelegs on Harry's shoulders, and looking Harry in the eye when Harry goes off to school in *Order of the Phoenix*). Nor is Padfoot still a man: many of the things Padfoot does (for example, chasing his tail) are more appropriate for a dog than for Sirius. The transformed person isn't wholly the object he's transformed into or wholly the person he was before he transformed. Obviously, then, the answer is that Padfoot is part man and part dog.

Since the time of René Descartes (1596–1650), who is generally considered to be the father of modern philosophy, there has been a natural way to think of how people might be divided: we think of each individual as being made up of two distinct parts—namely, a mind and a body. So perhaps when we say that Padfoot is part Sirius and part dog, we mean that he has the mind of one of them and the body of the other. There are four possibilities here:

1. Padfoot has the mind of Sirius and the body of a dog.
2. Padfoot has the mind of a dog and the body of a dog.
3. Padfoot has the mind of Sirius and the body of Sirius.
4. Padfoot has the mind of a dog and the body of Sirius.

The last two options would seem to be nonstarters: we can tell by looking at Padfoot that he doesn't have the body of Sirius. He looks nothing like Sirius—or any other man, for that matter. But this dismissal is too superficial: If Padfoot doesn't have Sirius's body, then what happens to Sirius's body when he transforms? Where does it go? It's all very well for Professor

McGonagall to assert that vanished objects go "into non-being, which is to say, everything," but it seems implausible that Sirius's body will go into nonbeing when he transforms into Padfoot and then will come out of nonbeing when he transforms back.[5] What's more plausible is that Sirius's body itself changes. Before he transforms, it is the physical body of a man, and afterward it is the body of a dog. But it is the same physical stuff, somehow rearranged. That is, if the body has an effect on what Padfoot does, the effect isn't going to come from his having Sirius's human body, because even if Padfoot does literally have Sirius's body, it is physically the body of a dog.[6]

What of the other two options? Both are problematic, for similar reasons. Why, if Padfoot has the mind of Sirius, does he chase his tail? And why, if he has the mind of a dog, does he stand on his hind legs at King's Cross Station? (Mrs. Weasley chastises him, hissing, "For heaven's sake act more like a dog, Sirius!"[7]) These are the questions with which we started. Thinking about Padfoot as divided between mind and body doesn't get us anywhere.

Whose Reasons?

Sirius has no reason to chase his tail, but perhaps Padfoot does. When Lupin is human, he has no reason to attack his students, but perhaps when he's a werewolf, he does have reason to do so. Perhaps it would be helpful to recast our inquiries in terms of reasons. Thus, we might wonder not whether the mind involved is Sirius's or Padfoot's, but whether the reasons causing the action are Sirius's or Padfoot's. This sort of strategy is a good one: usually, asking specific questions rather than general questions will yield answers that are helpful rather than vague. For that reason, asking questions about reasons, rather than about minds, is likely to provide more interesting answers. Unfortunately, no sooner do I make this suggestion than I start to see problems.

First, the answer to this question seems to lead us in the wrong direction: if anyone has reason to chase his tail, it's Padfoot, not Sirius. But, surely, if anything of Sirius is left after he becomes a dog, it would be his reasons for acting. It would be bizarre to say that in transforming, one loses one's reasons for acting. One transforms presumably as a means of achieving one's goals, as an expression of one's reasons. If transforming were to cause you to no longer act to achieve your goals, why would you ever transform?

We can see this more clearly in considering some of the examples of Polyjuice transformation. We expect the transformed individual to act for his or her reasons, not for those of the being he transformed into. This indeed is what we find. If the shape one takes when one transforms is the source of one's reasons for acting, then we might have expected Harry and Ron to act to achieve whatever goals Crabbe and Goyle have when Harry and Ron transform in *Chamber of Secrets*. But they don't; they act for their own reasons. Similarly, when they transform in *Deathly Hallows*, Harry transforms into Albert Runcorn, a Death Eater, and Ron transforms into Reginald Cattermole, a man whose wife is on trial for "stealing magic." Runcorn and Cattermole have no reason to cooperate and every reason to hate each other. As Runcorn, Harry has no reason to remove Moody's mad eye from Dolores Umbridge's door or to warn Arthur Weasley that he's being watched, but Harry does have reason to do these things, and so he, as Runcorn, does them. As Cattermole, Ron has reason to accompany his wife to her hearing, but he doesn't do this. Ron and Harry act according to their own reasons, not according to the reasons of Runcorn and Cattermole. So why would Padfoot act for doggy reasons, rather than for Sirius's reasons? Framing the puzzle in terms of reasons moves us no closer to solving it.

Finally, reasons have nothing to do with Sirius's tail-chasing behavior. Dogs don't chase their tails when they're excited because they have reason to do so; they chase their tails when they're excited, because, I assume, it's fun or it feels good. (Perhaps they do so because they think their tails are foreign objects, but Sirius knows better than that!) Similarly, I suspect that Lupin doesn't acquire a reason to attack Harry, Ron, and Hermione when he transforms. Instead, he would attack them because it's in his blood to do so. His reasons would lead him to refrain from attacking them. Any solution to our puzzle in terms of reasons will fail to explain Sirius's and Lupin's behaviors.

A Step in the Right Direction

Let's reconsider the distinction between mind and body. In the current context, this distinction suggests an explanatory strategy: some of our acts can be explained by talking about our minds, about the mental causes of the action. Other actions can be explained by talking about our bodies, about the physical causes of the action. In this light, perhaps the reason Padfoot chases his tail has to do with his having the body of a dog. Not everything that Padfoot does is explained by talking about his—Sirius's—mind; some of the things he does are properly explained by talking about his doggy body.

Consider this alternate history. Suppose that while at Hogwarts, when Sirius had learned that his friend Lupin was a werewolf and so decided to become an Animagus to keep Lupin company when he transformed, Sirius decided to become a bear. (Sirius's main concerns would have been met had he been a bear: bears are different from humans, so the werewolf bites presumably wouldn't infect him while transformed, and a bear would have been powerful enough to keep the werewolf in check.) Now, imagine him in *Order of the Phoenix*, outside for the first time in months. Would he have chased his tail? That seems unlikely. He would have done whatever it is that bears do when they are excited and feeling particularly good. He might have—if Winnie the Pooh is any guide—written a song and indulged in some honey. But as Padfoot, as a dog, he chases his tail. So, perhaps the correct explanation of Padfoot's behavior is that his body is a dog's body, and dogs chase their tails when they're excited.

Let's pause for a moment and review the ground we've covered. I started by wondering about certain of Padfoot's behaviors. We might think that transformation is just a really good disguise, that it's like putting on a costume. In that case, Padfoot would actually be Sirius looking like a dog. These behaviors tell us otherwise: they are behaviors that Sirius would never engage in, no matter what clothing he was wearing. So, we can draw one conclusion already: transformation is not just a really good disguise. Somehow, transformation simply transforms you. But we still wonder, why does Padfoot do these things? One possibility is that the reasons the transformed individual has for acting become the reasons that his chosen embodiment had. In that case, Padfoot would act for a dog's reasons. But some of the things Padfoot does are things that Sirius—the man, but not the dog—has reason to do. So much for that solution. Another possible solution is that Padfoot is part man and part dog. I rejected this solution earlier because it doesn't make sense of Padfoot's humanlike behaviors. But perhaps I was too hasty: if we first adopt the theory that some of the things one does can be explained by one's body and some by one's mind, then we can say that dogs—dogs' bodies—sometimes chase their tails, and because Padfoot has a dog's body, he chases his tail.

Let's push a bit deeper here. This theory brings with it other costs and commitments, some of which we may not like. According to this theory, we're able to explain the oddities in Padfoot's behavior because he has a dog's body. Presumably, Padfoot's having a dog's body explains his behavior because for animals the physical body sometimes trumps reason. That seems odd to me. Perhaps you think that some animals, including dogs, don't reason very well or don't do things for reasons, so, for them, talk of the reasons for their behavior is misplaced. If that's what you think, then you think that the things those animals do is best explained by facts about their bodies. But how could this explain Padfoot's behavior? He has a mind—a human mind—and we think that some of the things he does he performs as a consequence of having this mind (such as standing on his hind legs when saying good-bye to Harry at King's Cross Station). What is it about having the body of a dog that apparently makes it hard for Sirius to control that body?

Consider as well what we have to say to fully explain Padfoot's behavior. Remember, the idea here is that some behavior is caused by one's mind and some by one's body. Because Padfoot is a dog, he chases his tail, as dogs do. But why do dogs chase their tails? Presumably, because it feels good. But what could feeling good mean in this case? To whom does it feel good? Does it feel good to Sirius, the human being? I doubt it; Sirius never chases his tail. Does it feel good to Padfoot, the dog? It might. After all, it feels good to other dogs to chase their tails. But Padfoot has a human mind. Isn't it in the mind that his feeling resides? If so, then this explanation tells us that Padfoot chases his tail in order to cause good feelings in Sirius's mind. And this is odd because, as we noted, Sirius never chases his own tail (or, for that matter, his own rear end). But if feeling resides in the body, then we have to say that Padfoot's body has reasons for acting as it does, and Padfoot's mind (which is Sirius's mind) has reasons for acting as it does. It's possible, then, that these reasons could clash. Sirius might end up later saying to Harry, "I didn't want to chase my tail—I wanted to walk with you—but my body wanted to chase my tail." This would be quite odd, to say the least.

A Unified Self

So, I don't think this theory—that minds and bodies are distinct and that some of the things one does can be explained by one's mind and other things by one's body—is a good explanation for Padfoot's odd behavior. The problem, I think, stems from the way the theory invites us to think about minds and bodies. I've been talking about the relation between Sirius's mind and his body (as Padfoot) in a way that comes naturally when we adopt this distinction: that the mind directs the body like a captain directing a ship. That is, that they are wholly distinct entities and the mind must somehow bring the body to obey its will. This is what it feels like sometimes. For example, athletes talk of asking their bodies to run faster or jump higher. But even Descartes, the author of this distinction, rejects this way of thinking about the relation between mind and body. "I am not only lodged in my body, like a pilot in his ship. But, besides, . . . I am joined to it very closely and indeed so compounded and intermingled with my body, that I form, as it were, a single whole with it."[8] Even Descartes, that is, rejects the idea that the body and the mind are completely distinct. They are interwoven entities, not distinct, but really a unit, so that details about one have an effect on the other. Think of how you feel when you are sick, or how you felt when you were learning to ride your bike. The physical state of your body has a direct effect on how you think about the world, on the state of your mind. I don't think it would be an exaggeration to say that your body has a direct effect on who you are.[9]

How can this be? Let me draw your attention to a couple of details from *Deathly Hallows*. First, when Ron, Harry, and Hermione take the Polyjuice Potion and sneak into the Ministry of Magic, Harry is now in the body of Runcorn, a much larger and more physically intimidating man than Harry. He proceeds to act in un-Harry-like ways. He "thunders" with a "powerful voice," dominating the Atrium and causing the wizards there to freeze. He also punches a wizard with "an enormous fist." What's noteworthy here is not that Harry/Runcorn's body is large and so has the enormous fist and the powerful voice that naturally go with a large man. What's noteworthy is that these are Harry's acts, done for Harry's reasons—remember, Runcorn is in league with the Death Eaters—but the acts are natural only in Runcorn's body. In his own body, Harry wouldn't have "thundered" "Stop!" He might have yelled it, but he probably would have chosen some other, more productive action, given that his voice doesn't convey the same power that Runcorn's does. Nor would striking the wizard seem to be such an obvious choice. These are the right choices for Harry to make in this situation, given Harry's reasons and Runcorn's body. (Contrast this with a detail that, I suggest, Rowling gets wrong: when Harry transforms into Runcorn, he judges "from his well-muscled arms" that he is "powerfully built."[10] My suspicion is that Harry would feel powerfully built; he would have no need to observe his well-muscled arms in order to judge that he is powerfully built. On the other hand, Rowling's descriptions of Harry's feelings in other similar situations, such as the natural feeling he has when submerged in the lake after he eats gillyweed, are spot on.)[11]

Second, even though Harry has taken Polyjuice Potion before Bill Weasley and Fleur Delacour's wedding, Luna Lovegood is able to recognize him. She sees Harry in "Barny Weasley's" facial expression. This shouldn't be possible if there is a distinction between Harry's mind and Barny's body. Barny's facial expressions should be his own; they should be the facial expressions his body makes, even when it's Harry's mind that's causing them. Consider this thought experiment: suppose we were able to hook up your brain to someone else's body, so that your brain, your thoughts, controlled the other person's body. Likewise, the sensory inputs that the body receives would be relayed to your brain. Then suppose we tell you (via the other person) a shocking secret, but one that the other person already knew. What will happen? First, you will be surprised, but your host will not be surprised. Second, your host's face will register the surprise that you feel (not the surprise that your host feels, for she is not surprised). Will that face look like your face, surprised? No; it's not your face. It will look like your host's face, surprised. Friends of your host will remark on this: "Why does Mary look surprised? She knew such-and-such already." They won't wonder why Mary is making that peculiar expression (your surprised expression), because Mary won't be making that expression; she'll be making her normal surprised expression. But when Harry transforms into Barny, Barny's expression becomes Harry's. Similarly, when Harry and Ron run into Arthur Weasley while infiltrating the Ministry of Magic, Harry realizes that Ron is not looking his father in the eyes for fear that his father will recognize him if he does so.

The first scenario is an example of one's new body affecting how one thinks and acts. The second is an example of one's mind affecting how one's new body looks. I'm suggesting that the mind and the body of the transformed person is a unified whole, not a pairing of discrete elements. Otherwise, we cannot make sense of the behaviors in which the transformed person engages. Does this help with understanding Padfoot's behaviors? It seems that it does: Padfoot is neither man nor dog, but a combination of the two, so he chases his tail because it feels good, as do other dogs.

What about Crouch and Moody? One thing we might notice about Animagi and werewolves is that they become different kinds of beings when they transform. It's no wonder that some of Padfoot's behaviors are odd. When he behaves like a human, he's doing odd things for a dog, and when he behaves like a dog, his behavior is odd for a human. When someone uses Polyjuice to transform, however, he or she remains human, and so that person's body doesn't engage in such odd behavior. But I'll bet that some behaviors that didn't feel right before would feel right after transforming. Think about the transformations we Muggles undergo: activities that felt right before we lost a lot of weight feel odd afterward (and vice versa). Riding a bike feels alien and awkward until one learns how, and then it feels like the most natural thing in the world. We do things that change our bodies, and as a result, we change how we interact with the world. When we change our bodies in this way, we are at root changing who we are. I think at least part of the explanation for Crouch's behavior when he is Moody is that certain actions just feel right for him. Crouch/Moody is like Padfoot and like the rest of us: an indivisible whole, made up of mind and body, both of which contribute to the identity of the whole.

So, is Sirius a man or a dog?[12] That depends on what he looks like. When he looks like a man, he's a man. When he looks like a dog, he's neither. Padfoot—Sirius, when he looks like a dog—is a third kind of thing, reducible to neither a dog nor a man. He's a unique kind of being—a man-dog—that combines features of both humans and dogs. This view, I claim, makes the most sense of Rowling's text and accords well with our best contemporary theories of the self. As Descartes said, mind and body truly do form a "single whole." The nature of this entity is determined by both one's mind and one's body, even if one's body happens to be the body of a dog.

NOTES

1. The Resurrection Stone being irretrievably lost, we can't use that avenue of inquiry. Of course, you might think there's a more fundamental problem: Sirius is a fictional character. Details, details. Regardless, I think we can learn something about real people if we pay careful attention to this mystery about Sirius. So I plan to ignore the pesky detail that Sirius is fictional and instead treat Rowling as if she were a historian of a previously unknown part of reality. I'll take what she says to be relatively accurate, with the goal of making sense of Sirius's behavior and perhaps shedding some light on ourselves in the process.

2. Unlike the rest of these transformers, boggarts are not examples of humans transformed into other shapes.

3. Tolkien fans will recognize similarities between Rowling's Animagi and J. R. R. Tolkien's "skin-changers," such as Beorn in *The Hobbit*. Tolkien clearly presents Beorn as a human who can magically transform his human body into the body of a large bear. His behavior as a bear is quite unhuman. Interestingly, in contrast to the way Rowling typically portrays Animagi, Beorn has bearlike habits when he is in human form, such as a taste for honey, a lack of interest in wealth or jewels, and an "appalling" temper.

4. You might agree with me that Crouch/Moody's behavior is out of character for Crouch. If so, then you are likely to find his behavior just as puzzling as Sirius's

behavior. Or you might think that Crouch is simply trying to make himself fit in better at Hogwarts. Unscientific polling tells me that I am in the minority. So be it. I'll touch, but not dwell, on Crouch/Moody's behavior further on.

5. *Deathly Hallows*, p. 591.

6. Polyjuice cases are much clearer; when Harry becomes Gregory Goyle, it's not the case that Goyle has two bodies, one in the closet, the other in the Slytherin common room. Instead, Harry's body now looks like Goyle's, as if they were identical twins.

7. *Order of the Phoenix*, p. 183.

8. René Descartes, *Meditations*, translated by F. E. Sutcliffe (Harmondworth, UK: Penguin Books, 1968), p. 159.

9. As an aside, I don't want to leave the impression that Descartes had this view. His view was quite the opposite, for although he did think the mind and the body were "tightly joined," he also thought that the mind and the body were essentially distinct. The view I am proposing is that the mind and the body together form a whole that is the self. The mind, I suggest, cannot exist without the body.

10. *Deathly Hallows*, p. 240.

11. When Harry takes Polyjuice in *Chamber of Secrets*, Rowling reports that "Goyle's low rasp of a voice issued from his mouth" (p. 217). Compare this to the movie, which depicts Harry as trying to imitate Goyle's voice. I hope that you agree with me that Rowling is more accurate on this point than the movie is: the voice with which Harry speaks is determined by his body. If his body is shaped like Goyle's, then his voice should sound like Goyle's.

12. There are other related questions particular to the world of Harry Potter that are worth investigating. For example, notice that even when adopting the body of a Muggle, witches and wizards retain their magical powers. So, what's the source of one's magical powers? And how does the shape a boggart takes affect its identity? In *Prisoner of Azkaban*, Harry's Patronus only prevents the boggart-dementor from bothering him, but (unlike the portrayal in the movie), Lupin needs to use the Riddikulus charm to force the boggart back into the chest. This suggests that while the boggart might be affected by the body it adopts (the boggart as Severus Snape moves the way Snape moves), something of its boggart-ness remains; one needs magic appropriate to boggarts to deal with it completely. These questions are worth pursuing, but we don't have time here. Those of you pursuing your N.E.W.T.s in Transfiguration should write eighteen inches on these questions.

DESTINY IN THE
WIZARDING WORLD

Jeremy Pierce

The Potter stories portray Professor Sybill Trelawney, Hogwarts' Divination teacher, as an "old fraud" whose sooth-saying comes in pseudoscientific trappings. She teaches various techniques for predicting the future, including tea leaves, planetary orbits, palm reading, dream interpretation, tarot cards, and crystal balls. Each method has rules for students to follow, but they have little scientific basis. Trelawney's predictions often turn out wrong, such as her constantly repeated forecast of Harry's premature death. She also accepts others' fabricated predictions that fit her preconceived ideas, for example, when she awards Harry and Ron Weasley top marks for predicting tragic misfortunes in their immediate futures.

Nevertheless, at least two of Trelawney's prophecies are different. Professor Dumbledore calls them her only two "real predictions."[1] Normally, Trelawney speaks in such elastic generalities about common-enough occurrences that she'll usually find something that fits. A science-minded Muggle like Vernon Dursley might reject divination as a reliable predictor. What do the alignment of the planets and the random assignment of tarot cards in a deck have to do with the processes that lead to certain events happening rather than others? But this is a magical world, even if the Dursleys don't like it. Couldn't magic connect tea leaves or dreams with actual future events?

Unfortunately, Trelawney usually comes across as a complete fraud, and her usual methods are probably either nonmagical or unreliable magic. Professor McGonagall tells Harry's class that divination "is one of the most imprecise branches of magic. I shall not conceal from you that I have very little patience with it. True Seers are very rare, and Professor Trelawney—."[2] She stops short to avoid speaking ill of a colleague, but the point is clear. Sybill Trelawney isn't a true Seer.

Similarly, the centaur Firenze distinguishes between Trelawney and genuine Seers. "Sybill Trelawney may have Seen, I do not know. . . . But she wastes her time, in the main, on the self-flattering nonsense humans call fortune-telling."[3] He respects and practices prophecy, despite acknowledging its fallibility, but he distinguishes it from the nonsense of fortune-telling. That raises a question about genuine prophecies. What does it mean to say they're real, and how are they different from the others? Even Dumbledore, skeptical about most divination, acknowledges two of Trelawney's predictions as different, and Firenze also admits the possibility. So, what is this distinction?

Varieties of Prophecy

Do "real predictions" derive from what will actually happen? Is the future "fixed" so that there's just one future? Aristotle (384–322 B.C.E.) gets credit for first raising this issue.[4] Is it true when Harry first attends Hogwarts that he'll have a final face-off with Voldemort seven years later?

If the future is fixed, there's only one future, and it will happen. This isn't to say that it will happen no matter what anyone does. It could happen *because* of what they do, and if they did something else, a different future would happen. But part of the fixed future is what they'll do. Being fixed also doesn't necessarily mean the future is predetermined. People who believe the future is fixed may not be determinists, although some are.

Prophecies can be fallible or infallible. An infallible prophecy is guaranteed to be true. It couldn't have been wrong. By contrast, fallible prophecies could be wrong. False prophecies are fallible because they're actually wrong, but true prophecies can also be fallible. All it takes is possibly getting it wrong. Fallibility isn't about how sure we can be of whether a prophecy will come true. I might be very unsure of an infallible prophecy if I don't understand its secure basis. I might be very sure of a fallible prophecy, even a false one, if I lack crucial facts.

Exactly how does a Seer gain access to information in a prophecy? Here are several possibilities:

1. A prophecy might be a fallible prediction based on human observations through the five senses. Muggle weather reports and Trelawney's prophecies are like this.
2. If the future isn't fixed, all of the information in the universe wouldn't be enough to guarantee a correct prediction. But there might be enough to expect probabilities. Perhaps the Seer gains access to possible or likely futures. Maybe Trelawney sees possible futures but can't discern the most likely ones and must speak in vague generalities. Dumbledore says, "The consequences of our actions are always so complicated, so diverse, that predicting the future is a very difficult business indeed. . . . Professor Trelawney, bless her, is living proof of that."[5]
3. A prophecy might be a fallible prediction based on a limited understanding of a deterministic world. If the future

is predetermined by the current state of the world and the laws of nature, and the Seer has imperfect access to it through signs of what causes it, then the Seer views a fixed future. Magic derives information from the natural forces that lead to that future, but it may not give perfect information. Or the Seer might magically behold a fixed future without interpreting it correctly, perhaps because of partial information.

4. A soothsayer may be skilled at using predictions to make people do things. Such a "Seer" could influence people by knowing how an audience is likely to respond to a prophecy. As we'll see shortly, Dumbledore thinks Trelawney's first "real prediction" led Voldemort to choose Harry to kill, marking Harry as his equal. Trelawney didn't intend anything, but the prophecy plays a role in its own fulfillment.

5. An infallible prediction might come from a complete understanding of the deterministic processes that guarantee an outcome. This would need an all-knowing being or magical forces influenced by deterministic processes.

6. An infallible prediction might come from infallible access to the actual future. This might be by magic or through someone who has direct contact with the future, perhaps a divine being or a person with cross-time communication. Or a Seer might have the ability to see into the actual future (not merely into possible futures).

7. Finally, a prophecy could combine fallibility and infallibility, with infallible access to some fixed fact about the future and fallibility about another aspect. The fallibility might come either from imperfect access to a fixed fact or from information about likely futures.

So, the question before us is what kind of prophecy Professor Trelawney's genuine prophecies are, as opposed to her usual fortune-telling.

Fallible Prophecies

Most of Trelawney's predictions are perfect examples of the first category—fallible predictions based on sensory experience. They're usually vague or open-ended enough to find something to fit them, but there may be no guarantee, and it won't always fit well.

It's easy to see how general prophecies might at best be only probable, even if some are *very* likely. Trelawney's predictions don't come from an infallible source but from her ability to predict likely enough things, sometimes based on background information. Many of her predictions are easy to fulfill. Others may happen to be right by accident. Some are false, such as her forecasts of Harry's imminent death.

Dumbledore seems to treat all prophecies as fallible when he tells Harry that the first of Trelawney's real prophecies didn't have to come true:

> "The one with the power to vanquish the Dark Lord approaches. . . . Born to those who have thrice defied him, born as the seventh month dies . . . and the Dark Lord will mark him as his equal, but he will have power the Dark Lord knows not . . . and either must die at the hand of the other for neither can live while the other survives."[6]

Dumbledore suggests to Harry that some prophecies turn out to be false. "Do you think every prophecy in the Hall of Prophecy has been fulfilled?"[7] He continues, "The prophecy does not mean you *have* to do anything! . . . In other words, you are free to choose your way, quite free to turn your back on the prophecy!"[8] Voldemort's obsession with the prophecy will lead him to seek out Harry, and as a result, they'll almost certainly face off, but not because this was "fated" by the prophecy.

So, prophecies can vary in likelihood. Is that the distinguishing factor between "real predictions" and Trelawney's usual sayings? Some are likely to be true because they're based on her perceptions of what tends to happen, and she makes them vague enough to be likely. Others are more genuine because they're more likely. This is a difference of degree. They're both matters of likelihood, although some are more likely. But when Dumbledore treats two prophecies as special, doesn't it seem as if they're more special than that? Indeed, there's still something different about them. The two "real predictions" were purely involuntary and have a magical source. They aren't category 1, which involves actively paying attention. Trelawney must have had a stronger connection with the future, an occasional ability to connect with an actual, fixed future (category 3) or possible futures (category 2).

There are also some indications that Professor Trelawney has inconsistent access to the future or to possible futures, even when conscious. Consider the following example when Harry is heading to his first private lesson with Dumbledore in *Half-Blood Prince*:

> Harry proceeded through deserted corridors, though he had to step hastily behind a statue when Professor Trelawney appeared around a corner, muttering to herself as she shuffled a pack of dirty-looking playing cards, reading them as she walked.
>
> "Two of spades: conflict," she murmured, as she passed the place where Harry crouched, hidden. "Seven of spades: an ill omen. Ten of spades: violence. Knave of spades: a dark young man, possibly troubled, one who dislikes the questioner—" She stopped dead, right on the other side of Harry's statue. "Well, that can't be right," she said, annoyed, and Harry heard her reshuffling vigorously as she set off again, leaving nothing but a whiff of cooking sherry behind her.[9]

What she says could easily apply to Harry, but she has no inkling of his presence. Is that likely to be a coincidence?

Harry encounters her again on his way to his last appointment with Dumbledore before they leave for Voldemort's cave:

> "If Dumbledore chooses to ignore the warnings the cards show—" Her bony hand closed suddenly around Harry's wrist. "Again and again, no matter how I lay them out—" And she pulled a card dramatically from underneath her shawls. "—the lightning-struck tower," she whispered. "Calamity. Disaster. Coming nearer all the time."[10]

This is so vague that it might just be category 1, but the tower is significant in light of the book's finale, which not only includes Dumbledore's death but even leads to a bigger disaster, as the Death Eaters seize power.

Self-Fulfilling Prophecies

Dumbledore suggests that Trelawney's first real prediction might be self-fulfilling. He tells Harry, "It may not have meant you at all," because Neville Longbottom had been born a day earlier, and his parents had also thrice defied Voldemort.[11] But then a few paragraphs later, he tells Harry, "There is no doubt that it *is* you," because Voldemort's choice to go after Harry, rather than Neville, led to his marking Harry as his equal. According to Dumbledore's interpretation, the prophecy didn't itself determine whether it was about Harry or Neville. Voldemort's choice of Harry made it true of Harry. He wouldn't have attacked Harry had there not been a prophecy, and so the prophecy led him to fulfill that part of itself.

Alexander of Aphrodisias, a philosopher during the late first and early second centuries, discussed self-fulfilling predictions. In the story of Oedipus, Apollo makes a prophecy to King Laius that his future son will kill him. Some of Alexander's contemporaries believed that Apollo's prophecy caused Laius to try to kill his son, which eventually led Oedipus to kill his father (without knowing it was his father). Alexander gives a number of arguments against this position, but one response is telling:

> Well, if someone says these things, how does he . . . preserve prophecy . . . ? For prophecy is thought to be prediction of the things that are going to happen, but they make Apollo the author of the things he predicts. . . . How is this not the deed of him who prophesied, rather than revelation of the things that were going to be?[12]

We can imagine someone *seeming* to foretell the future but really just causing the events that lead to the predicted future. Alexander says it's not a genuine prophecy unless it's already true that those events are going to happen, and the speaker predicts them because he knows they'll happen. If the words are simply an attempt to manipulate events, they're not a genuine prophecy.

A real prophecy could cause what it describes, but this isn't true of Trelawney's first prophecy. It didn't *cause* Voldemort to go after Harry. He could have gone after Neville, but Dumbledore notices he chose Harry as a "half-blood, like himself. He saw himself in you before he had ever seen you."[13] What made him choose Harry wasn't the prophecy, which didn't cause him to go after *anyone*. Dumbledore suggests that if Voldemort had heard the whole prophecy, he might not have been so hasty. When Harry asks why Voldemort hadn't waited to figure out which one it was (or, I might add, killed both), Dumbledore says Voldemort had incomplete information because his spy (later revealed as Severus Snape) was thrown out of the room halfway through the prophecy:

> "Consequently, he could not warn his master that to attack you would be to risk transferring power to you— again marking you as his equal. So Voldemort never knew that there might be danger in attacking you, that it

might be wise to wait or learn more. He did not know that you would have 'power the Dark Lord knows not.'"[14]

The prophecy by itself couldn't have *made* Voldemort do anything. He heard some of the prophecy, but it didn't *ensure* anything. It couldn't control how much Snape heard. If Voldemort had heard the rest, he might not have chosen to do anything. So, it doesn't seem as if the self-fulfilling interpretation of prophecies is a good way to distinguish "real predictions" from Professor Trelawney's usual prophecies.

Destiny

In a 2007 interview with a Dutch newspaper, J. K. Rowling said that her use of Professor Trelawney reflected her view that there's no such thing as destiny.[15] What does this denial of destiny amount to?

A *compatibilist* about freedom and predetermination thinks we can be free even if our choices are determined by things outside our control. Some compatibilists say there's just one possible outcome, the actual future. Other compatibilists speak of possible choices, meaning we can consider various options and then pick one, even if our deliberation is predetermined by things outside our control. A *libertarian* about freedom holds that we have options because there's nothing that guarantees our choices ahead of time. This is more than compatibilism allows, because the libertarian considers predetermined choices unfree.

Some libertarians believe in a fixed future, meaning there are truths *now* about what *will* happen. You might have many *possible* futures open to you, even if there's only one *actual* future that will happen.[16] Other libertarians, thinking that such truths about future choices would threaten our freedom, insist on an open future, where statements about our future free choices are neither true nor false (until those choices are made).

The most natural denial of destiny is the open future view. No future statements about people's free choices are true or false. Yet someone denying destiny could mean that there are possible futures open to us, without denying that only one of them is the actual future. It's possible Rowling means just that, in which case she might even be a compatibilist, although this kind of language is more typical of a libertarian.

Dumbledore tells Harry that the prophecy about him doesn't have to be fulfilled just because it's a real prophecy. Does Dumbledore mean there's no fact about whether it will be fulfilled, and it becomes a genuine prophecy only when the foretold event occurs or is guaranteed to happen? Or does he mean the prophecy doesn't *make* Harry or Voldemort do anything? What it predicts is the actual future, but other futures are possible. We need to delve more deeply into the Potter books to see what kind of destiny there is and isn't in Harry's world.

A Rodent's Destiny

In *Prisoner of Azkaban*, Professor Trelawney makes a second "real prediction":

> "The Dark Lord lies alone and friendless, abandoned by his followers. His servant has been chained these twelve years. Tonight, before midnight . . . the servant will break free and set out to rejoin his master. The Dark Lord will rise again with his servant's aid, greater and more terrible than ever he was. Tonight . . . before midnight . . . the servant . . . will set out . . . to rejoin . . . his master."[17]

If the prophecy that one of Voldemort's followers would go to him that night was overwhelmingly likely, then Wormtail must have been extremely likely to escape that night. Other followers who were capable of going were unlikely to try. If Remus Lupin had remembered to take his Wolfsbane potion to manage his werewolf transformation or someone had responded more quickly when Wormtail transformed, Wormtail might not have escaped. If a "real prediction" involves greater likelihood, this should be a likely outcome. It doesn't seem likely, so this particular prophecy is hard to see as fallible but likely.

The earlier prophecy is similar. Even if Voldemort was likely to go after Harry, how probable was it that Wormtail would become secret-keeper at the last minute? Voldemort wouldn't otherwise have marked Harry and given him power "the Dark Lord knows not." If Voldemort hadn't told Snape his plan, Snape wouldn't have begged for Lily Potter to be spared, and Lily wouldn't have had to make a voluntary protective sacrifice. Again, Harry wouldn't have been marked. Thus, this prediction also seems to be "real" in some stronger sense than simply being "likely but fallible."

Time Travel and Fixed Time

To make sense of Rowling's views on prophecy and destiny, we must consider what she says about time travel. If time travel can change the past, it allows serious paradoxes, such as the case Hermione Granger mentions of killing your past self before you could travel back and kill yourself. If you did that, you wouldn't have lived long enough to go back in time to have done it. You can't change the past according to the fixed-time theory, and that means you won't kill yourself. You already survived, so it won't happen because it didn't happen. In Harry's one instance of time travel, Hermione and he travel back in time three hours, carefully avoiding being seen. They accomplish what they set out to do, saving Buckbeak and Sirius Black. There's never any indication of a change. The entire account fits nicely with what we already knew about that three-hour period.

We find out the second time around that later-Harry cast the stag Patronus that saved earlier-Harry from the dementors. A fixed view of time fits this best. If Harry is saved by the

Patronus stag the first time around and then casts it the second time around, the best explanation is that Harry's later self was there all along. Yet future events cause those present actions, which means the future must happen a certain way for Harry and Hermione to have been able to travel back in time to do these things. A fixed view of time allows for this.

Nevertheless, Hermione describes time travel in a way that allows changing the past. "We're breaking one of the most important wizarding laws! Nobody's supposed to change time, nobody!"[18] She adds later, "Professor McGonagall told me what awful things have happened when wizards have meddled with time. . . . Loads of them ended up killing their past or future selves by mistake!"[19] If we trust a trustworthy character reporting on another trustworthy character's statements, then in Harry's world the past can be changed. That would mean time isn't fixed.

It's highly unlikely that McGonagall is lying or that Hermione misinterprets her or lies about it to Harry. It's possible (but still unlikely) that the Ministry of Magic has spread misinformation about a guarded magical subject and that even McGonagall doesn't know the truth. Some may find that a stretch. But the alternative, if the stories are to be consistent, is to take "time travel" in cases of changing the past as possibility-travel and not time travel.[20] They travel to another possible time line. The one time-travel case in the novels does seem to be genuine time travel, so it's not clear what mechanism would make it possibility-travel in only past-changing cases.

Aside from these puzzles about time travel, perhaps the most compelling argument for fixed time is that it fits best with current physics. Absolute space-time is often considered incompatible with special relativity. An open future requires an absolute present moment, after which little is fixed. But there is no absolute present. What we call the present is relative to a frame of reference. There can't be an absolute future if special relativity is correct.[21]

With a fixed future and prophetic access to it, Trelawney's first prophecy doesn't just happen to get it right, despite being unlikely. It is guaranteed to be right, even if many of the events along the path to fulfilling it seem unlikely. We might even conclude something stronger than simply that the future is fixed. Many unlikely events happen to lead to a prophesied event. A lot of chance events could have gone the other way to prevent the prophecy's fulfillment.

Harry and his friends defeat Voldemort and his follow-ers, despite overwhelming odds, partly from sheer luck, and it fulfills a prophecy. That's hard to make sense of without a stronger connection between the prophecy and the actual future. It seems lucky that Harry and his friends have spent time in Moaning Myrtle's bathroom making Polyjuice Potion, which helps them locate the entrance to the Chamber of Secrets. They might have tried something different to figure out what Draco Malfoy knew or might have brewed the potion elsewhere. Their choice of that bathroom allows Harry to find the Chamber, save Ginny Weasley's life, destroy a Horcrux, make the Sword of Gryffindor capable of destroying further Horcruxes, leave behind the basilisk fang to destroy the Cup Horcrux, and alert Dumbledore to the fact that Voldemort must have made more than one Horcrux. A fair amount depends on where they happen to choose to brew that potion.

Many other events that could have gone otherwise are crucial to things working out in the end. Harry's luck from Felix Felicis accomplishes a lot more than he realizes, including seemingly unlucky things such as Dumbledore's death but also his obtaining Horace Slughorn's memory of Voldemort wanting to divide his soul into seven pieces by making exactly six Horcruxes. Harry had that potion because he had received Snape's former Potions book, and that occurred only because Dumbledore failed to inform Harry that he could take Potions, and Harry's change in circumstances with Potions depended on Slughorn coming back to teach.

In the second half of *Deathly Hallows*, Harry and his friends happen to be captured by the group that had Griphook. They arrive at Malfoy Manor during Voldemort's absence, after the fake Sword of Gryffindor was stored with a Horcrux whose location they didn't know. Snape had gotten the real sword into their hands for it to be there for Bellatrix Lestrange to see it and freak out, leading Harry to suspect that the hiding place of the fake sword also contains a Horcrux.

Harry later arrives at the Shrieking Shack just as Voldemort is about to kill Snape, allowing Snape to convey Dumbledore's last message to Harry. All of these events rest on luck. You might wonder whether some force guided things along to ensure that the prophecy would be fulfilled. The fact that so many chance events led to the prophecy's fulfillment might suggest the influence of some divine being.

This would be a stronger destiny than merely a fixed future, because it involves the deliberate intentions of an intelligent being. Many Christians, for example, have interpreted the Potter books to reflect a strong view of divine providence, with God having a plan for the universe. That might mean God predetermines all of our actions by means of prior events causing them. But it could as easily involve libertarian freedom, as long as God knows what people would do in all possible circumstances and therefore knows infallibly what free choices they may make.

These lucky circumstances seem far too easy if there isn't someone guiding events toward certain outcomes. Such a view may not fit what Rowling intended to say when she denied destiny and what Dumbledore says when he insists that Harry or Voldemort could have done something contrary to the prophecy. It's hard to be sure what Rowling meant (and what she meant Dumbledore to mean). But the story makes better sense if there is a deeper, providential explanation of the lucky occurrences. If not, Harry and his friends are just incredibly lucky![22]

NOTES

1. *Prisoner of Azkaban*, p. 426.

2. Ibid., p. 109.

3. *Order of the Phoenix*, p. 603.

4. "On Interpretation," chap. 9, reprinted in *Aristotle: Introductory Readings*, edited by Terence Irwin and Gail Fine (Indianapolis: Hackett, 1996), pp. 11–15.

5. *Prisoner of Azkaban*, p. 426.

6. *Order of the Phoenix*, p. 841.

7. *Half-Blood Prince*, p. 510.

8. Ibid., p. 512.

9. Ibid., pp. 195–196.

10. Ibid., p. 543.

11. *Order of the Phoenix*, p. 842.

12. Alexander's "On Fate," 30–31, reprinted in *Voices of Ancient Philosophy: An Introductory Reader*, edited by Julia Annas (New York: Oxford University Press, 2000), p. 46.

13. *Order of the Phoenix*, p. 842.

14. Ibid., p. 843.

15. *Volkskrant*, November 2007. The interview is in Dutch, but it has been translated into English at www.the-leaky-cauldron.org/2007/11/19/new-interview-with-j-k-rowling-for-release-of-dutch-edition-of-deathly-hallows (or http://tinyurl.com/ypazb4). My discussion relies entirely on that English translation.

16. For an excellent defense of the compatibility of foreknowledge and libertarian freedom, see Gregory Bassham's chapter, "The Prophecy-Driven Life: Fate and Freedom at Hogwarts," in *Harry Potter and Philosophy: If Aristotle Ran Hogwarts*, edited by David Baggett and Shawn E. Klein (Chicago: Open Court, 2004), pp. 223–225.

17. *Prisoner of Azkaban*, p. 324.

18. Ibid., p. 398.

19. Ibid., p. 399.

20. For a more in-depth discussion of time travel in the Potter novels, see Michael Silberstein, "Space, Time, and Magic," in *Harry Potter and Philosophy*, pp. 192–199.

21. This objection is developed in much more depth in Theodore Sider, *Four-Dimensionalism: An Ontology of Persistence and Time* (New York: Oxford University Press, 2002), pp. 42–52. This chapter also discusses other difficulties that arise if you deny the fixed view of time.

22. Thanks to Winky Chin, Jonathan Ichikawa, Peter Kirk, Ben Murphy, Tim O'Keefe, Samantha Pierce, Rey Reynoso, and Brandon Watson for comments at various stages of this chapter's development.

PART TWO

THE MOST POWERFUL
MAGIC OF ALL

CHOOSING LOVE

The Redemption of Severus Snape

Catherine Jack Deavel and David Paul Deavel

Although Harry "felt a savage pleasure in blaming Snape" for Sirius Black's death, easing his own sense of guilt, he can't get Professor Dumbledore to agree.[1] In fact, Dumbledore finds Severus Snape completely trustworthy, despite all appearances to the contrary. It might be tempting to chalk up Harry's suspicion to emotional immaturity, but, other than Dumbledore, *no* members of the Order of the Phoenix trust Snape wholeheartedly. After Snape kills Dumbledore, Professor McGonagall murmurs, "We all wondered . . . but [Dumbledore] trusted . . . always."[2] She continues, "He always hinted that he had an ironclad reason for trusting Snape. . . . Dumbledore told me explicitly that Snape's repentance was absolutely genuine."[3] With so many lives at stake, how could Dumbledore be so certain that Snape is loyal and trustworthy?[4]

In a word, the answer is love—not Dumbledore's love for Snape, nor Snape's for Harry, but Snape's love for Lily Potter, Harry's mother. Although Lily doesn't reciprocate Snape's romantic love, Snape never stops loving her, and that love eventually leads, however circuitously, to his redemption.

Enlightened contemporary readers might smile indulgently at the rhetoric of love and redemption, chalking it up to J. K. Rowling's sentimentality. After all, why think that love is a good reason to trust Snape? Clearly, Snape dislikes, even hates, Harry, Sirius, and others. Shouldn't Dumbledore worry that this malice might win the day? Furthermore, why think that Snape has been redeemed? Isn't his hate already evidence to the contrary? If he were redeemed, one might argue, then these feelings would be gone. Appeals to love and its transforming power are, of course, ubiquitous in literature, but aren't such notions, at root, just old-fashioned, quaint, and simplistic? What would a philosopher say about such a thing? As it happens, philosophers have had quite a lot to say about love. They have explored the nature of love, the varieties of love, and even the way love can blind us and lead to mistakes in judgment. The Potter series, and Snape in particular, offers us a chance to explore these issues as well.

Snape and the Many-Splendored Thing

From Plato (around 428–348 B.C.E.) to C. S. Lewis (1898–1963), love has been a recurring and prominent theme among great thinkers. Whatever its source or ultimate significance, the many-splendored thing of love has served as the inspiration for poets and playwrights, novelists and essayists, philosophers and theologians. The prominence of love as a theme in the Potter books is hard to miss. Lily's love saves and protects Harry. Harry's love defeats Professor Quirrell and prevents Lord Voldemort from possessing Harry's soul. And Voldemort's fatal weakness, Dumbledore tells us, is that he never understood that love is the most powerful magic of all.

In her refusal to water down love to something merely rhetorical or sentimental, Rowling joins some elite philosophical company. Greek philosophers distinguished between three kinds of love: *eros, philia*, and *agape* Eros, or erotic love, is the type of love found in romantic relationships. Mr. and Mrs. Weasley, Ron Weasley and Hermione Granger, and Harry and Ginny Weasley are good examples of such love. In Western philosophy, the most famous analysis of erotic love is contained in Plato's *Symposium*, where Plato seeks to show how crude physical desires can be progressively refined to draw the soul upward to things beautiful and divine. Philia is friendship love. It's important to see that friendship is indeed a kind of love—rendering poignant and sad Dumbledore's observation that Voldemort never had a friend or even wanted one. In fact, for ancient Greeks and Romans, friendship was generally believed to be superior to romantic love.[5] The third type of love, agape, is universal, self-giving, and unconditional love. When the Gospel writers tell us that "God is love," it is agape that they have in mind.

Traditional philosophical accounts of love help us make sense of Snape's complicated character because they emphasize that love is not primarily a feeling but a choice, an act of the will. Ideally, our emotions will be in harmony with what we understand to be the good, but we can act for the good even when our emotions rebel. The fact that Snape continues to have conflicted emotions does not prove that he has not been transformed by love. To the contrary, Snape's ability to act consistently for the good of others, despite his emotional indifference to or even dislike of these individuals, testifies to the strength of his love for Lily.

The Abandoned Boys

Snape is an intriguing character, in part because he shares origins similar to Voldemort's and Harry's. Like Harry and Voldemort, Snape hails from a mixed bloodline, which raises suspicions and hatreds in parts of both the Muggle and the wizard worlds. Desperate to associate himself with his mother's family, the Princes, and downplay his Muggle ancestry, Snape dubs himself "the Half-Blood Prince." Having grown up in a home with feuding parents, Snape finds his first real taste of home at Hogwarts—again like Harry and Voldemort—using his magical powers and forming alliances in the wizard world. As Harry observes, he and Voldemort and Snape, "the abandoned boys, had all found home there [at Hogwarts]."[6] All three also tended toward Slytherin, with only Harry not ending up there.

Of course, Harry and Voldemort took very different paths. Voldemort opted for power over love, selfishness over altruism, conquest over the vulnerability of friendship and genuine relationships of any sort. In sharp contrast, Harry opened his heart to friends and was willing to sacrifice himself for those he loved. Rather than choosing a fragmented psyche like Voldemort's, Harry allowed his friends to make him a better person of integrity and wholeness.

Much ink has been devoted to the patterns of good and evil that Harry and Voldemort respectively represent, but what about this third lost boy, that complicated amalgam of darkness and light, Dumbledore's double agent and killer, Harry's protector and adversary? What makes Snape tick?

Snape the Occlumens

Snape is a complicated character not simply because he is a double agent, but because his loyalties truly have been divided in the past, and his reason and emotions continue to be divided. Initially, Snape had been a Death Eater; after Snape's repentance, Dumbledore asks him to play the dangerous role of informant when the Dark Lord returns. To do so, Snape must gain Voldemort's complete trust. He must betray neither his loyalty to Dumbledore nor his pledge to protect Voldemort's enemies, especially Harry. His anger at and sometimes hatred of Harry (and others) are real, but equally real are his constant self-risk and courage in fighting Voldemort.

Snape doesn't choose to protect Harry and the other enemies of Voldemort because of great personal affection for them—the warm fuzzies associated with today's often watery and superficial notions of "love." On the contrary, he chooses to act for what he knows to be their good despite strongly disliking many of them. Love that is understood as the desire for the good of the other can be found not only in Rowling's depictions, but in writers on love who range from Aristotle to Aquinas to M. Scott Peck, despite the cultural and temporal distances among them. They share in common an understanding of love expressed in friendship as willing the good of another for the other's own sake.[7] Over and over, the decision is stark in the Potter books between the option of furthering one's own apparent good at the expense of others or sacrificing it for the good of others. Love requires self-sacrifice, binds one's happiness to the good of another, makes one vulnerable to loss and grief, and strengthens one's commitment to the good.

These thinkers also emphasize that strong feelings become morally good or bad when they influence our reason and will, that is, when feelings affect both our understanding of what is good or bad and how we act. Particularly in Snape's case, love is not primarily found in feelings but in actions. Love changes the course of his beliefs, alliances, and actions; he repents because of love, and he finds redemption by choosing to act for love.[8] In short, it is Snape's love for Lily that primarily motivates the actions leading to his redemption.

Once Dumbledore realizes that Voldemort and Harry can share each other's thoughts and emotions, he asks Snape to teach Harry Occlumency, a magical technique for sealing "the mind against magical intrusion and influence."[9] Voldemort is remarkably accomplished at gaining access to others' thoughts and memories, making the detection of lies almost certain. "Only those skilled at Occlumency," Snape says, "are able to shut down those feelings and memories that contradict the lie, and so utter falsehoods in his presence without detection."[10] As Dumbledore's double agent, Snape regularly achieves what few manage even once: successfully lying to Voldemort's face. Snape succeeds not only by intelligence and cunning, revealing enough information to appear to be a valuable informant while withholding the most significant points, but also by sheer magical prowess.

Snape's skill at Occlumency reveals both his strength and his weakness of character. The successful Occlumens empties personal emotion, something Harry can't do. Snape fumes, "Fools who wear their hearts proudly on their sleeves, who cannot control their emotions, who wallow in sad memories and allow themselves to be provoked this easily—weak people, in other words—they stand no chance against [Voldemort's] powers!"[11] Snape survives not by giving up his love for Lily the way Voldemort had renounced love and friendship. Rather, Snape conceals his love from Voldemort. Although this ability to hide memories and emotions is crucial to his role as a double agent, it also isolates Snape from friendship. The final chapters of *Deathly Hallows* reveal the depth of Snape's sacrifice and courage. As he lays dying from Nagini's bite, Snape transmits to Harry a flood of memories chronicling both Snape's love for Lily and his secret protection of Voldemort's enemies. Snape remains the consummate Occlumens. His memories cannot be taken; they must be offered freely. Only while dying does he permit Harry access to his thoughts and feelings, revealing that Harry is a Horcrux and showing him what must be done to defeat Voldemort.

Snape's Choice

From childhood, Snape loves Lily Evans, although selfishly at first. He watches her with "undisguised greed," while dreaming of Hogwarts as an escape from his family and a way of gaining acceptance in the wizarding world, despite his half-Muggle bloodline.[12] At Hogwarts, though, he is still an awkward outsider, now fighting with James Potter, for whom everything, especially magic and Quidditch, comes so easily. Worse, Snape knows that James is also in love with Lily.

Snape's love for Lily begins to redeem him, ever so slowly at first. When Lily is a child, she asks Snape whether it makes a difference being Muggle-born, to which, after hesitating, he answers no. When Lily is a teenager, having refuted Snape's earlier false belief in the superiority of wizard blood, she defends Snape against James and his friends, only to have the mortified Snape call her a Mudblood. He apologizes, but Lily refuses to defend him anymore. With the friendship broken, Snape chooses Dark Magic and the Death Eaters. Later, though, he would remember this painful and costly lesson and, as headmaster, rebuke Phineas Nigellus's portrait for referring to Hermione Granger as a Mudblood.

After dutifully reporting to Voldemort the prophecy he overheard about the child who would challenge the Dark Lord, Snape begs Dumbledore to protect Lily. Dumbledore asks, "Could you not ask for mercy for the mother, in exchange for the son?" Snape assures Dumbledore he has tried, to which Dumbledore responds, "You disgust me. . . . You do not care, then, about the deaths of her husband and child? They can die as long as you get what you want?"[13] Snape's love is not yet pure; he does not love Lily as what Aristotle calls a "second self."[14] Rather, he desires Lily's good as it relates to him. If he had desired Lily's good for her own sake, he would want to protect those most precious to her, too. Snape relents, promising "anything" in return for Dumbledore's protection of the family. After Lily's murder, Dumbledore asks Snape to act on his love for Lily by protecting her beloved son.

Snape's romantic love for Lily is tainted with selfishness at first, but his love deepens as he accepts the role Dumbledore proposes. Plato reflects on a similar deepening of love in the *Symposium*, which presents various characters attempting to describe and praise love. In the *Symposium*, Socrates' teacher, Diotima, claims, "Love is wanting to possess the good forever."[15] This "possession" of the good is not the satisfaction of selfish desire in a superficial eros, which values the beloved for what he or she provides to the one who loves, but is instead a relationship to the beloved that draws the one who loves toward the beloved as a free-standing good. Someone who loves seeks "giving birth in beauty," either to children or to ideas and virtue.[16] Love opens itself to the eternal by extending the love of parents to their children or by building virtue and love of what is transcendent in the one who loves. Rowling gives examples of both. Out of love, James and Lily willingly sacrifice themselves for each other and for Harry. Snape's romantic love for Lily, though unrequited, gradually does "bring to birth" virtue in Snape. After Snape commits himself to fighting Voldemort, the earlier selfishness eventually fades.

Reflecting on the refinement of romantic love in the context of the Christian tradition, Pope Benedict XVI comments that "love looks to the eternal. Love is indeed 'ecstasy,' not in the sense of a moment of intoxication, but rather as a journey, an ongoing exodus out of the closed inward-looking self towards its liberation through self-giving."[17] Snape's love for Lily pushes him beyond selfish desire and changes him fundamentally. Snape's ongoing love for Lily, even after her death, spurs him to choose actions that gradually make his love more like hers, turned toward the good of others and capable of self-sacrifice. His love for Lily makes him place himself, like James and Lily, between Voldemort and Harry.

A Work in Progress

Snape's decision to fight Voldemort and shield Harry remains steadfast, but his character doesn't change instantly. Here we see the damage of vice and the work of virtue: both are habits, built up over time. Changing one's feelings and behavior requires vigilance and effort. Demanding that Dumbledore keep his role secret, Snape still rages at his school-day tormentors, seeing in Harry all of James's arrogance and reveling in Harry's failures and detentions.[18] Harry's physical resemblance to James blinds Snape to the shared character traits between Harry and his mother. Snape's patterns of behavior and emotion continue to block friendships, but at least his actions unite him to the cause of those battling Voldemort.

Snape also continues to share, partially, Voldemort's false assessment that those who guide their actions by love are weak. Snape spits this insult at Harry during Occlumency lessons: Harry is weak because he cannot lock away thoughts and feelings of love. Likewise, when Snape encounters Nymphadora Tonks's changed Patronus, he sneers, "I think you were better off with the old one. . . . The new one looks weak."[19] On rare occasions, "a great shock . . . [or] an emotional upheaval" can alter a Patronus.[20] Tonks has fallen in love with Remus Lupin (a werewolf), and her Patronus is now a wolf. Presumably, the wolf itself doesn't "look weak." Instead, the change is evidence of her love, or, alternately, evidence that love has transformed her. It is this love—particularly of the despised Lupin—that Snape finds weak. But Snape's own Patronus, a doe, offers eloquent testimony against his assertion. Snape's love for Lily altered his Patronus to match hers. His strongest defense against magical threats is now an emblem of his beloved and his transformation by love—despite Snape's ability to block out his emotions and memories.

Snape's Patronus reflects Aristotle's notion of the beloved as a second self; it is both a magical extension of himself and a manifestation of his love for Lily. Similarly, Harry is protected by the love of his parents: his Patronus is James's stag, and Lily's self-sacrificial love literally becomes part of his body, protecting him from Voldemort. In contrast, Voldemort protects himself by making Horcruxes. In love, one entrusts part of one's soul to another, in a fashion: a friend shares another's joys and sorrows and acts for his good, even when sacrifice is required. Friendship strengthens the soul's integrity: friends become better people by acting for the other's good and building virtue. In short, loving makes us more fully human. But Voldemort entrusts his soul to objects, which cannot share his joys and sorrows or require anything of him. With the Horcruxes, Voldemort has eight "selves," but each division of his soul makes Voldemort less human.

Snape can act courageously not because his previous beliefs and emotions have been thoroughly purged, but because he deliberately chooses to act according to love—in the sense of doing what's best for the other. Here, Harry's and Snape's courage are similar because, for each, an act of the will is required to forgo what he wants and consciously choose self-sacrifice instead. Harry shows that love conquers death by freely sacrificing himself. Rather than simply reacting (even virtuously), Harry chooses consciously. Harry observes how much easier a death chosen in the moment—like throwing himself in front of a curse, as his parents did—would have been.[21] Similarly, Snape hasn't made his sacrifice for good in a single dramatic act.[22] He has consciously chosen for years the perilous balancing act of protecting Harry while masquerading as a Death Eater. This task is all the more difficult (and clearly an act of will) because Snape acts primarily for the love of Lily, not of Harry. He wills Harry's good for the mother's sake, but he acts to protect Harry nonetheless.

Finally, love is the key to Snape's redemption because it allows him to feel remorse, an emotion he shares with Harry but not with Voldemort. Evil acts damage the soul, but remorse can begin to knit it together, heal it, and make it whole. Snape's remorse does not in itself eradicate years of resentment; the difference is that he doesn't allow anger and hatred to decide his actions. Despite these feelings, he can choose to act for the good. These actions are a testament both to his love for Lily and to the substance of his redemption. Snape's love and remorse are manifest not primarily in his emotional states but in his ongoing acts of the will to pursue the good of another.

Harry shows remorse in forgiving Snape, purifying himself as well. Throughout the series, Snape and Harry wage a private battle, marked by guarded suspicion and outright loathing. After Sirius's death, Harry blames Snape for goading Sirius into rushing to the fight at the Ministry: "Snape had placed himself forever and irrevocably beyond the possibility of Harry's forgiveness by his attitude toward Sirius."[23] In the final scenes of *Deathly Hallows*, however, we see that Harry has forgiven Snape. Years later, Harry tells his middle child, "Albus Severus . . . you were named for two headmasters of Hogwarts. One of them was a Slytherin and he was probably the bravest man I ever knew."[24] Harry and Ginny name their children for people who fought Voldemort and chose to sacrifice their own good for that of others—James, Lily, Dumbledore, and Snape.

Love does not transform easily or immediately. But what we see in Severus Snape is that love can radically transform a life. Snape doesn't get the girl, but his deep love for Lily changes his beliefs and actions. This love motivates Snape to persevere in his dangerous and lonely role of double agent. Through love, Snape is capable of self-sacrifice, like Lily—and Harry.

NOTES

1. *Order of the Phoenix*, p. 833.

2. *Half-Blood Prince*, p. 615.

3. Ibid., p. 616.

4. It is also possible, of course, that Dumbledore attained "ironclad" proof of Snape's loyalty through Legilimency (perhaps with Snape's consent).

5. Aristotle, for example, devotes about a fifth of the *Nicomachean Ethics*, his great work on human happiness and fulfillment, to the topic of friendship.

6. *Deathly Hallows*, p. 697.

7. Aristotle states, "[T]hose who desire the good of their friends for the friends' sake are most truly friends, because each loves the other for what he is, and not for any incidental quality," *Nicomachean Ethics*, 1156b10. Thomas Aquinas cites Aristotle explicitly when he claims, "to love is to will the good of another," *Summa Theologica*, I–II, 26, 4 ad. In a similar vein, the late M. Scott Peck defines love as the "the will to extend one's self for the purpose of nurturing one's own or another's spiritual growth." See M. Scott Peck, *The Road Less Traveled: A New Psychology of Love, Traditional Values and Spiritual Growth* (New York: Simon & Schuster, 1978), p. 81.

8. Of course, not all of Snape's actions are good, judged either from an external or an internal criterion. From an external standpoint, Snape's killing of Dumbledore is not objectively good, but within the logic of the books, it seems to be presented as good in at least some sense, or at least permissible. Moreover, Snape's continued hostile action toward Sirius is clearly not good, nor is his bullying of students. But the argument is not that Snape becomes perfect through love, but that, overall, Snape eventually acts for the good of others.

9. *Order of the Phoenix*, p. 530.

10. Ibid., p. 531.

11. Ibid., p. 536.

12. *Deathly Hallows*, p. 663.

13. Ibid., p. 677.

14. Aristotle, *Nicomachean Ethics*, 1166a31.

15. *Symposium*, 206a, translated by Alexander Nehamas and Paul Woodruff, in *Plato: Complete Works*, edited by John M. Cooper (Indianapolis: Hackett, 1997).

16. *Symposium*, 206b. See also 208e and the following paragraphs. The general points about the nature of love cited earlier fit well with the portrayal of love in the Potter books. Lily Potter's mother-love is the central example of love in the series. Note, too, that Molly Weasley's duel with Bellatrix Lestrange, in which she fights expressly to protect her children (and the children of others), is given pride of place in the final battle, second only to Harry's duel with Voldemort.

17. *Deus Caritas Est*, paragraph 6. Benedict continues his Christian analysis of love, claiming that this self-gift offers both "authentic self-discovery and indeed the discovery of God: 'Whoever seeks to gain his life will lose it, but whoever loses his life will preserve it' (Luke 17:33)" (ibid.). Harry's sacrifice of his life at the end of *Deathly Hallows* appears to operate on this same principle.

18. Resigned, Dumbledore agrees: "I shall never reveal the best of you," *Deathly Hallows*, p. 679.

19. *Half-Blood Prince*, p. 160.

20. Ibid., p. 340.

21. The Christian allusions, especially in *Deathly Hallows*, are unmistakable, among them the hero who conquers death by sacrificing his life willingly to save others, the Scripture verses on the tombstones in Godric's Hollow, the affirmation of immortal souls, and the choice of King's Cross Station as Harry's between-worlds destination.

22. Despite insisting on secrecy about his role, Snape becomes enraged at Harry's accusation of cowardice, presumably because of the purpose and the on-going risk of his task.

23. *Half-Blood Prince*, p. 161.

24. *Deathly Hallows*, p. 758.

LOVE POTION NO. 9¾

Gregory Bassham

In the Muggle world people spend vast sums of money on perfumes, body sprays, cosmetics, jewelry, pheromones, body-sculpting, skimpy clothing, gym memberships, tanning salons, diet programs, and other means of increasing physical attractiveness and stirring romantic interest. In the wizarding world there are far more powerful and reliable attractants: magical love potions. Yet there are obvious ethical issues regarding the use of such potions, particularly the *nonconsensual* use, as occurs in two key episodes in the Harry Potter stories. So, what do magical love potions have to teach us about love, infatuation, and the ethical treatment of others? In particular, what can we learn from Merope Gaunt's use of a love potion to ensnare Tom Riddle Sr. (Voldemort's father), and her eventual decision to stop using the potion, at great cost to herself and her unborn son?

Violently Pink Products

Love potions not only make for fascinating thought experiments, they're also an important part of the Harry Potter plot.

In *Chamber of Secrets*, Professor Lockhart at one point jokingly encourages the students at Hogwarts to ask Professor Snape how to whip up a love potion, and in *Prisoner of Azkaban*, Mrs.Weasley tells her daughter, Ginny, and Hermione Granger about a love potion she made as a young girl.

But in *Half-Blood Prince*, we find several significant references to love potions. The first happens in Diagon Alley, at Weasleys' Wizard Wheezes, Fred and George's magic shop:

> Near the window was an array of violently pink products around which a cluster of excited girls was giggling enthusiastically. Hermione and Ginny both hung back, looking wary.
>
> "There you go," said Fred proudly. "Best range of love potions you'll find anywhere."
>
> Ginny raised an eyebrow skeptically. "Do they work?" she asked.
>
> "Certainly they work, for up to twenty-four hours at a time depending on the weight of the boy in question . . ."
>
> ". . . and the attractiveness of the girl," said George, reappearing suddenly at their side.[1]

So, in Harry's world, love potions are legal, apparently work only on males (although this isn't explicitly stated), vary in potency depending on the weight of the boy and the attractiveness of the girl, and work for only a limited time without a fresh dose.

The next appearance of love potions comes at Hogwarts, in the newly installed Professor Slughorn's Potions classroom, where Hermione's showing her stuff:

> "Now, this one here . . . yes, my dear?" said Slughorn, now looking slightly bemused, as Hermione's hand punched the air again.
>
> "It's Amortentia!"

"It is indeed. It seems almost foolish to ask," said Slughorn, who was looking mightily impressed, "but I assume you know what it does?"

"It's the most powerful love potion in the world!" said Hermione.

"Quite right! You recognized it, I suppose, by its distinctive mother-of-pearl sheen?"

"And the steam rising in characteristic spirals," said Hermione enthusiastically, "and it's supposed to smell differently to each of us, according to what attracts us, and I can smell freshly mown grass and new parchment and—"

But she turned slightly pink and did not complete the sentence.[2]

On the next page, Slughorn reveals more about this love potion:

"Amortentia doesn't really create *love*, of course. It is impossible to manufacture or imitate love. No, this will simply cause a powerful infatuation or obsession. It is probably the most dangerous and powerful potion in this room—oh yes," he said, nodding gravely at Malfoy and Nott, both of whom were smirking skeptically. "When you have seen as much of life as I have, you will not underestimate the power of obsessive love."[3]

Later in *Half-Blood Prince*, we learn just how dangerous and powerful a love potion can be, when Ron unwittingly eats a box of Chocolate Cauldrons spiked with love potion and becomes madly infatuated with Romilda Vane. From that episode, we discover that love potions act almost instantaneously; that they cause obsessive thoughts, intense excitement, and violent emotions; that they can strengthen over time; and that they can be cured by means of a simple antidote.

So, what kind of person would actually use a love potion? In our final snippet from *Half-Blood Prince*, we are introduced to one: Voldemort's mother.

Little Hangleton

Merope Gaunt, the local tramp's daughter, harbors a secret, burning passion for Tom Riddle, the wealthy squire's son. An unlikely pair, but Merope is a witch whose powers give her a chance to plot her escape from the desperate life she has led for eighteen years under the subjugation of her father and brother. "Can you not think of any measure Merope could have taken to make Tom Riddle forget his Muggle companion, and fall in love with her instead?"[4] Albus Dumbledore asks Harry. To which Harry offers two guesses: the Imperius Curse and a love potion.

The Imperius Curse, of course, is one of the three "unforgivable curses" in the magical world; it robs victims of their will and is, as a result, a prime example of how magic in Harry's world *can* but *must not* be used to manipulate and exploit others, especially the most vulnerable. Love potions, we've seen, aren't illegal in Harry's world. Perhaps they're not considered as dangerous as the Imperius Curse, because they don't last as long, produce only romantic feelings (as opposed to, say, homicidal intentions), and don't result in total control of the affected person. But it's instructive that Harry sees a particular effect and correctly narrows down the likely causes to either the Imperius Curse or a love potion, reminding us of Slughorn's sober warnings of the love potion's dangers.

After Harry's two guesses, Dumbledore continues,

"Very good. Personally, I am inclined to think that she used a love potion. I am sure it would have seemed more romantic to her, and I do not think it would have been very difficult, some hot day, when Riddle was riding alone, to persuade him to take a drink of water. In any case, within a few months . . . the village of Little Hangleton enjoyed a tremendous scandal. You can imagine the gossip it caused when the squire's son ran off with the tramp's daughter, Merope."[5]

Dumbledore continues by engaging in some guesswork:

"You see, within a few months of their runaway marriage, Tom Riddle reappeared at the manor house in Little Hangleton without his wife. The rumor flew around the neighborhood that he was talking of being 'hoodwinked' and 'taken in.' What he meant, I am sure, is that he had been under an enchantment that had now lifted, though I daresay he did not dare use those precise words for fear of being thought insane."[6]

After Harry asks why the love potion stopped working, Dumbledore adds,

"Again, this is guesswork . . . but I believe that Merope, who was deeply in love with her husband, could not bear to continue enslaving him by magical means. I believe that she made the choice to stop giving him the potion. Perhaps, besotted as she was, she had convinced herself that he would by now have fallen in love with her in return. Perhaps she thought he would stay for the baby's sake. If so, she was wrong on both counts. He left her, never saw her again, and never troubled to discover what became of his son."[7]

Harry then asks again whether it's important to know all of this about Voldemort's past, to which Dumbledore replies, "Very important, I think," and "It has everything to do with the prophecy." What does this love potion narrative add to the story, and what might it have to do with the prophecy about Harry's defeat of Voldemort?[8]

Real Love or Mere Infatuation?

So, here's a question: Did Merope Gaunt, Voldemort's mother, love Tom Riddle Sr.? She was certainly infatuated with him, attracted to him, willing to go to extraordinary lengths to have him. But did she love him?

Dumbledore says she did, but another possible answer is no, and here's the case for it: She didn't love him, or at least she didn't love him very deeply, *exactly because* she was willing to use a love potion on him. Presumably, a love potion, after all, robs a person of his free will. This is what makes love pills or potions an ideal thought experiment to elicit the recognition that real freedom requires more than doing what we want to do. Doing what we want to do may be necessary for freedom, but it's not sufficient; we must also have the *freedom to do otherwise*. Tom lacked such "libertarian" freedom.

Some philosophers, including Harry Frankfurt, deny that the ability to do otherwise is necessary for genuine freedom. This view especially appeals to those who think that everything we do is strictly determined by the laws of the physical universe or by the sovereign plan of God. They typically accept *compatibilism*: the idea that free will is consistent with strict determination of all of our actions and choices. Yet even compatibilists will likely deny that Tom Riddle Sr. freely loved Merope. Why? Because even if Tom was doing what he wanted by loving her, he wouldn't have wanted to love her as a result of a magical inducement.

How much *could* Merope have loved Tom if giving him the potion deprived him of his freedom? It wasn't that she loved him *too much*; she didn't love him *enough*, if at all. It was selfish of her. She wanted what was in *her* interests, not *his*. She may have felt amorous affection or entertained an unhealthy obsession for him, but clearly she did not feel the deep love that respects the true interests and considered preferences of the beloved.

Not only did she take away Riddle's freedom, enslaving him by the potion, she robbed him of the chance to grow in the "relationship," and I use that term loosely, for although love can be one-way, relationships by their nature are not. Merope didn't create a relationship that provided a context for Riddle to remain committed despite fluctuating feelings, to grow more in love as time goes on, to attain love's deeper reaches after the physical attraction and the initial excitement fade, or to become a better person as the rough edges of his personality get smoothed out in the mutual self-giving of a real and reciprocal loving relationship. No, she subjected him to magic that coerced his will into becoming obsessed with her. She could have treated him like dirt after that, and still he'd go on stupidly relishing and accepting whatever she dealt him, for that's the nature of the potion. This is surely a situation that invites abuse, but it's hardly a paradigm of love.

Incidentally, this shows us what's wrong with using a love potion even on oneself to develop feelings for another, a person we perhaps deem worthy of loving. We're inclined to think it's at least not as bad to use a potion on oneself as it is to administer it to another person, because the issue of free will doesn't arise in the same way. By choosing to take the potion, our free will is intact. This isn't obviously correct, but suppose we grant it. Still, there's the other issue of becoming a certain kind of person. Think how easy it would be to take the potion—rather than working hard in the relationship to remain committed despite challenges and to grow as a person through relational hardships. With all of the challenges removed, we would lose terrific opportunities to become better persons through the relationship.[9]

Not His Mother's Son

I could imagine that sort of story for Merope, and it's the direction I originally anticipated this chapter to go. It's no shock,

I had figured, that a character so thoroughly evil and despicable as Voldemort would hail from such troubled beginnings. It's not a stretch that a man who never loved would have come from a loveless union generated and sustained by magic alone. Nor would it be surprising that a character who from his earliest years harbored such fondness for cruelty and domination would have a mother willing to coerce the will of her mate and a father who would so callously neglect his child after the enchantment lifted.

This view of Merope and Voldemort seems to make a good deal of sense. Its only drawback, so far as I can see, is that it's wrong. Especially where Merope is concerned, the *contrast* between her and Voldemort is far more important than the *comparison*. Voldemort's problem is not that he's his mother's son, which in many ways he isn't. No, the problem is that Voldemort is more like his grandfather Marvolo Gaunt and his ancestor Salazar Slytherin. My point in excluding Merope from the list is that she illustrates how, in Harry's world, choices—not innate talent or biological ancestry or magical pedigree—most shape characters and destinies.

Merope is a character who ought to elicit from us compassion and no small amount of respect. What she did to win Riddle was wrong, and radically so, but good people sometimes do bad things. It's not the occasional misdeed that defines us but the habitual practice, the settled character, the persistent pattern of choices that put us on our life's trajectory. We are what we *consistently* do, as Aristotle put it. Her action was wrong, yes, but I'm not convinced she was very bad at all. To the contrary, she shows a remarkable character, all the more so in the face of all the obstacles she had to overcome and the temptations she had to resist. What matters is not merely where she ended up, but also the distance she had to travel to get there.

What matters is the ultimate trajectory her life took and not merely the projected track of her worst decisions.

Unfortunately, Voldemort, if anything, ended up following in the footsteps of where his mother *was* headed until she came to her senses. Whereas *she* eventually stopped going in the direction of the dark side, *he* embraced it wholeheartedly. The blood of Slytherin coursed through each of them, but their lives went in diametrically opposite directions. If nothing else, this illustrates, once more, the primacy of choice in Harry's world.

Critics have sometimes complained about the shortage of redeemed characters in the Potter books, but Merope is a prime example of one: a character whose background was as tragic as anyone's, whose capacity for misusing magic was as great as anyone's, whose temptations to engage in the Dark Arts were as strong as anyone's, yet whose life showed that not even a person like that is destined for darkness. And if even *she* wasn't, then *Voldemort* wasn't, for his upbringing was no more tragic than hers. If his destiny ended up beyond redemption, it was because his own choices, over time, forged a mutilated character from which there was no escape. Character may be destiny, but this makes more sense and is more just if character is the culmination of a truly free set of choices, rather than the inevitable outcome of "blood" or fate. This possibility of true freedom, of goods potentially but needlessly lost, imbues the Potter books with an element of tragedy that's often a feature of great literature.

Consider again Merope's tragic home life: physical, verbal, and emotional abuse; a condition of virtual domestic slavery; an absence of love and affirmation; an abundance of violence and meanness. None of this makes her ensnarement of Riddle right, but—and this is part of Rowling's nuanced moral analysis—it ought to soften our critical judgment of Merope, especially since, of her own volition, she eventually gave up using the potion. At the risk of losing the love of her life, her unborn child's father, and perhaps the first happiness she ever experienced, at the risk of rejection and terrible pain—pain that did in fact practically kill her with a broken heart—she did the right thing, choosing character over power, reality over appearance, forgiveness over resentment. And she chose love over hate, letting Riddle leave because that was his choice, despite her continued love for him, indeed, *because* of her love for him. And despite Riddle's abandonment of her, she still named her son after him, so gracious was her character, which reminds us of Dumbledore's eventual gracious response to Muggles, despite their cruel and devastating mistreatment of his sister. Voldemort, in contrast, chose to exact revenge for his father's abandonment by killing both his father and his grandparents and by rejecting his Muggle name and heritage.

The contemporary philosopher William Hasker offers an analysis of freedom quite relevant to Merope's predicament:

> All sorts of experiences and relationships acquire a special value because they involve love, trust, and affection that are freely bestowed. The love potions that appear in many fairy stories (and in the Harry Potter series) can become a trap; the one who has used the potion finds that he wants to be loved for his own sake and not because of the potion, yet fears the loss of the beloved's affection if the potion is no longer used.[10]

Merope came to a crossroads in her short, tragic life: through magic she could continue to manipulate Riddle, or she could stop, though at great personal cost. Merope did the right thing. She gave up using her magical powers altogether after Riddle left her, refusing to use them even to save her own life. It might have been grief that led to the loss of her powers, but Dumbledore is virtually certain that instead, she no longer *wanted* to be a witch. Perhaps she saw its potential for abuse, especially within herself, and she refused to indulge it anymore. She may have recognized within herself the call to the dark side, as it were, and realized that the best way to avoid it was by renouncing magic altogether, never again subjecting another to the sort of tyranny that she herself had been subjected to by her family. She had experienced firsthand what that led to and no longer wanted any part of it.

Certain behavior can skip a generation. The child of an alcoholic not uncommonly sees the ugliness of the addiction and reacts against it, perhaps by becoming a rigid teetotaler, and then *his* children react against *that*, and the pattern recurs. Merope so reacted against magic and its abuses and retained such potential for love that she was willing to suffer and be vulnerable. Exhibiting what Voldemort could only think of as weakness, she was willing to fall prey to what he considered the worst thing of all: death. Merope chose the death of her body, rather than the death of her character and her own pain before the domination of another. Her love for Riddle had made her vulnerable to hurt and rejection, as all love does, and her aversion to hurting others the way she herself had been hurt contributed to her premature death. Not surprisingly, given her horrible upbringing, she lacked some of the good qualities that Harry's mother had. But nonetheless, Merope did all that she could to battle the forces of unforgiving fate to break free from the pattern of magical manipulation and coercion.[11]

In this sense, Voldemort is radically unlike his mother, who, despite her tragic history, still retained tenderness of heart and the capacity for love, whereas Voldemort never loved another, never even had a genuine friend or wanted one. And this wasn't because of his tragic beginnings and certainly not because of his mother's moral failing but, among other reasons, because he rejected the pain, vulnerability, and weakness that caring for another as much as for himself inevitably involves. He wanted to be untouchable, and he got his wish, losing his very humanity in the process.

Remember that Dumbledore said that he wasn't as concerned about the young Voldemort's ability to speak to snakes as he was about his obvious instincts for cruelty, secrecy, and domination. Voldemort's abilities didn't define him; his choices did, and sowing his choices reaped a character and a destiny of darkness.[12] He might have chosen not to love in order to avoid dependency or weakness, but his habitual unwillingness to open his heart to another led to the loss of his capacity to do it altogether.[13] What we see in Voldemort is a picture of where the definitive choice of evil and the rejection of love lead: a character in love only with himself but who ends up harming and fragmenting himself in irremediable ways.

Tragically, Voldemort learned from the *worst* his mother did, rather than from the *best*, hating what he should have loved, and imitating with reckless abandon what she herself rejected. All of this, of course, only bolsters the contrast between Voldemort and Harry. So much of what distinguishes Harry from Voldemort is that Harry, despite his troubled past and tragic life, never loses his ability to love. He doesn't harden his heart and start to care only about himself. He doesn't cut himself off from others. Far more than Voldemort, he remains his mother's son—the mother whose courage and sacrificial love keep Harry safe from the worst Voldemort can dish out.[14] Her love unleashes a more ancient and powerful magic than any potion can hope to imitate or Voldemort can hope to defeat or even understand.[15]

NOTES

1. *Half-Blood Prince*, pp. 120–121.

2. Ibid., p. 185.

3. Ibid., p. 186. One wonders why, in Harry's world, love potions remain legal if they're so dangerous and potentially manipulative. They aren't allowed at Hogwarts, but they can be lawfully bought, sold, and used, apparently even by the underaged. This is an example (one of many) of how dangerous things are permitted in the wizarding world that would never be allowed in our own. (Of course, wizards might well say the same about our dangerous firearms, automobiles, and nuclear weapons.)

4. Ibid., p. 213.

5. Ibid.

6. Ibid., p. 214.

7. Ibid.

8. In *The Tales of Beedle the Bard* (New York: Scholastic, 2008), pp. 56–57, Dumbledore's commentary on "The Warlock's Hairy Heart" includes this reference to love potions:

> [The tale] addresses one of the greatest, and least acknowledged, temptations of magic: the quest for invulnerability. . . . To hurt is as human as to breathe. Nevertheless, we wizards seem particularly prone to the idea that we can bend the nature of existence to our will. . . . Of course, the centuries-old trade in love potions shows that our fictional wizard is hardly alone in seeking to control the unpredictable course of love. The search for a true love potion continues to this day, but no such elixir has yet been created, and leading potioneers doubt that it is possible.

Dumbledore even adds this footnote: "Hector Dagworth-Granger, founder of the Most Extraordinary Society of Potioneers, explains: 'Powerful infatuations can be induced by the skillful potioneer, but never yet has anyone managed to create the truly unbreakable, eternal, unconditional attachment that alone can be called Love.'"

9. Here's an analogy: Sometimes people need medication to deal with psychological struggles. But imagine a case in which a depressed patient has a chance to become medicated to deal with the problem, when what he really needs is to work through issues of anger or resentment. How tempting it would be for such a patient simply to pop a pill, rather than to deal with the underlying causes. The pill would certainly be easier, but it wouldn't offer the real solution required. It would deal only with the symptoms, not with the real cause. Pulling out weeds at their roots may be harder than simply spraying them to make them temporarily go away, but, ultimately, it's more effective and enduring.

10. William Hasker, *The Triumph of God over Evil: Theodicy for a World of Suffering* (Downers Grove, IL: InterVarsity Press, 2008), p. 156. Hasker continues, "For that matter, individuals without free will would not, in the true sense, be human beings at all; at least this is the case if, as seems highly plausible, the capacity for free choice is an essential characteristic of human beings as such. If so, then to say that free will should not exist is to say that we humans should not exist. It may be possible to say that, and perhaps even to mean it, but the cost of doing so is very high." Ibid.

11. Merope, Dumbledore says, gave up, leaving her child behind. Surely, it would have been better had she not given up but rather persevered, at least for the child's sake. Perhaps Voldemort wouldn't have emerged if she had. Although this is true, Merope's giving up was likely not enough in Rowling's universe to ensure that Voldemort would emerge. Presumably, he had a choice in the matter and could have chosen a different path, despite the loss of his mother. So even if Merope's death was a contributing factor, it was only one among others. The nature of how Merope gave up is also an interesting question. If she committed suicide, for example, then my speculative argument in this chapter for her redemption, admittedly a redemption only partial and imperfect, would be undermined. But she may have simply been tired, having lost the will to live; she may have done the best she could. And in contrast to Voldemort's doing all in his power to avoid death, Merope's willingness to accept it seems practically virtuous. She's not responsible for doing more than the best she could, and it does good to remember that Dumbledore himself says not to judge her too harshly.

12. For more on this theme, see my chapter on abilities versus choices in this volume, "Choices vs. Abilities: Dumbledore on Self-Understanding."

13. It's a function of literature, the philosopher Noël Carroll reminds us, to magnify and thereby clarify the patterns that shape human affairs in order that we may discern such regularities when they appear less diagrammatically in the flesh. See Noël Carroll, "*Vertigo* and the Pathologies of Romantic Love," in *Hitchcock and Philosophy: Dial M for Metaphysics*, edited by David Baggett and William Drumin (Chicago: Open Court, 2007), p. 112.

14. In the final book, Snape casts Harry in negative terms, concluding, "He is his father over again." To which Dumbledore replies, "In looks, perhaps, but his deepest nature is much more like his mother's," *Deathly Hallows*, p. 684.

15. Thanks to Mark Foreman, Laura Jones, Noah Levin, and especially Dave Baggett for their insightful comments on an earlier draft.

HARRY POTTER, RADICAL FEMINISM, AND THE POWER OF LOVE

Anne Collins Smith

Love is a force in the Potter universe that crosses hierarchical boundaries and defeats the powerful. And, curiously, love is most efficacious in combating evil in J. K. Rowling's world when it makes no attempt to compete at all. Self-sacrifice and kindness bring unexpected rewards; love and compassion overwhelm greed and ambition, overcoming them without attempting to defeat them. In other words, Rowling's world resonates with the values of radical feminism. Perhaps that sounds strange. So, to demystify this claim, we'll begin with a survey of contemporary feminist scholarship on Harry Potter en route to an understanding of radical feminism, culminating in an examination of the role of love in the Potter books.

The Feminist Debate So Far

Feminist commentators are divided on Rowling's series. Two general schools of interpretation prevail: those who consider the series sexist, and those who consider it progressive.

Some writers, such as Christine Schoefer, Elizabeth Heilman, and Eliza Dresang, have argued that the Potter books perpetuate traditional gender stereotypes and reinforce negative gender portrayals in the minds of young readers.[1] Ximena Gallardo-C. and C. Jason Smith, in their joint article "Cinderfella," offer a startling and exciting feminist interpretation of the motifs and symbolism in the series, but they, too, claim that the books are sexist, at least on the surface.[2]

Others writers, for example, Edmund Kern, Mimi Gladstein, and Sarah Zettel, have claimed that Rowling provides a balanced view of the sexes that includes strong female characters and an egalitarian magical society.[3] They argue that the books are not sexist and indeed offer good role models for young readers.

Although these two schools of interpretation are generally opposed, they are not completely black-and-white. Dresang, for example, offers a highly nuanced perspective on Hermione Granger's capacity for self-determination even within a society that Dresang considers patriarchal; Kern willingly admits that the books are slanted toward male characters, even as he disputes the fairness of some accusations of sexism.

This dispute between the two schools of interpretation primarily focuses on the portrayal of female characters in the series. In "Harry Potter's Girl Trouble," Christine Schoefer observes that there are no female characters in the series who approach the level of the male characters: "No girl is brilliantly heroic the way Harry is, no woman is experienced and wise like Professor Dumbledore."[4] Elizabeth Heilman argues that the books "replicate some of the most demeaning, yet familiar, culture stereotypes for both males and females."[5] Gallardo-C. and Smith claim that "the Harry Potter books resonate with gender stereotypes of the worst sort."[6]

In response, Kern, Zettel, and Gladstein offer eloquent pleas for the importance of context. They acknowledge the existence of female characters who display negative traits traditionally associated with feminine stereotypes, but they also observe that there are numerous parallel depictions of male characters who display negative masculine traits. Kern observes, for example, that "the 'silliness' of Lavender and Parvati mirrors the juvenile antics of Dean and Seamus," and that Hermione's accident with the Polyjuice Potion should be read in parallel to Ron's accident with the slug-eating spell.[7] Zettel points out that "Madam Pince the librarian goes irrational when she thinks a student has written in a book. But then, Filch the caretaker wants the students whipped and chained for littering."[8] Gladstein juxtaposes "incompetent Trelawney" with "fake Gilderoy Lockhart."[9] Expanding on their point by referring to characters not available to some earlier commentators, these authors also point to villains such as Dolores Umbridge and Bellatrix Lestrange, who command as much fear and respect as any of the male Death Eaters.

Among the various negative feminine stereotypes, the act of giggling is a lightning rod for feminist commentary. Dresang comments that "[t]he pervasive description of girls as silly, giggling, and light-headed undermines [Rowling's] more gender-balanced depiction of girls' opportunities in the patriarchal hierarchy."[10] Heilman states that this giggling undermines the sportsmanship of the girls who play Quidditch: "Even as sports team members, the girls exhibit girlish behavior by giggling at the possibility of playing with the handsome new captain and seeker, Cedric Diggory. . . . Quidditch is not the only context for giggling. The second two books are littered with references to giggling girls."[11] Zettel acknowledges such criticisms and offers a pointed comeback:

> Critics deride the girls at Hogwarts because they are shown to giggle and shriek and generally make a lot of noise. Some real live girls do giggle and shriek. Some are quiet and serious. Some like pink and ruffles.

Some like athletics and blue jeans. We see them all at Hogwarts. *I reject the notion that we must tell girls that the only way to be valid human beings is to turn themselves into boys.*[12]

Radical vs. Liberal Feminism

Although Zettel does not identify herself as a radical feminist, her response to these critics highlights a major point of disagreement between liberal and radical feminism. Liberal feminism, historically grounded in the writings of Mary Wollstonecraft (1759–1797), Harriet Taylor Mill (1807–1858), and John Stuart Mill (1806–1873), holds the once-controversial view that women are people—that is, intelligent, autonomous beings—and should be treated as such. Sometimes characterized as "first-wave feminism," the feminism of the eighteenth and nineteenth centuries drew inspiration from Enlightenment philosophers, emphasizing individual rights and responsibilities and arguing that these should be applied to women as well as to men.[13]

The liberal-feminist view that women are people may seem entirely reasonable but in actuality is surprisingly problematic. There's an inherent assumption in liberal feminism that "people" is a gender-neutral term, but in fact our concept of what "people" means has been shaped by a society whose intellectual life has long been dominated by men. Moreover, while liberal feminism is optimistic in its belief that women, given equal opportunity, will achieve equal status with men socially, politically, and economically, it overlooks the possibility that women may have interests, strengths, and abilities different from those of men, which may lead women to prefer different measures of success.

There are examples of liberal feminism among both the supporters and the detractors of the Potter series. Gladstein, a supporter of the series, praises Professor McGonagall, who has succeeded in rising to a powerful position within the Hogwarts hierarchy; she also speaks in support of Hermione, whose logical acumen and love of learning fall into a traditionally masculine pattern of rationality and inquiry. These characters have succeeded on masculine terms, and their successes are rightly praised. Characters who have achieved different sorts of success, however, may not receive their full due within the context of liberal feminism. Gladstein, for example, highlights Molly Weasley's "active and assertive" participation in the Order of the Phoenix in the later books but only briefly mentions her earlier role as a mother.[14]

We can also see a tendency toward liberal feminism in some of those who take a more negative view of the series. Heilman, for example, comments on Rowling's tendency to depict girl students in groups: "This repeated grouping . . . reinforces the idea of the sociological construct of the communal and friendly girl compared to the individual and competitive boy." She claims that this reinforces "the inferior position of females," which suggests that she considers being communal rather than individual, friendly rather than competitive, as an indication of actual or perceived inferiority.[15]

This tendency of liberal feminism to downplay roles and traits traditionally associated with women is part of the reason that a different form of feminism, radical feminism, evolved as part of the "second wave" of feminism in the 1960s and the 1970s. Radical feminism takes its name from the Latin word *radix*, meaning "root," and holds that the root cause of women's oppression is the "sex/gender system," a set of social expectations that force identities onto people in such a way that a person's physical sexual identification necessarily determines that person's personality, permissible social roles, and acceptable economic occupations. In a patriarchal society, these expectations will tend to privilege men and disempower women.[16] For example, in the United States within living memory, women used to be shunted into a handful of acceptable "pink-collar" jobs such as nurses, secretaries, and schoolteachers.

Although radical feminists disagree on exactly how to fix the problem, they often focus on the characteristics that are traditionally labeled masculine or feminine by society and consider ways in which these characteristics can be freed from rigid categorizations, such as the following contrasted pairs:

Traits Traditionally Considered Masculine	Traits Traditionally Considered Feminine
control	love
independence	interdependence
individualism	community
hierarchy	networking
domination	sharing
competition	cooperation
aggression	compassion
reason	emotion

Some radical feminists feel that our society would benefit from people in general becoming more androgynous, so that men and women could freely mix and match whatever characteristics appeal most to them individually. In this way, both men and women would become "people," but our understanding of what people are would no longer be limited to the guidelines laid down by a male-dominated society. Other radical feminists feel that the values traditionally considered feminine would benefit our society most and should be adopted by men and women alike, thus shifting the definition of "people" to a more feminine-centric model.[17]

Some scholarly commentaries on the Potter series exemplify radical feminism. For example, Zettel emphasizes the importance of Molly Weasley's household management, pointing out that "she's successfully raising seven kids on a tight budget. Honestly, the woman should get a medal."[18] In a more serious vein, Zettel argues that for "an author to show that only traditional male power and place matter is to discount and belittle the hard and complex lives of our peers and our ancestresses."[19] Zettel's willingness to praise female characters who have succeeded on terms other than traditional masculine ones would be welcomed by radical feminists.

Another article that offers a radical-feminist perspective on the Potter series is Gallardo-C. and Smith's "Cinderfella." Although these authors criticize the gender stereotypes present on the surface of the series, they move to a deeper level to present a radical-feminist interpretation of the good and evil sides of the conflict. The evil characters, they point out, display "phallic power and ambition" and are "aggressive and power-hungry."[20] This would apply even to female characters such as Umbridge, who, despite her stereotypically feminine taste in clothing and office decoration, demonstrates an ongoing obsession with traditionally masculine values such as control, hierarchy, and structure in her takeover of Hogwarts in *Order of the Phoenix* and in her creation of her own bureaucracy to persecute Muggle-born magic users in *Deathly Hallows*. On the other hand, Harry's own choices and decisions "belie a preference for the feminine," and his compatriots exhibit traditionally feminine characteristics such as "kindness, selflessness, a desire for intimacy with others, and responsibility."[21] In this way, these authors argue that Rowling associates good with values traditionally considered feminine and evil with values traditionally considered masculine.

This association of good with qualities such as love and compassion is something radical feminists have in common with earlier philosophers and theologians, who also felt that such traits needed to be integrated into our understanding and practice of humanity. From St. Gertrude the Great's emphasis on loving-kindness as an essential feature of God's nature and a crucial one for humans to imitate, to Gandhi's campaign of nonviolent civil disobedience in which he proclaimed that "life without love is death," to C. S. Lewis's careful analysis of each of the various types of love as necessary for the fulfillment of humanity, many thinkers have emphasized the importance of traits such as love, kindness, and compassion.[22]

Radical feminists argue not only that these traits have been traditionally assigned to women, rather than valued by society as a whole, but that this has been done in a particularly harmful way. Women are encouraged to be so altruistic that they don't stand up for themselves, and they submit meekly to traditional forms of oppression for fear that any attempt at assertiveness will be seen as a lack of femininity.[23] Meanwhile, men are damaged as well, because living up to a macho ideal that emphasizes competition and independence is a stressful and incomplete way to be human. As Heather Booth, Evi Goldfield, and Sue Munaker wrote, "As long as artificially constructed, mythically based images of masculine and feminine are the only alternative, both men and women are going to find conflict between their imposed sexual identity and their goals as human beings."[24]

More Wonderful and More Terrible than Death

As mentioned at the outset, love, traditionally identified as a feminine characteristic, occupies a position of particular importance in Rowling's universe, and her depiction of it resonates with radical feminism. Again and again, we see Harry's capacity to love and be loved protect him from evil and enable him to protect others.

We learn about the importance of love in the first book, when the love imprinted on Harry's skin by his mother's sacrifice saves Harry's life. Professor Quirrell, whose body Lord Voldemort inhabits, finds that he cannot bear to touch Harry because of the invisible mark left by the love of Harry's mother. This is the first example in the series in which we see that love resists evil effortlessly, without deliberate action on Harry's part. We then learn from Dumbledore that this same love saved Harry from Voldemort's earlier attempt to kill him in infancy. Love is not wielded as a weapon; it simply overwhelms evil by its very existence.[25]

This love, however, is extrinsic to Harry's own nature. In *Sorcerer's Stone*, he is saved by his mother's love for him, not by his own love for others. It is significant that this love is literally in his skin, on the outside, rather than, say, in his heart, on the inside. As the books progress, however, we see Harry's intrinsic ability to love others become more and more important.

In *Prisoner of Azkaban*, Harry saves the life of Peter Pettigrew, not out of love for the traitor who betrayed Harry's parents, but out of love for Remus Lupin and Sirius Black. Harry does not want his father's friends to become murderers; he cares more about them than about his own desire for vengeance. The consequences of this deeply unselfish action are multiple; ultimately, Pettigrew's debt to Harry saves Harry's life, although that was not Harry's motivation for saving him.

In the later books, Rowling continues to emphasize Harry's love for others. In *Order of the Phoenix*, near the end of the confrontation at the Ministry of Magic, Harry is briefly possessed by Voldemort. Harry is not strong enough to repel Voldemort, and he resigns himself to the possibility of death. The thought enters his mind that death would reunite him with his beloved godfather: "*And I'll see Sirius again.* And as Harry's heart filled with emotion, the creature's coils loosened, the pain was gone."[26] Harry does not deliberately set his love for Sirius against Voldemort's will; had he done so, love would take its place as another weapon in the arsenal of masculine competition. Instead, Voldemort simply cannot bear to be in its presence; once again, love overwhelms evil without effort.

In explaining the incident in the Ministry of Magic, Dumbledore describes "a force that is at once more wonderful and more terrible than death, than human intelligence, than forces of nature. . . . It is the power . . . that you possess in such quantities and which Voldemort has not at all. That power . . . saved you from possession by Voldemort, because he could not bear to reside in a body so full of the force he detests."[27] This power, of course, is love. As Dumbledore explains, "In the end, it mattered not that you could not close your mind. It was your heart that saved you."[28] Dumbledore's explanation demonstrates a preference for traditionally feminine characteristics over traditionally masculine ones, because reason, the power of the mind, is traditionally identified as masculine, while emotion, the power of the heart, is traditionally considered feminine.

In *Half-Blood Prince*, Dumbledore states that love is the "power the Dark Lord knows not" that is mentioned in the prophecy about Voldemort and his self-chosen enemy.[29] Dumbledore further explains that this power is what kept Harry from succumbing to the temptations of the Dark Arts and from yielding to the more ordinary temptations of using his magical abilities to obtain selfish goals such as wealth or immortality. He is forced to explain these things to Harry because Harry does not realize them; again, love has not functioned as a conscious barrier that Harry has deliberately raised in order to fight against these temptations, but as a quality within himself that keeps him from even being tempted in the first place.

Love achieves even greater importance in the final volume, *Deathly Hallows*, functioning at multiple levels in different parts of the book. Harry's ability to love unselfishly is not confined to humans but extends to loving other beings as well, which bears unexpected benefits. Remembering Dumbledore's critical remarks in *Order of the Phoenix* about Sirius's neglectful treatment of the house-elf Kreacher, moved by Kreacher's story of his dreadful journey with Regulus Black to replace the Horcrux locket with a replica, and stirred by Hermione's sympathetic explanation of Kreacher's psychology, Harry begins to treat Kreacher with kindness. As a result, Kreacher eagerly assists Harry in locating the real locket by tracking down the thief, Mundungus Fletcher, who is able to tell Harry its where-abouts. Harry's respectful treatment of the goblin Griphook also makes possible the recovery of an object that can be used to destroy Horcruxes, the Sword of Gryffindor. And, of course, Harry's constant kindness toward Dobby is rewarded when Dobby saves Harry's life at the cost of his own.

Harry's most surprising act of love, however, is his attempt to redeem Voldemort himself. Harry's plea to Voldemort to feel remorse, with the recognition that this would enable him to heal and reunite the surviving fragments of his shattered soul, is an astonishing act of compassion that shocks Voldemort "beyond any revelation or taunt."[30] "'It's your one last chance,' said Harry, 'it's all you've got left. . . . I've seen what you'll be otherwise . . . be a man . . . try . . . try for some remorse.'"[31] Of course, Voldemort does not recognize Harry's appeal as an act of compassion. A hypermasculine figure obsessed with domination and control, he fails to understand the genuine power of traditionally feminine values, a flaw that has already caused him to overlook the capabilities of house-elves and the true motivation of his supposed ally Severus Snape.

Harry's choice of words here reveals a remarkable aspect of Rowling's worldview. When Harry urges Voldemort to "be a man," he is implicitly claiming that Voldemort's actions to date have *not* demonstrated manhood, that Voldemort's hypermasculinity is not in fact true manhood at all. Instead, Harry's understanding of manhood is one that is fully human, incorporating traditionally feminine traits as well as tradi-tionally masculine ones. As Terri Doughty wrote in her essay comparing the Potter series to other contemporary books aimed at adolescent males, "The Harry Potter books do not problematize masculinity."[32] In contrast to the protagonists of contemporary books that depict young men struggling with little guidance toward a violent and alienated adulthood, Harry has a number of positive adult male role models, such as Dumbledore, Rubeus Hagrid, and Lupin, who do not hesitate to express traits such as reassurance or sympathy, and who are able to assure Harry "that he is growing into the right sort of boy."[33] In the Potter books, the right sort of boy, indeed, the right sort of man, is not only strong and brave, but kind and loving as well.

Less surprising than Harry's attempt to redeem Voldemort is his willingness to yield his own life to protect the ones he loves. The outcome of this act, however, is also surprising to Voldemort; Harry is not, in fact, killed, and his act of sacrifice offers magical protection to his compatriots. Meanwhile, Harry's mastery of the Elder Wand contrasts sharply with the attempts by other wizards to obtain it; he never sets out deliberately to acquire it, and he does not intend to use it for destructive purposes. The only spell he casts in the final showdown is defensive. Harry does not engage in a "duel to the death" with Voldemort. The fact that he is successful without attempting to compete shows again that in this series, love is more important than aggression.

The Triumph of Love

In Rowling's world, love does not enter into combat, which would mean that it was participating in and implicitly promoting the masculine structure. From a radical-feminist perspective, when love overcomes hatred, it does so without deigning to enter into any sort of contest, but simply and naturally overwhelms evil by its very presence. Although the successes of Hermione and McGonagall may mark the presence of liberal feminism in Rowling's creation, the ultimate triumph of love and compassion over selfishness and ambition clearly provides an overarching worldview that is more in line with radical feminism.

NOTES

1. Christine Schoefer, "Harry Potter's Girl Trouble," on Salon.com, January 12, 2000, http://archive.salon.com/books/feature/2000/01/13/potter/index.html; Elizabeth E. Heilman, "Blue Wizards and Pink Witches: Representations of Gender Identity and Power," in *Critical Perspectives on Harry Potter*, edited by Elizabeth E. Heilman (New York: Routledge, 2003), pp. 221–239; Eliza T. Dresang, "Hermione Granger and the Heritage of Gender," in *The Ivory Tower and Harry Potter*, edited by Lana Whited (Columbia: University of Missouri Press, 2002), pp. 211–242.

2. Ximena Gallardo-C. and C. Jason Smith, "Cinderfella: J. K. Rowling's Wily Web of Gender," in *Reading Harry Potter: Critical Essays*, edited by Giselle Liza Anatol (Westport, CT: Praeger, 2003), pp. 191–203.

3. Edmund M. Kern, *The Wisdom of Harry Potter: What Our Favorite Hero Teaches Us about Moral Choices* (Amherst, NY: Prometheus Books, 2003); Mimi R. Gladstein, "Feminism and Equal Opportunity: Hermione and the Women of Hogwarts," in *Harry Potter and Philosophy: If Aristotle Ran Hogwarts*, edited by David Baggett and Shawn E. Klein (Chicago: Open Court, 2004), pp. 49–59; Sarah Zettel, "Hermione Granger and the Charge of Sexism," in *Mapping the World of the Sorcerer's Apprentice*, edited by Mercedes Lackey and Leah Wilson (Dallas: Benbella Books, 2005), pp. 83–99.

4. Schoefer, "Harry Potter's Girl Trouble," p. 1.

5. Heilman, "Blue Wizards and Pink Witches," p. 222.

6. Gallardo-C. and Smith, "Cinderfella: J. K. Rowling's Wily Web of Gender," p. 191.

7. Kern, *The Wisdom of Harry Potter*, p. 149.

8. Zettel, "Hermione Granger and the Charge of Sexism," p. 99.

9. Gladstein, "Feminism and Equal Opportunity: Hermione and the Women of Hogwarts," p. 59.

10. Dresang, "Hermione Granger and the Heritage of Gender," p. 237.

11. Heilman, "Blue Wizards and Pink Witches," p. 226.

12. Zettel, "Hermione Granger and the Charge of Sexism," p. 98 (emphasis added).

13. Sondra Farganis, *Situating Feminism: From Thought to Action*, volume 2 in the series *Contemporary Social Theory* (Thousand Oaks, CA: SAGE, 1994).

14. Gladstein, "Feminism and Equal Opportunity: Hermione and the Women of Hogwarts," p. 58.

15. Heilman, "Blue Wizards and Pink Witches," p. 228.

16. Rosemarie Putnam Tong, *Feminist Thought: A More Comprehensive Introduction*, 3rd ed. (Boulder, CO: Westview Press, 2009), p. 51.

17. Ibid., p. 54ff.

18. Zettel, "Hermione Granger and the Charge of Sexism," p. 90.

19. Ibid., pp. 91–92.

20. Gallardo-C. and Smith, "Cinderfella," p. 200.

21. Ibid., pp. 199, 200.

22. Gertrude of Helfta, *The Herald of Divine Love* (*Legatus Divinae Pietatis*), translated and edited by Margaret Winkworth (New York: Paulist Press, 1993); M. K. Gandhi, *The Way to God* (Berkeley, CA: Berkeley Hills Books, 1999), p. 56; C. S. Lewis, *The Four Loves* (New York: Harcourt Brace Jovanovich, 1960).

23. For a surprisingly recent example, see Shankar Vedantam's eye-opening article about research showing that contemporary working women are reluctant to ask for raises: "Salary, Gender and the Social Cost of Haggling," *Washington Post*, July 30, 2007, p. A07.

24. Heather Booth, Evi Goldfield, and Sue Munaker, "Toward a Radical Movement," in *Radical Feminism: A Documentary Reader*, edited by Barbara A. Crow (New York: New York University Press, 2000), p. 60.

25. This notion of achieving effects without striving, through "nonaction," is reminiscent of the Taoist concept of *wu-wei*.

26. *Order of the Phoenix*, p. 816.

27. Ibid., p. 842.

28. Ibid., p. 844.

29. *Half-Blood Prince*, p. 509.

30. *Deathly Hallows*, p. 741.

31. Ibid., p. 741; the ellipses are Rowling's.

32. Terri Doughty, "Locating Harry Potter in the 'Boys' Book' Market," in *The Ivory Tower and Harry Potter*, edited by Lana Whited (Columbia: University of Missouri Press, 2002), p. 253.

33. Ibid., pp. 253–254.

PART THREE

POTTERWATCH:
FREEDOM AND POLITICS

PATRIOTISM, HOUSE LOYALTY, AND THE OBLIGATIONS OF BELONGING

Andrew P. Mills

When you enter Hogwarts in your first year, the Sorting Hat assigns you to one of four "Houses": Gryffindor, Slytherin, Hufflepuff, or Ravenclaw. Each House has its own colors, mascots, and traditions, and the Houses form the social structure of the school. House members live together, eat together, take classes together, and compete together—on and off the Quidditch field—to win honor and glory for their Houses.

Being in a House at Hogwarts affects the way you treat other people. After all, we think that as a good Gryffindor, Hermione Granger should support the Gryffindor Quidditch team, help Gryffindor earn points toward the House Cup by doing well in class (and by helping Ron Weasley and Harry with their homework), and in other ways give preferential treatment to the other Gryffindors. Indeed, if Hermione were not to care about the welfare of her fellow Gryffindors, or if she weren't upset when she cost the House points, we'd count that as a moral failing of hers. And worse, if she were to help Vincent Crabbe and Gregory Goyle—members of Slytherin— with *their* homework or were to sabotage Harry's Nimbus 2000 so that Hufflepuff would win that week's Quidditch match, Hermione would rightly be accused of betraying her House and of being a disloyal and unpatriotic Gryffindor. One of the many things we admire about Hermione, Ron, and especially Harry is that they are loyal and dedicated to one another and to their friends. That they are "patriotic Gryffindors" is one of their virtues.

But is patriotism of this sort really a virtue? Many of us think that it is. What else would explain why we demand that our political leaders be patriotic, why we raise our children to love their homeland, and why we admire soldiers who risk their lives in service to their country? Yet in spite of this, there are some powerful arguments that claim that patriotism is a *vice*—that if we're in favor of patriotism, we're similar in important ways to Voldemort and the Death Eaters. So, which is it? Is patriotism a virtue? A vice? Or does it depend on the circumstances?

The Dangers of Patriotism

Those who consider patriotism a virtue may be thinking that to lack patriotism is to be selfish. Patriotism, as the U.S. politician and presidential candidate Adlai Stevenson (1900–1965) once wrote, "means putting country before self."[1] A patriot might risk her life to defend her country and thus sacrifice her personal interests so that her nation might prosper. That a patriot should put her country's interests ahead of her own is admirable, but what should her attitude be toward the interests of *other* countries? Here, too, it seems the patriot should give preference to her own country's interests. Being a patriotic Gryffindor means that Hermione should sacrifice some of her free time to help Ron and Harry with their homework (so that the House won't lose any more points!), but it also means that Hermione should put the interests of Gryffindor ahead of the interests of the other Houses. Similarly, being a patriotic American means preferring America's well-being over the well-being of all other countries—thus, the injunction to "buy American" and so support the U.S. economy. But it's just this aspect of giving preference to our own country over all others that causes the problems and makes patriotism look like a vice.

The Russian author Leo Tolstoy (1828–1910) called patriotism "the desire for the exclusive good of one's own nation" and thought it was this very desire that produced war.[2] Emma Goldman (1869–1940), a Lithuanian-born social activist who spent much of her life working and writing in America, felt similarly. She wrote,

> [C]onceit, arrogance, and egotism are the essentials of patriotism. . . . Patriotism assumes that our globe is divided into little spots, each one surrounded by an iron gate. Those who have had the fortune of being born on some particular spot, consider themselves better, nobler, grander, more intelligent than the living beings inhabiting any other spot. It is, therefore, the duty of everyone on that chosen spot to fight, kill, and die in the attempt to impose his superiority upon all the others.[3]

Patriotism thus seems to involve, if Tolstoy and Goldman are right, a Voldemort-like sense of superiority: our nation is the best, the citizens of our nation are better than the citizens of other nations, and those other nations must serve our interests by giving us resources we need or behaving in the ways we want them to behave—and if they won't do it voluntarily, we'll force them to do so at the tip of a wand. Or at the barrel of a gun.

Death Eaters and Discrimination

We can appreciate this criticism of patriotism even more by thinking about the Death Eaters. Those in league with Voldemort believe that some wizards—"purebloods," they call them—are morally more worthy than other wizards (whom they derisively call "Mudbloods"), and that Muggles barely register on the moral radar. But any such view, which counts some subset of the population as morally superior to the rest, runs counter to a long tradition in ethics according to which acting morally means treating everyone—man or woman, black or white, Christian or Muslim, Muggle or wizard—as having equal moral worth.

Utilitarians such as the English philosophers Jeremy Bentham (1748–1832) and John Stuart Mill (1806–1873) have some basic disagreements with the German philosopher Immanuel Kant (1724–1804) concerning the nature of ethics. Both camps, however, agree that a fundamental principle of morality is that all people are of equal moral worth. Utilitarians hold that actions are to be judged according to their effects on the sentient creatures (creatures who can feel pleasure and pain) who are affected by them. And all such creatures count equally. "Each to count for one, and none for more than one," as Bentham famously put it. The Minister of Magic's pain or pleasure is no more important than that felt by the lowliest house-elf or the ugliest Blast-Ended Skrewt.

Although Kant disagreed with the utilitarians over what it takes for a being to count morally (mere sentience wasn't enough for him), he did agree that everyone who matters morally matters equally. To act morally, you must, Kant said, "act in such a way that you always treat humanity, whether in your own person or in the person of any other, never simply as a means, but always at the same time as an end."[4] *All* people must be treated as beings whose life projects—their "ends"—are equally valuable, and no one should be used merely to serve the ends of someone else. Harry's allies know this: in the dark days described in *Deathly Hallows*, the hosts of the underground radio program *Potterwatch* remind their listeners to save their Muggle neighbors from Death Eater attacks, on the grounds that "[e]very human life is worth the same, and worth saving."[5] Hermione goes even further, extending this principle to nonhumans, as part of her tireless and thankless effort to liberate the Hogwarts house-elves. Recall her horror when she realizes that the meals at Hogwarts are prepared by house-elves or, as she puts it, "slave labor." To do something about the situation, she starts S.P.E.W., the Society for the Promotion of Elfish Welfare.

This principle of equality, however expressed, explains what's wrong with racism, sexism, anti-Semitism, and all other forms of discrimination. Each of these views violates the idea that everyone deserves equal moral consideration. White racists think the suffering of black people is of less importance than the suffering of white people. Male sexists think that it's all right for women to be subservient to men, and so on. But, as Goldman and Tolstoy see it, patriotism is no different. After all, how is giving preferential treatment to your countrymen—which is what patriotism seems to require—any different from giving preferential treatment to those who share your ancestry or skin color or gender? Doesn't the idea that we should treat all people as having equal moral worth conflict with the idea that some people are to be given preferential treatment because of some characteristic (such as race, gender, or ancestry) they had no control over? It's justifiable to morally discriminate against someone because of something he or she has done (like using one of the Unforgivable Curses), but it seems unjustifiable to base moral worth on something he or she can't control, such as whether either of the person's parents is a Muggle or which country the parent was born in.

The Sorting Hat Speaks: Division and Divisiveness

So far, then, it looks like we must view patriotism as a vice—as the moral equivalent of racism or sexism—and that we must view the loyalty that Gryffindors show to their House not as something admirable, but as a position morally equivalent to the Death Eaters' view that only pureblood wizards are morally worthy, and that wizards of mixed parentage and Muggles are morally inferior. But there's another problem with patriotism, one that even the Sorting Hat could see: patriotism divides us when we should be united. Solving global crises requires international cooperation, but such cooperation is difficult when we see other countries as our rivals. The Sorting Hat recognizes the problem with, well, *sorting* Hogwarts students at the beginning of Harry's fifth year:

> Though condemned I am to split you
> Still I worry that it's wrong,
> Though I must fulfill my duty
> And must quarter every year
> Still I wonder whether sorting
> May not bring the end I fear.
> Oh, know the perils, read the signs,
> The warning history shows,
> For our Hogwarts is in danger
> From external, deadly foes
> And we must unite inside her
> Or we'll crumble from within.[6]

With division comes divisiveness, and what may have started out as harmless sorting for noble ends will end up as the basis for opposition and hatred.

Think, too, of the Triwizard Tournament. As Albus Dumbledore describes it, the tournament is "a friendly competition" and is "a most excellent way of establishing ties between young witches and wizards of different nationalities."[7] But after it gets underway, Ron is unable to see Hermione's friendship with Viktor Krum, the champion from the foreign Durmstrang school, as anything other than disloyal behavior. Because Hermione is friendly with Krum, Ron accuses her of helping Krum solve his egg, part of the second task of the tournament:

> "I'd *never* help him work out that egg!" said Hermione, looking outraged. "*Never*. How could you say something like that—I want Harry to win the tournament. Harry knows that, don't you, Harry?"
>
> "You've got a funny way of showing it," sneered Ron.
>
> "This whole tournament's supposed to be about getting to know foreign wizards and making friends with them!" said Hermione hotly.
>
> "No it isn't!" shouted Ron. "It's about winning!"[8]

With views like Ron's, it's no wonder that Dumbledore has to remind everyone of the point of the tournament—and that winning isn't it. "The Triwizard Tournament's aim was to further and promote magical understanding. In light of . . . Lord Voldemort's return, such ties are more important than ever before," Dumbledore says. Indeed, Dumbledore sees that it is this very division that Voldemort banks on: "[W]e are only as strong as we are united, as weak as we are divided. Lord Voldemort's gift for spreading discord and enmity is very great. We can fight it by showing an equally strong bond of friendship and trust."[9] Dumbledore could just as easily be talking about the environmental threat posed by global warming or the wars that grow out of many nations' thirst for more oil. Strong bonds of international friendship and trust are just as necessary in the fight against global crises as they are in the fight against Tom Riddle. The formation of Dumbledore's Army—which includes students from all of the Houses except Slytherin—shows that House (or national) divisions matter little when everyone is affected equally by an external threat, and that unifying in the face of that threat can be an effective response to it.

Patriotism and Global Conflict

Let's consider one more possible problem with patriotism before we look for a way to make sense of it. Many people think being patriotic simply requires you to "love your country." That's good as far as it goes, but what does someone who loves her country do? Here's one possible answer. If you love your country, doesn't that mean wanting your countrymen to live well and to have all of the trappings of the good life? Yet living the typical American middle-class life (with a large house in the suburbs, cars, vacations, large TVs, high-calorie meals, and so forth) costs a lot of money and consumes a significant amount of the world's scarce resources. It looks like the only way to maintain this "good life" for us and our countrymen is either to exploit the people of other countries—they have to work cheaply, so that we can afford the goods they make, and they have to go without cars and large houses, so that the price of oil and other essential resources stays low for us—or for us to use more than our fair share of the world's resources, thus denying them to others. Either way, it might be thought that our well-being depends on other people living much less well than we do. (Think again of the house-elves at Hogwarts: how much does the well-being of the students depend on the horrid working conditions of the enslaved elves?) If this line of thought is right, and if we agree that everyone counts equally, it seems to follow that we will have to significantly curtail our lifestyles and dial down our high standards of living so that others can climb out of backbreaking poverty. So, then, if "loving your country" means endorsing the high standard of living that your countrymen enjoy, this will mean taking steps to exploit the citizens of other countries, and that is tantamount—isn't it?—to thinking that the well-being of your fellow Americans is more important than the well-being of other people. And that sounds pretty close to the idea that the people of your country are morally superior to the people of other countries.

Of course, there are a number of "ifs" in this line of reasoning and quite a few possible objections. You might think that raising the standard of living in other countries actually serves to benefit our economy—the more money that people in other countries have, the more stuff of ours they can buy, and the less foreign aid from us they will need. But even so, the issue of scarce resources helps us see the possible conflict between patriotism and the moral point of view that gives equal moral standing to all persons. Accordingly, if we wish to maintain the view that patriotism is a virtue, we have to figure out a way to understand patriotism so that it doesn't conflict with the powerfully attractive view that all people—of whatever nationality—are of equal moral worth. Let's now look at how we can do that.

Patriotism Restored

We've seen some major dangers of patriotism: it promotes an unjustified sense that *we* are morally better than *them*, it may lead to economic imperialism, and it may prevent united action in situations where working across national boundaries is crucial to solving shared problems. But let's not write off patriotism just yet; maybe we just haven't understood it properly. Martha Nussbaum, a leading contemporary American philosopher, tries to find room for national bonds and loyalties in what she calls a "cosmopolitan" worldview: one in which we see ourselves as citizens of the world and recognize our obligations to all people, not only to our neighbors and countrymen. Because Nussbaum's cosmopolitanism embraces the equal moral worth of all people in different clothing, she might offer us a way to be patriotic but not join the Dark Lord.

To see how Nussbaum finds room for patriotism within a moral view that says all people are of equal moral worth, let's think back to the Hogwarts Houses again. Imagine that we think that all Hogwarts students are equally deserving of an education, and we need to figure out the most effective way to provide them with the best education we can. We want *all of them* to be properly housed and fed, to learn their subjects, and to grow into responsible, educated wizards. The education of each student is as important as that of every other student. Yet this very desire—rooted, as it is, in the equal moral worth of all students—might lead us to endorse sorting the students into Houses. Small Houses, with their more intimate common rooms and dormitories, may be the best way to keep an eye on everyone, administer Hogwarts, and foster the friendship and mutual support that are necessary for students to succeed at school. The competition for the House Cup will motivate students to do well in their classes: because they will want their House to win, they will study hard so that they can answer their teachers' questions correctly and earn their House points toward the Cup. In other words, we might reasonably think that as in a family, fostering a sense of House loyalty, pride, and patriotism will be the most effective way to meet our goal of providing a quality education for all students. The reason, in other words, that Hermione should give special preference to the other Gryffindors is not because Gryffindor students are somehow morally superior to the students of other Houses—of course, they aren't—but rather because if every student gives this sort of preferential treatment to the members of his or her own House, then all students will succeed and receive the education they deserve. Nussbaum makes the point in terms of parents caring for their children:

> To give one's own sphere special care is justifiable in universalist terms, and I think this is its most compelling justification. To take one example, we do not really think

our own children are morally more important than other people's children, even though almost all of us who have children would give our own children far more love and care than we give others'. It is good for children, on the whole, that things work this way, and that is why our special care is good, rather than selfish.[10]

So, we may endorse the special regard for our own countrymen that patriotism involves, but we are justified in doing so, according to Nussbaum, only to the extent that such an attitude serves the interests of all people and doesn't require that others suffer so that we may prosper. If Americans give special care and attention to other Americans, and Chinese give that same sort of care and attention to other Chinese, and similarly with all of the citizens of each country, then everyone will (at least, in theory) be taken care of and prosper. Patriotism can thus be a virtue when it serves the interests of the citizens of all countries; it becomes a vice when it fosters and promotes injustice and inequality. Figuring out when this occurs can be difficult, as Ron's struggles with the point of the Triwizard Tournament demonstrate, but it seems that Nussbaum leaves us a good deal of room to be patriots while still respecting the rights of people in other countries.

The Importance of Community

Being a loyal and patriotic member of a group doesn't necessarily mean that you regard the members of your group as morally superior to everyone else. That is the difference between the patriotism of a Gryffindor and the bigotry of a Slytherin. But what is the value of group membership itself? Is your well-being dependent on your being a member of a well-defined community with clear boundaries and an unsullied connection to its historical traditions? Or might life in a community whose rich cultural traditions are insulated from the rest of the world be stifling and an inauthentic response to our modern situation?

It's pretty clear how the Death Eaters, with their mantra of preserving the purity of wizarding blood, would answer this question. To thrive, wizards must keep their kind free from any intrusion from the nonwizarding world. So afraid of the outside world are they that Voldemort kills the Hogwarts Muggle Studies teacher, whose crime, aside from liking Muggles, was advocating cultural mixing and "the dwindling of the pure-bloods."[11] The Death Eaters clearly think that flourishing as a wizard—living the good wizard life—requires being a member of the wizarding community, a community they believe must be kept pure and undiluted.

The idea that human flourishing requires membership in a community that is united by common traditions and cultural practices—an idea taken to violent extremes by the Death Eaters—is known in political philosophy as "communitarianism." Communitarians believe that participation in the life of some particular community provides meaning for our lives and is the source of our value systems. Indeed, drawing on Aristotle's claim that human beings are "political animals" and so can't achieve their full humanity outside of a "polis" (roughly, a small political community), some communitarians assert that our very identities are tied to the community we are a part of. To understand how our identities are "constructed" by our membership in communities, think of Harry's identity as "the Boy Who Lived." This is central to how Harry sees himself, how everyone else sees him, and what he takes as his obligations and values. Nearly everything about Harry is centered on this role he has played in the wizarding world. Removed from that world, with its history, alliances, family relations, and traditions, Harry wouldn't know who he is or what he should do. Indeed, we get a sense of how Harry is *without* the wizarding community when we see his life lived "under the stairs," before he enrolls at Hogwarts. His misery could be ascribed to his removal from his home community.

Strong versions of communitarianism see community membership as a basic human need—like the need for food and shelter—which can seem reasonable once we recognize the importance of having a sense of who we are, a set of values, a meaning, and a life purpose. The crucial point is that according to communitarians, we get these only from belonging to groups united by common traditions, memories, cultural practices, and so on. If such communities are so essential to our well-being, there's good reason to think that we should work to preserve these communities and ensure that they do not disappear into the cultural melting pot. According to communitarians, our well-being is threatened when we are removed from these meaning-conferring communities or when our community is threatened from outside by the forces of assimilation or modernity.

But, of course, communitarians would have problems with the Death Eaters' tactics. Preserving strong cultural bonds is all well and good, but, surely, that doesn't require violence and acts of domination. Surely, the mixed-blood wizards and other magical creatures need not be persecuted, and Muggles need not be killed in order for the wizarding community to preserve its identity. Matters get a little trickier when preserving cultural traditions involves violations of the liberty of members of that culture. Recent debates about the treatment of women in certain cultures—from female genital mutilation in certain traditional African cultures to the social oppression of women in certain Islamic cultures, just to name two—turn on the question of whether preserving cultural traditions or safeguarding individual liberty is more important. If we can't figure out how to preserve our culture without oppressing others, we may have a good reason to rethink communitarianism.

Human Flourishing and the Preservation
of Dying Cultures

Let's say we figure out a way to draw this line and decide to preserve certain cultures that are under threat of dying out or being assimilated. Is that a good thing? Is it worth our time and effort to do so? Does something bad take place when a minority culture (such as the Amish or Native American tribes) gets swamped by the relentless tide of modernity? Would it be bad if all of the centaurs left the Forbidden Forest and assimilated into the wizarding world, taking jobs at Hogwarts (as Firenze did), in the Ministry of Magic, or at Zonko's Joke Shop? Should special steps be taken to preserve dying or threatened cultures? Communitarianism provides one reason for doing so: the well-being of the people of that culture depends on its continued preservation. The implication is that if a culture dies out, its people will be cast adrift in the modern world and will suffer as a consequence of no longer belonging to their home culture, with its history and ancestral traditions. Is that right? Do people really, as the contemporary philosopher Jeremy Waldron puts it, "need their rootedness in the particular culture in which they and their ancestors were reared in the way they need food, clothing, and shelter"?[12]

So, which view of human well-being is correct? The communitarian view that people need rootedness in a traditional culture in order to live full human lives? Or the cosmopolitan view that true human flourishing requires being a sort of cultural immigrant who moves among many cultures, mixing and integrating bits and pieces of different traditions?

According to some philosophers, one powerful reason in favor of the cosmopolitan view of the good life is that it is the only reasonable response to life in the modern world. Perhaps centuries ago, when human communities were largely isolated from one another, the good life required continual membership in some traditional community. But in a modern, interconnected world, where people of different faiths, ethnicities, races, and nationalities mix every day, whether online or on the streets of London, Mumbai, or New York, human flourishing requires an ability to move comfortably among different traditions. As Waldron puts it, the

> hybrid lifestyle of the true cosmopolitan is the only appropriate response to the modern world in which we live. We live in a world formed by technology and trade; by economic, religious, and political imperialism and their offspring, by mass migration and the dispersion of cultural influences. In this context, to immerse oneself in the traditional practices of, say, aboriginal culture might be a fascinating anthropological experiment, but it involves an artificial dislocation from what actually is going on in the world.[13]

Earlier, we saw cosmopolitanism as a view about the equal moral worth of all persons; here, cosmopolitanism is being offered as a view about what is necessary for human flourishing. It's more a view about the value of mixing and moving between cultures than it is about the moral worth of people, but the Harry Potter books make strong arguments in favor of both kinds of cosmopolitanism. In rejecting the racist view of Lord Voldemort, the books take a stand in favor of the equal moral worth of all persons. But when we think about how Harry was able to defeat Voldemort, we see that much of his success was due to his ability to move among cultures and his willingness to work together with people from different ethnic groups. Harry can move as easily in the Muggle world as he can in the wizarding world; his best friends are the pure-blood wizard Ron, the Muggle-born wizard Hermione, and the half-human, half-giant Rubeus Hagrid. He talks to snakes, works with centaurs and goblins, and even befriends a house-elf, a hippogriff, and a phoenix. Intercultural fluency is perhaps best demonstrated by the many characters who are part-this and part-that. In addition to Hagrid, there's the werewolf Remus Lupin, the Animagus Sirius Black, the part-veela Fleur Delacour, and the half-human, half-horse Firenze. If there's a moral lesson at the heart of the Harry Potter books, it is an endorsement of both sorts of cosmopolitanism—the idea that all people are of equal moral worth, and that flourishing in the modern world requires an embrace of other cultures and an ability to navigate among them.[14]

NOTES

1. Adlai Stevenson, "The Nature of Patriotism," in *Lend Me Your Ears: Great Speeches in History*, edited by William Safire (New York: W. W. Norton, 1992), p. 70.

2. Leo Tolstoy, "Patriotism or Peace," in *The Complete Works of Count Tolstoy*, vol. 20, edited and translated by Leo Wiener (London: J. M. Dent & Co., 1905), p. 472.

3. Emma Goldman, "Patriotism: A Menace to Liberty," in *Anarchism and Other Essays* (New York: Mother Earth Publishing Association, 1910), pp. 134–135.

4. Immanuel Kant, *Groundwork for the Metaphysic of Morals*, translated by H. J. Paton (New York: Harper Torchbooks, 1964), p. 96.

5. *Deathly Hallows*, p. 440.

6. *Order of the Phoenix*, pp. 206–207.

7. *Goblet of Fire*, p. 187.

8. Ibid., pp. 422–423.

9. Ibid., p. 723.

10. Martha Nussbaum, "Patriotism and Cosmopolitanism," in *For Love of Country* (Boston: Beacon Press, 2002), p. 13.

11. *Deathly Hallows*, p. 12.

12. Jeremy Waldron, "Minority Cultures and the Cosmopolitan Alternative," *University of Michigan Journal of Law Reform* 25, no. 3–4 (1991–1992): 762.

13. Ibid., p. 763.

14. Thanks to Anne Gilson LaLonde for helpful comments on an earlier draft of this essay.

DUMBLEDORE'S POLITICS

Beth Admiraal and Regan Lance Reitsma

Political libertarianism teaches that the primary value that government should protect and respect is the personal liberty of each of its citizens. According to standard libertarian thinking, personal liberty is of such significant moral value that the only morally justifiable political state is highly restricted. Its only legitimate task is to protect its citizens from force, fraud, and theft.

Is Albus Dumbledore a political libertarian? Even more, does the Harry Potter series support a libertarian political agenda? Several Potter commentators seem to think so. In *Harry Potter and Imagination*, Travis Prinzi argues that "it is not difficult to see" in Dumbledore's behavior and attitudes a small-government libertarian."[1] And Prinzi describes the Potter series as a "political fairy tale," with an "embedded" political philosophy, whose "libertarian element" is "crucial to the plot and morality of Harry Potter."[2] In the article "Harry Potter and the Half-Crazed Bureaucracy," Benjamin Barton, a law professor at the University of Tennessee, argues that the Potter series contains "an impregnable invective against government," an attack that he encourages the libertarian movement in America to take advantage of.[3] (Listen up, ardent lovers of liberty.)

Potter fans might wonder why Prinzi and Barton make these claims. The Potter series doesn't read like a libertarian manifesto. Wouldn't an extended argument for a libertarian political philosophy need to speak overtly and often, as many libertarians do, about the virtues of the free market and the vices of the modern, liberal welfarist state, not to mention about the folly of engaging in "entangling alliances" with international organizations akin to the United Nations?[4] But market deregulation, antiwelfarism, and a conspicuously robust conception of national sovereignty simply aren't major themes in the Potter books.

Also, there isn't any direct evidence that Dumbledore favors a minimal "nightwatchman" state. Though he at various times holds several very influential positions within the wizarding world—Headmaster of Hogwarts School of Witchcraft and Wizardry, the Supreme Mugwump of the International Confederation of Wizards, and the Chief Warlock of the Wizengamot—at no point does he advocate any general political philosophy: monarchist, communist, fascist, liberal democratic, libertarian, anarchist, or other. And nowhere does Dumbledore spout any of the stock slogans commonly associated with libertarian theorizing. He never pronounces, for instance, that "the government that governs least governs best" or that each person has "a natural right to full self-ownership."

On what grounds, then, do Prinzi and Barton base their libertarian interpretations?

Is Dumbledore a Libertarian?

Prinzi gives three basic arguments for the thesis that Dumbledore is "libertarian-minded."[5] First, Dumbledore is suspicious of political power. Second, he advocates personal freedom and political equality. Third, he has a "hands-off management style" that fits with a libertarian belief in a hands-off, laissez-faire government. Let's consider these three arguments.

First, Prinzi points out that Dumbledore clearly distrusts political power. How could he not, since he so often sees it misused? The Ministry of Magic, instead of being a help in time of need, is often an obstacle to defeating Voldemort. The Ministry was completely ineffective in preventing Voldemort's reign of terror during the Dark Lord's first rise to power. And as Voldemort's evil forces steadily and ominously gather again in *Goblet of Fire*, Percy Weasley and others at the Ministry are hard at work writing an officious policy about cauldron-bottom thickness. All the while, Dumbledore must work behind the scenes to undermine the Dark Lord's plans. Also, the Ministry operates unjustly in suspending Dumbledore from his duties in *Chamber of Secrets*, in condemning Buckbeak in *Prisoner of Azkaban*, in charging Harry with underage use of magic in *Order of the Phoenix*, and in trying to impose Ministry control over Hogwarts that same year. Each time, Dumbledore must find a way to steer the course of events to a just conclusion. Dumbledore is, no doubt, smart enough to draw the conclusion that people in power often cannot be trusted.

What's more, Dumbledore clearly understands first-hand how corrupting power can be. In *Deathly Hallows*, he admits that "power was my weakness and my temptation" and says that he turned down the post of Minister of Magic several times because he had "learned that I was not to be trusted with power."[6]

Do these considerations show that Dumbledore is "libertarian-minded"? No. This argument is a non sequitur. The conclusion simply doesn't follow from the supporting evidence, for libertarians do not have a monopoly on the idea that power corrupts. Political theorists of a variety of persuasions accept this claim. The U.S. political system, which today is far from libertarian, attempts to limit the "corrupting influence of power" by implementing a system of "checks and balances." No one branch of the federal government—the executive, the judicial, or the legislative—is allowed to have overriding power over the other two. The point is that there are mechanisms to limit the power of any one person or any one government agency, other than by implementing a libertarian political system. In fact, Lord Acton, who coined the famous saying that "power corrupts, and absolute power corrupts absolutely," was a traditional Catholic who did not favor a minimal, nonmoralistic state.

Prinzi's second argument is that Dumbledore shares with the libertarian tradition a strong devotion to the value of personal liberty. No doubt, he does. It is one of his most notable and praiseworthy traits. For instance, Dumbledore's treatment of the enslaved house-elves who work at Hogwarts reflects such devotion. Dumbledore thinks the institution of house-elf servitude should end. As Prinzi is right to emphasize, Dumbledore happens to favor, for strategic reasons, a gradual approach to changing the system.[7] He chooses not to call for the immediate emancipation of house-elves because the elves, having been educated (or, as Hermione says, "brainwashed") to take pride in their identity as servants, would be deeply offended by the idea that they want to be free. Dumbledore understands this and offers the house-elves the right to be paid for their work and to receive time off but doesn't compel them to accept payment or vacation time. Dumbledore's policy allows the house-elves to live with the idea of greater freedom and, when they are ready, to decide for themselves when they would prefer to be free. This gradualism itself can be seen as a way of respecting the personal freedom of the house-elves (though it amounts to letting them, for the time being, choose to be less free).

Like libertarians, Dumbledore is tolerant of unpopular minority groups, and he often speaks up for victims of discrimination. For example, he works to save the lives of the last giants of Britain. The giants, given their brutish natures, do present a serious threat to the safety of both Muggles and wizards, and so Dumbledore takes it upon himself to learn what is necessary to interact with these slow-witted and impulsive creatures, find a place for them to live, and suppress a "safety movement" to have them killed. Dumbledore is also willing to hire teachers at Hogwarts who belong to despised minorities, such as the half-giant Rubeus Hagrid, the werewolf Remus Lupin, and the centaur Firenze. Finally, Dumbledore consistently opposes purebloodism and wizarding claims of superiority, saying that "it matters not what someone is born, but what they grow to be!"[8] Dumbledore has, Prinzi concludes, a libertarian attitude toward personal freedom and the equality of each member of the wizarding world.

Dumbledore clearly does place a high value on protecting the individual autonomy of each person. But again, libertarians aren't the only political theorists who sing the praises of liberty. Many political theorists—liberals, for instance—would endorse the emancipation of house-elves and equal rights for minority groups. If Prinzi wants to convince us that Dumbledore has the heart and the mind of a libertarian, he should provide evidence that Dumbledore's personal outlook has content that is *distinctly* libertarian. What sets political libertarianism apart from other strands within the liberal tradition is its commitment to the *primacy* of personal liberty. A libertarian not only believes in a moral right to personal liberty, but construes this right in a strikingly robust way.[9] Let's consider three notable ways that libertarians restrict government interference with personal liberty, then ask whether Dumbledore advocates similar restrictions. Prinzi seems to think he does.

First, libertarians oppose laws that restrict people's liberty "for their own good." Liberal regimes often require the use of seatbelts or motorcycle helmets, prohibit steroid use by athletes, forbid people from swimming at certain beaches without a lifeguard, and extract money for retirement savings.

They justify these practices, at least in part, on the grounds that these rules prevent people from harming themselves. But a properly respectful government, libertarians believe, will not be paternalistic; it will let its citizens make their own decisions, even if those choices will predictably have negative consequences. Second, libertarians oppose laws that outlaw "victimless crimes" or "harmless immoralities" such as prostitution, gay sex, recreational drug use, and gambling. They believe that a government should not limit freedom simply because an act is considered immoral. A state is under a positive obligation to protect the liberty and the property of its citizens, but as John Locke might have put it, a "civil magistrate" should not concern himself with the "care of souls."[10] Third, libertarians are deeply critical of bureaucratic attempts to help the disadvantaged or to redistribute wealth in order to reduce economic inequality. When a state takes money from the "haves" and gives it to the "have-nots," libertarians see this as "state-sanctioned theft" or "forced labor." Many libertarians would agree that a private act of charity—a personal donation to Oxfam, say—is morally praiseworthy. But if a government forcibly takes your hard-earned money and gives it out as "welfare," that's simply robbery by another name.

At its heart, political libertarianism has a muscular conception of the moral life. It thinks in radically individualistic terms; strongly admires personal intelligence, creativity, strength, and initiative; views freedom as the "master" political value; is strongly skeptical of government power and bureaucratic solutions; and places considerable faith in the "invisible hand" of the market to create wealth and prosperity.

With this brief sketch of libertarianism in hand, let's return to our discussion of Dumbledore's political views. Prinzi's third argument—his appeal to Dumbledore's "hands-off management style"—could be construed as his strongest attempt to reveal that Dumbledore not only shares several values in common with libertarianism, but has a notably libertarian mind-set. Dumbledore has, as Prinzi puts it, a "willingness to let the people under his charge live and be free."[11] Libertarians, as we've seen, believe that the state should not legislate paternalistic rules; rather, it should permit its citizens to make their own decisions, however unwise. Dumbledore, Prinzi claims, also takes this view. As headmaster, Dumbledore largely permits faculty and students to "do as they please," despite the many poor decisions they often and predictably make. Dumbledore presumably doesn't endorse Professor Binns's deadly dull lecturing, Hagrid's use of dangerous magical creatures, or Professor Sybill Trelawney's wacky teaching methods. Nor, even more significantly, does Dumbledore intervene to protect students against humiliation, bias, and cruelty. For instance, he permits Severus Snape to hang Neville Longbottom upside down in front of class, to take significant points from Gryffindor unjustly, and to withhold medical treatment from Hermione Granger when one of Draco Malfoy's spells inadvertently makes her teeth grow humiliatingly long. Dumbledore can't be accused, to say the least, of being a meddling headmaster.

Even more conspicuous than the many unfortunate things that happen at Hogwarts under Dumbledore's watch is his approach to Harry. It seems to us, as we read through the series, that one of Dumbledore's most striking features is his absence. Dumbledore doesn't raise and educate orphaned Harry. He hardly contacts a lonely Harry during his painful summers with the Dursleys. He doesn't stand by eleven-year-old Harry's side as the boy confronts Voldemort for the first time—or, for that matter, the second and third times, in the Chamber of Secrets and in the graveyard at Little Hangleton. Dumbledore does give Harry, true enough, the tools necessary to fight Voldemort. But these tools do not guarantee young Harry's victory; they leave so much for Harry himself to do. Why isn't Dumbledore there, right beside Harry? Even when Dumbledore is physically present, Harry often finds Dumbledore terse and emotionally distant. What does all of this say about Dumbledore?

Harry isn't the only one who finds Dumbledore inexplicably distant and disengaged. Amycus Carrow, the Death Eater, mocks Dumbledore: "Always the same, weren't yeh, Dumby, talking and doing nothing, nothing."[12] Red Hen, a popular Potter commentator, calls Dumbledore "one of the very biggest (non-chocolate) frogs" in the wizarding world, who has squandered the chance to reform wizarding society for decades.[13]

Prinzi has a more charitable interpretation. He thinks Dumbledore makes a *principled choice* not to micromanage other people's lives or to constantly Apparate in to save the day. It isn't that Dumbledore is lazy, weak, or indifferent. Instead, Dumbledore believes that a leader is under significant restrictions against the use of coercive power, and he is willing to work within these self-imposed moral constraints. Dumbledore has, Prinzi thinks, a very robust conception of personal autonomy, one that implies that leaders ought to refrain from interfering with the choices other people make. Prinzi is even willing to claim that the motive that leads Dumbledore to stand by as Hogwarts teachers mistreat students is deeply libertarian. Dumbledore has, Prinzi thinks, the libertarian's "muscular" view of human life; he admires self-reliance and views life as a testing ground that gives people the opportunity to learn the life skills and develop the personal resolve necessary to make it in a tough world. As Dumbledore says to Severus Snape, "It has been essential . . . to let [Harry] *try his strength.*"[14]

Prinzi's argument that Dumbledore's management style reflects a libertarian mind-set is unconvincing, though. For one thing, as libertarians would point out, managing a school is very different from running a government. Although libertarians oppose the government's use of coercion, they often find coercion appropriate within the family and within private institutions like Hogwarts. And the idea that personal freedom should be the "master value"—whether or not it makes sense in politics—makes no sense in running a school for teens and preteens. Libertarian ideals are grounded in the idea that adults should be permitted to govern their own lives, because they have the ability to deliberate and make their own choices. But this reasoning can't sensibly be applied to eleven-year-old children whose intellectual powers are still developing.[15]

For the sake of argument, though, let's permit the analogy between Hogwarts and a political society, and let's take Dumbledore to be the head bureaucrat of this society of teachers and students. Even if we grant this assumption, Prinzi's argument doesn't succeed. For libertarian thinking wouldn't lead a person to do what Dumbledore did, namely, stand by as students are bullied, mistreated, and endangered by faculty. Libertarianism is not anarchism.[16] According to libertarian thinking, a person in a position of political power is under a moral obligation to intervene to protect those under his supervision from abuse. This is the central purpose of a political state. A clear-thinking libertarian bureaucrat would have intervened to prevent teachers from endangering students or treating them cruelly or unfairly. Also, a good libertarian leader would have required professors to live up to their contractual obligations to educate students. Dumbledore's failure to address the abusive behavior and the lousy pedagogy of bad teachers doesn't reflect standard libertarian thinking.

Prinzi claims that Dumbledore permits faculty to mistreat pupils because doing so will foster self-reliance in students and so strengthen their moral fiber. But this reasoning is deeply inconsistent with libertarian thinking. Libertarians believe that the political state should not take it upon itself to make its citizens into better people. The state is not charged with making its citizens decent, responsible, tough, courageous, or anything else—only safe. The reason that libertarians praise the virtue of self-reliance is not because they want bureaucrats to teach it, but because they recognize that in a society in which people do not receive significant protection from a well-intentioned, paternalistic state, this virtue is crucial. It's clear that Dumbledore does think he has the obligation or at least the prerogative to inculcate moral virtues in his students. But then it's important to notice that his "management style" does not reflect beliefs about the proper structure of a government. It reflects his views about the proper behavior of headmasters.

Barton's Libertarian Interpretation of the Potter Series

Prinzi's arguments do not stand up to analysis. So, what about Barton's libertarian interpretation? He argues that "J. K. Rowling's strikingly negative portrait of the Ministry of Magic and its bureaucrats" is evidence that the Potter series as a whole has an implicit libertarian political agenda. Is this true?

As Barton persuasively argues, the Potter books offer a scathing portrait of the Ministry. It's difficult to imagine a more hard-hitting indictment than Barton's own point-by-point analysis:

> What would you think of a government that engaged in this list of tyrannical activities: tortured children for lying, designed its prison specifically to suck all life and hope out of the inmates; placed citizens in that prison without a hearing; ordered the death penalty without a trial; allowed the powerful, rich or famous to control policy; selectively prosecuted crimes (the powerful go unpunished and the unpopular face trumped-up charges); conducted criminal trials without defense counsel; used truth serum to force confessions; maintained constant surveillance over all citizens; offered no elections and no democratic lawmaking process; and controlled the press?[17]

When confronted with political leadership as brutal and oppressive as this, it's easy to find yourself wondering, exasperated, whether the proper cure isn't to strip government of its power. But if this is the cure Barton means to encourage, his argument is unsound. A justifiable sense of exasperation at the Ministry of Magic is not an "invective against government" itself. More to the point, there isn't any compelling reason to think that the Potter series succumbs to this exasperation.

To start with, the Ministry of Magic is not altogether corrupt. It includes good people and good laws. Arthur Weasley, though hampered by a very sketchy grasp of how Muggle artifacts work, is hardworking and honest. Dumbledore himself, except for a brief hiatus, holds the position of the Chief Warlock of the Wizengamot, a bureaucratic position, and he is not a bungling incompetent. In *Order of the Phoenix*, the majority of the members of the Wizengamot, a judicial body, vote in Harry's favor when he is brought up on bogus charges. The Ministry of Magic, although it includes many Orwellian-sounding bureaus, has been largely effective in keeping the existence of wizards secret from Muggles for many centuries and in restraining wizards from using their magical powers to rule the world. The Ministry also supports and enforces many sensible rules. For instance, when Harry is charged with violating the rule against underage wizardry in the presence of a Muggle, the rule makes a sensible exception for cases of self-defense. Not to mention, it is the Ministry that had the wisdom to appoint Dumbledore to the post of Headmaster of Hogwarts.

No doubt, the Ministry of Magic is far too often bungling, incompetent, and even positively corrupt. Several top Ministry officials, including Minister of Magic Pius Thicknesse, become Voldemort's puppets by being placed under the Imperius Curse. Many high-ranking officials, such as Minister of Magic Cornelius Fudge and ex-Head of Magical Law Enforcement Barty Crouch Sr., are autocratic and power-hungry. Others, such as Dolores Umbridge and Albert Runcorn, are downright evil. And some are just "doddery old fools," like the members of the Committee on the Disposal of Dangerous Creatures.[18] In summary, the premise of Barton's argument is an exaggeration but very close to the truth—the Ministry of Magic is a lousy bureaucracy.

The most questionable aspect of Barton's argument, though, is not its premise but its inference. Why conclude, from the fact that the Potter series presents a portrait of bad governance, that the series advocates a minimal, "nightwatchman" libertarian government? Is it that Barton assumes that less of a bad thing is better, and so a smaller Ministry would be better? If so, his reasoning should lead him to favor political anarchism, which calls for the total abolition of government. Even if we set this glib retort aside, why think that when it comes to government, smaller is necessarily better? If seven of the Justices on the Supreme Court were corrupt and demonstrably biased in their judgments, the proper response would be to replace the judges, not to down-size to a two-justice court. In brief, the proper antidote to bad governance is better governance, and it would take an argument, a very complex argument, to show that a government with a libertarian structure is the proper cure for the types of corruption and inefficiency evident in the Ministry of Magic. Does the Potter series make or even gesture at this argument?

We are willing to grant that a careful evaluation of the Ministry of Magic provides strong grounds for thinking that a good government would put in place stringent safeguards to protect citizens from torture, barbarous punishments, unfair trials, and bureaucrats wielding truth serum. But it is a further question, once these safeguards are in place, whether a good government would do *no more than* protect the liberty, the property, and the bodily integrity of its citizens. Where is the evidence that the Potter series accepts a right to liberty as robust as the libertarian theory does? Or that the series, as a whole, is antiwelfare, or antipaternalism, or anti–United Nations, or as confident in the free market as standard libertarianism?

Barton claims—rather exuberantly—that J. K. Rowling "will do more for libertarianism than anyone since John Stuart Mill."[19] Who knows? His prediction, though not particularly plausible, could turn out to be true. But if a considerable number of readers do happen to infer, from the Potter series, that libertarianism is the best political theory, they will be guilty of the same leap in logic as Barton.

It's worth noting that if there is a libertarian agenda in the Potter series, it is not likely to be there because of the author's intent. Rowling began writing the Harry Potter series while she was on welfare and has expressed no regret for that. Indeed, in voicing her own political views, Rowling has not supported libertarian values. On the contrary, she supported Barack Obama and Hillary Clinton in the 2008 U.S. presidential election, donated £1 million to the British Labour Party, and has said that her real-life hero is Robert F. Kennedy—hardly a paragon of "small government"![20]

The Potter books do raise important questions about what a good government and good political leadership would be like. No doubt, the Ministry fails to respect, among other things, freedom and equality, and it would be very interesting to ask, "What's the best way to fix the Ministry of Magic?" But libertarians will have to do more than point to the poor example set by the Ministry or to the good example set by humble Dumbledore to argue soundly for a libertarian philosophy.

NOTES

1. Travis Prinzi, *Harry Potter and Imagination: The Way between Two Worlds* (Allentown, PA: Zossima Press, 2009), p. 236.

2. Ibid., p. 239. At times, Prinzi stresses the importance of the libertarian threads in the Potter series. For example, in his "succinct summary of the political philosophy underlying the Harry Potter series," Prinzi lists Fabian gradualist, libertarian, and Christian themes (p. 241). At other times Prinzi speaks more modestly: there is, in the Potter series, "plenty to make a libertarian happy" (p. 233), and "libertarian elements

are evident in the series" (p. 238). We will be evaluating the less modest claims. In a personal communication, Prinzi notes that he does not claim that Dumbledore is a *political* libertarian in any robust or overt sense. His claim, rather, is that Dumbledore is broadly libertarian in his personal interactions with people, in his respect for individual moral choice, and in the way he holds positions of power, and that this "lends credence to an intentionally libertarian reading of the series." We are grateful to Prinzi for this clarification. As this chapter makes clear, we think of libertarianism as essentially a *political* view and thus find it misleading to speak of "libertarian elements" in the Potter books that have no reference to small government, individual freedoms, economic liberties, foreign entanglements, or other political themes characteristic of classic and contemporary libertarianism. For Prinzi's own, more fully articulated take on Dumbledore's politics, see his *Harry Potter and Imagination*, chapters 11 and 12.

3. "Harry Potter and the Half-Crazed Bureaucracy," *Michigan Law Review* 104 (May 2006):1523–1538, available online at www.michiganlawreview.org/archive/104/6/Barton .pdf. See also Andrew Morris, "Making Legal Space for Moral Choice," *Texas Wesleyan Law Review* 12:1 (2005): 473–480.

4. The full quotation, from Thomas Jefferson's first inaugural address, is "Peace, commerce and honest friendship with all nations. Entangling alliances with none." The phrase has been used more recently as the title of several essays by the U.S. representative and libertarian presidential candidate Ron Paul.

5. Prinzi, *Harry Potter and Imagination*, pp. 236, 239.

6. *Deathly Hallows*, pp. 717, 718.

7. Especially in comparison to Hermione Granger. When Hermione learns that Hogwarts has house-elves, she forms S.P.E.W., the Society for the Promotion of Elfish Welfare, which advocates for fair wages and working conditions. A house-elf is freed from servitude if his master gives him an article of clothing, so Hermione begins to leave socks and woolly hats for the house-elves.

8. *Goblet of Fire*, p. 708.

9. Libertarians are often described as being against "big government." This description, though true, isn't very precise. Perhaps it is more illuminating to situate libertarianism between anarchism and modern liberalism. Anarchists, libertarians, and modern liberals each agree that there is a moral right to liberty but disagree—significantly—about how robust this right is. The anarchist believes in the strongest conception of this right. He claims that any political state, by its very nature, violates individual rights so significantly that a political state is morally unjustified. Freedom should reign; no person or group should be given the bureaucratic authority to restrict liberty in any way. A modern liberal, on the other hand, believes in a considerably weaker conception of the moral right to liberty. She thinks, first, that a political state should pursue political goals other than protecting and respecting personal liberty and, second, that the pursuit of some of these political goals justifies restricting the personal freedom of citizens. Libertarians stand between these two broad views; their conception of the right to liberty is less robust than the anarchist's, more robust than the modern liberal's.

10. John Locke, *A Letter Concerning Toleration* (Indianapolis: Hackett, 1983; originally published 1689), p. 26.

11. Prinzi, *Harry Potter and Imagination*, pp. 234–235.

12. *Half-Blood Prince*, p. 594.

13. Red Hen, "Case in Point: Albus Dumbledore," www.redhen-publications.com/Dumbledore.html.

14. *Deathly Hallows*, p. 687 (emphasis added).

15. Libertarians usually defend their conception of the nightwatchman state by appeal to a "natural right" to personal liberty, often interpreted as a "moral right to full self-ownership." If you have a property right to a material object—a laptop, say—that means that you get to decide who gets to use the laptop; you deserve compensation from anybody who steals or breaks it; and you have the right to sell or give the laptop to whomever you choose. Libertarians believe that people also have these same ownership rights over their own persons. A person has complete authority to decide what happens to her property, which includes her body. It is her right to decide whether to accept medical treatment, to take recreational drugs, to have sexual relations with another person, to join the military, and so on. If the state fails to respect this set of rights, it fails to treat the citizen with the dignity that she, as a person, deserves. The standard libertarian argument for a nightwatchman state takes this moral theory as a starting point. Libertarians believe that if there were no political state—if we were all living in "the state of nature," a world without any political institutions—violations of the right to personal liberty would be (far more) rampant, and so a political state is necessary to protect the moral right to full self-ownership of each and every person. But a government "bigger" than the nightwatchman state would itself significantly and consistently violate this same right. And so, with due trepidation, human society should establish a political state, endow it with powers—very limited powers—and keep a very wary eye on bureaucrats, to make sure they do not overstep their bounds. For a classic discussion, see Robert Nozick, *Anarchy, State, and Utopia* (New York: Basic Books, 1974).

16. Contrary to anarchists, libertarians believe that it is necessary to create a political state—with a legislature, a police force, a court system, and an army—and to give this political state the authority to exercise coercive power. A libertarian regime would support and enforce legal rules that prohibit serious rights violations such as theft, breach of contract, rape, and murder. Also, it would promote the security and the economic interests of its own citizens, for instance, by actively preserving free market conditions at home and by sending ambassadors, trade specialists, and military negotiators abroad.

17. Barton, "Harry Potter and the Half-Crazed Bureaucracy," pp. 1523–1524.

18. *Prisoner of Azkaban*, p. 292.

19. Barton, "Harry Potter and the Half-Crazed Bureaucracy," p. 1526.

20. "J. K. Rowling Wants to See a Democrat in the White House," available at www.earthtimes.org/articles/show/184525,jk-rowling-wants-to-see-democrat-in-the-white-house.html.

Prinzi admits that Rowling would not "identify herself politically as a libertarian, and that there are no deliberate links to libertarian political philosophers or activists" in the books (Prinzi, *Harry Potter and Imagination*, p. 238). His claim is that there are implicit libertarian themes in the Potter series and that these themes support a libertarian "reader response" interpretation (personal communication). Far be it from us to impose any hegemonic constraints on readers' ability to "respond" however they like to the Potter books. Our claim is simply that there is no explicit or implicit endorsement of political libertarianism in the books, and that any attempt to read libertarian themes into them is a stretch.

DUMBLEDORE, PLATO, AND THE LUST FOR POWER

David Lay Williams and Alan J. Kellner

> Those who are best suited to power are those who have never sought it.
>
> — Albus Dumbledore

> A city in which those who are going to rule are least eager to rule is necessarily best.
>
> —Plato

Lord Acton, in an oft-repeated phrase, observed that "power tends to corrupt and absolute power corrupts absolutely." This phrase neatly sums up what most would consider common wisdom. Yet the world finds itself persistently burdened by the abuse of power. Rulers continually find new and creative ways to line their pockets, privilege their friends, and secure and even bolster their own authority. The list of offenses would shock even many Death Eaters—or perhaps fill them with envy.

In an age that prides itself on its progress in technology and even in morals, why is it that we have progressed so little in protecting ourselves against the usurpations of our rulers? Perhaps it is because we have not learned the important lessons of the first Western political philosopher, Plato (C. 428–348 B.C.E.). Plato's solution to this problem is ingeniously simple: power should never reside in the hands of those who lust for it. Rather, it should be granted only to those who would prefer to occupy themselves with other matters. It is disinterest in power that paradoxically makes the best rulers. This lesson turns out to be central to the climax of the entire Harry Potter series.

Plato and Dumbledore: Separated at Birth?

Albus Dumbledore lived in a stormy age. He saw the rise and fall of the dark wizard Gellert Grindelwald, as well as Voldemort's reign of terror. He saw warfare, both with his wand and in the subtle forms of alliance building and intelligence gathering. He also had personal relationships with the most important players in the saga. Grindelwald was a close boyhood friend, and Voldemort was one of the most talented students at Hogwarts. These experiences taught Dumbledore about the precariousness of peace and the need for truly just rulers.

Plato likewise grew up in an age of remarkable political upheaval. His entire youth was consumed by the decades-long Peloponnesian War between his home city of Athens and the mighty city-state of Sparta. The war and its aftermath provided opportunities to observe both the best and the the worst in human nature. Like Dumbledore, Plato witnessed a power-hungry talented fellow pupil, the tempestuous Alcibiades, rise to high military and political positions, only to betray Athens by siding with her Spartan enemies.[1] Athens would go on to lose the war and suffer the indignity of having an imposed tyranny, known as "the Thirty," headed by the dreaded Critias.

Critias was a bloodthirsty tyrant, who just happened to be Plato's mother's cousin. Several years later, Plato was invited to travel to Syracuse in order to train the petulant son of the tyrant Dionysius I. Indeed, Plato, like Dumbledore, had once seriously contemplated a career in politics—a natural choice, given his talents, family connections, and personal experiences.[2] So, although Plato is sometimes regarded as a pie-in-the-sky philosopher, nothing could be further from the truth. His observations about politicians and their relationship with power are based on real-world experiences.

What did Plato learn from his encounters with political power? His most detailed reactions to his own personal experiences are recorded in his "Seventh Letter," addressed to the rulers of Syracuse. The letter recounts his own flirtations with political power, including the opportunity to join the Thirty at the end of the Peloponnesian War. At first, he was deeply tempted to join with them in forging a new society, perhaps to promote the "greater good," as the young Dumbledore and Grindelwald had desired. But he soon found that he could play no role in this new regime, which "made the former government seem in comparison something precious like gold."[3] The limitless power of the tyrants went to their heads and manifested itself in revenge killings, the settling of old scores, the confiscation of wealth, and ultimately, under the restored democracy, the unjust execution of Plato's beloved teacher, Socrates. This was enough to make Plato "withdraw in disgust" from a life in politics and ultimately dedicate himself full time to philosophy, just as the duel with Grindelwald that resulted in the death of Dumbledore's sister changed Dumbledore's mind about a political life.[4]

Like Dumbledore, Plato turned from politics to education. Dissatisfaction with politics led him instead to establish the Academy, the first university in Western civilization. The Academy is the root of our present English word *academic*, and it was here that Plato experienced some of his greatest personal triumphs. The Academy's notable alumni included Cicero and Plato's own pupil Aristotle. Plato would also write many of his most famous works while teaching there, on a wide range of subjects, including art, ethics, science, mathematics, philosophy, and even love. So, both Dumbledore and Plato found solace from the burdens and temptations of politics in teaching the young.

Plato's retreat from political life, however, was hardly a retreat from systematic thought about politics—in much the same way that Dumbledore remained integral to magical politics even as a professor at Hogwarts. Plato found the Academy the perfect place to reflect on the political world and to distill the wisdom he had acquired in experience. His political philosophy is most fully and artfully rendered in his work the *Republic*. Perhaps the most memorable proposal in this work is the office of the philosopher-ruler.[5] The ideal society Plato sketches in the *Republic* consists of three classes—a working class, soldiers, and rulers. It is this last class that possesses all policy-making powers, as well as the day-to-day oversight of state affairs. Plato's philosopher-rulers hold enormous power, and it is crucial that they be the best and most qualified persons to rule. In particular, they must possess each of the four "cardinal virtues": justice, courage, wisdom, and self-control. To ensure that only the wisest and most virtuous citizens become rulers, Plato proposes a rigorous and lengthy educational process designed to sort out the wheat from the chaff. This process puts even Hogwarts to shame, lasting until age thirty-five, followed by a fifteen-year internship in public service. By the end, Plato hoped, we should be able to distinguish the Potters from the Malfoys.

To be sure, paramount for Plato among the qualifications to rule is intelligence. He makes it repeatedly clear that rulers must be quick learners and possess an unusually good memory. It is often rightly said that Plato was the first philosopher to advocate openly the joining of political power with intellectual heft. Indeed, this is why he insists that the only qualified rulers are philosopher-rulers—those who exceed all others in their cerebral powers.

Although this is perhaps the most celebrated element of Plato's qualifications to rule, intelligence alone is not enough. From popular culture, we all know many brilliant criminals who employed their gifts for devious purposes—Lex Luthor from *Superman*, Hannibal Lecter from *The Silence of the Lambs*, Anakin Skywalker from *Star Wars*, and even Dr. Evil from *Austin Powers*. Mere intelligence may be an essential prerequisite for ruling, but Plato's demands transcend a super-sized cranium. Rulers must combine their brains with virtue. The question—in Plato and in Potter—is how to distinguish between the gifted who will use their power for good and those who will use it for selfish ends.

Most notably, those burdened by excessive self-love are unfit for ruling.[6] They are often among the most intellectually gifted of the students but have difficulties in resisting their impulses and those who would flatter them. Like Voldemort, they view political power as a means to feed one's desires, thus they lust after power. They crave it and climb all over themselves to secure it. But it is precisely this lust for power that suggests their unsuitability for wielding it, according to Plato: "When ruling is something fought over . . . civil and domestic war destroys these men and the rest of the city as well."[7] Tyrants like Critias usually live short lives and are capable of bringing the entire state down with them. Recall, for example, that Voldemort's life—in any corporeal or physical sense—is relatively short as well. In *Sorcerer's Stone*, he must drink unicorn blood to regain his strength; he must feed off the life of another until he can assume a physical form again. Even though Plato was assuming that magic could not be used to save oneself, his analysis of tyrants also holds true in Harry's world. We should therefore rather seek out rulers who are disinterested in holding political power: a "city in which those who are going to rule are least eager to rule is necessarily the best."[8]

Plato offered a useful test for readers to distinguish those who might succumb to the temptations of power from those who would resist, a tale known as the "Ring of Gyges," a legend that J. K. Rowling resuscitates and mirrors in the tale of the Deathly Hallows with Harry's invisibility cloak (more on this shortly). Plato's tale is delivered by the character Glaucon, who was Plato's brother in real life. According to the story, a shepherd finds a magical ring uncovered by an earthquake and discovers that by turning the ring toward himself, he becomes invisible. Possessed of this new talent, the formerly modest shepherd immediately sets out to seduce the king's wife, attack the king with her help and kill him, and seize the king's power for himself, all in rapid succession. Glaucon argues that "no one . . . would be so incorruptible that he would stay on the path of justice, or bring himself to keep away from other people's possessions and not touch them, when he could take whatever he wanted from the marketplace with impunity, go into people's houses and have sex with anyone he wished, kill or release from prison anyone he wished, and do all the other things that would make him like a god among humans."[9]

Plato's implicit reply is that Glaucon's conclusions apply only to those who lust after power. The truly just and good—those fit for political power—would conduct themselves in precisely the same way whether they were invisible or not. For those few qualified individuals, there is no ambition to promote one's selfish interests over that of friends and fellow citizens. So, there is no political benefit to invisibility. In the end, then, Plato wants political power to reside in the hands of the wise and virtuous. These qualities are best manifested in the indifference of rare individuals to the temptations of power. The Ring of Gyges is among the best tests to sort out those who can be trusted with this type of power. Indeed, this question of who can resist the great temptations of power is one of the central questions—if not *the* most important—to be investigated in the Harry Potter series.

Fudge and Umbridge: The Lessons of Obviously Unfit Power-Brokers

If Plato faced great challenges in securing incorruptible political power in his ideal republic, the challenges facing governance in the more practical, though magical, world of Harry Potter must be nearly insurmountable. With Dolores Umbridge's acts of umbrage in her year of tyrannical rule at Hogwarts, Cornelius Fudge's refusal to believe clear evidence of Voldemort's return, and Rufus Scrimgeour's tactless blandishments to Harry in exchange for his service, there is good reason to question whether proper rule in the wizarding community is even possible. Is the Ministry destined to be corrupt? Rowling's characters have much to teach about the nature of political power as we examine a few possible candidates for Minister of Magic: Umbridge, Fudge, Voldemort, Dumbledore, and Harry.

No fan of the Potter series would consider Dolores Umbridge a model citizen, let alone a just ruler. In fact, Umbridge's relentless onslaught of rules, vicious detention measures, and Gestapo-like tactics for gaining and maintaining control might make us wonder why she was not in Voldemort's cohort, rather than the Ministry's.[10] Nevertheless, she holds positions of power in the series—both at the Ministry and at Hogwarts. A Platonic evaluation of her time as a leader must be negative. She provides an object lesson in how *not* to rule.

Readers can understand Umbridge's unsuitability for rule from two simple facts. First, that she lacks all of the necessary virtues Plato discusses in the *Republic*—courage, wisdom, justice, and self-control. Umbridge's lack of self-restraint is a particular weak spot. All it takes is one snide remark, and her passive-aggressive rage is unleashed—hardly something Plato would expect of a successful philosopher-ruler. Second and more important, all of Umbridge's torment tactics reveal her inner lust for power. Take, for instance, Harry's detentions with Umbridge in *Order of the Phoenix*. She instructs him, "I want you to write '*I must not tell lies*,' . . . as long as it takes for the message to *sink in*."[11] This "sink in," as we all know, is quite literal. And her cruelty seems only to increase, relative to the amount of power she is given. As the year progresses and as she attains a more prominent role of authority at Hogwarts by the Ministry, her decrees multiply, as do her detentions. We might even speculate that her incremental increases in authority merely fuel her lust for more power. One thing is certain, though: Plato would have expelled her from his Academy.

Whereas Umbridge never rose to the position of Minister of Magic, the almost equally dangerous and inept Cornelius Fudge did. Part of what made him such a poor Minister was his perpetual fear of losing power. This concern fostered dictatorial tendencies that manifested in a control of the press. The Dark Lord's return to power was partly due to Fudge's failings as a leader. For example, when Harry announced that Voldemort had in fact returned, Fudge resorted to trashing Harry in the press in order to maintain his own public image— an image that only got worse once the truth came out.

Umbridge's position as the Hogwarts High Inquisitor is another example of Fudge's attempts to maintain power in unjust ways. Recall how at the beginning of *Order of the Phoenix* Harry is brought to court for producing a Patronus to protect himself and his cousin, Dudley, from dementors. The dementors were not supposed to be away from Azkaban. To cover up the Ministry's mistake, Fudge brings Harry to trial and does all that he can to tilt the scales against him. He moves the time of the hearing, for instance, in an attempt to make Harry late and to prevent Dumbledore from attending. All of this goes to show that Fudge's virtues as a ruler are at best dubious. He craves power, but his insecurity leads him to use that power for his own advantage, rather than for the public good. He stumbles over himself in his attempts to maintain power, which prevents him in the end from keeping it. So, like Umbridge, Fudge lacks the key features Plato described as necessary for successful ruling, particularly courage, wisdom, and self-control.

Voldemort and Dumbledore: Two Tempted by Power

Self-confidence and decisiveness are certainly not qualities lacking in Lord Voldemort. Even during his humble beginnings in the orphanage, Tom Riddle was drawn to power. "He was already using magic against other people, to frighten, to punish, to control. The . . . strangled rabbit and the young boy and girl he lured into a cave were most suggestive. . . . *'I can make them hurt if I want to.'*"[12] Contrary to the great Enlightenment philosopher Immanuel Kant's dictum never to use another person merely as a means to an end, Riddle used others as a means to feed his desires and ambitions. The fledgling Death Eaters, "a group of dedicated friends," were not friends at all—only followers.[13] "Riddle undoubtedly felt no affection for any of them," Dumbledore tells Harry.[14] Riddle's great intelligence and social cunning were a deadly pair. A great suck-up, as well as a skilled wizard, he was a star at Hogwarts not only with his cronies but with the faculty as well.

This attitude reveals Riddle's unwavering egocentrism— a trait that gets more pronounced as he becomes Lord Voldemort.[15] Two clear examples of this excessive self-love also reveal Voldemort's intense craving for power and his paradoxical ability to harm himself in securing it: the murder of Lily Potter and the creation of the Horcruxes. Despite his key follower's wishes, Voldemort kills Lily, Severus Snape's great love. Perhaps Voldemort feels that Snape will not leave his side, regardless of what he does; perhaps he does not care.

Voldemort's quest is his own, and others are valued by him only as tools to serve his own desires. His lust for immortality, even at the cost of splintering his own soul, is the ultimate proof of his evil and his propensity for tyranny. Finally, we cannot neglect Voldemort's schemes to gain power at the Ministry. Although he realizes that his reputation prohibits his direct seizure of power as Minister of Magic, he lusts after the office's powers and plants others there as instruments of his desires.

With his ruthless egotism, keen intelligence, and tyrannical tendencies, Voldemort fits perfectly into Plato's category of "least trustworthy rulers." Perhaps a character better fit to rule is Albus Dumbledore. He "was offered the post of Minister of Magic, not once, but several times," and he is, after all, the most philosophical character in the Harry Potter series, making him the obvious choice as *philosopher*-ruler.[16] Nearly every tale concludes with a lesson from the wise sage, brilliantly tying together the previous year's events with all of their manifold meanings. In *Half-Blood Prince*, while engrossed in the Pensieve, Dumbledore delves into questions regarding human nature and the moral psychology of evil, giving Harry and us important clues as to what a ruler ought to be like. Dumbledore even exhibits all of the key traits a philosopher-ruler must have. He is courageous, just, and wise, and has self-mastery—or does he? In *Deathly Hallows*, we learn that Dumbledore was tempted by power in his youth, along with his friend and soon-to-be dark wizard Gellert Grindelwald. He admits of this period that "I had learned that I was not to be trusted with power . . . that power was my weakness and my temptation."[17] Many years later, after having realized his dangerous will-to-power, he is tempted again by Marvolo Gaunt's ring, the ring that ultimately shortens his life.

What makes Dumbledore venerable, even with these flaws, is his self-knowledge.[18] Plato's teacher, Socrates, instructed his students to know themselves; Dumbledore had enough self-knowledge to know that he could not be trusted with power.

This simple realization makes the crucial difference. It prevents him from accepting the offer to be Minister of Magic, which would confer the power he so desires. And so, although unfit to rule, as it turns out, Dumbledore never reaches the dark lows of Grindelwald or Voldemort—although he potentially could have. Dumbledore promotes justice in the wizard community simply by knowing himself, resisting the power he craves, and passing his lessons on to his students. Had Dumbledore succumbed to his own temptations, Voldemort might have had a competitor as the most sinister character of Harry Potter. Dumbledore's Socratic self-knowledge and Platonic teachings reveal the qualities that virtuous Potter characters embody. They have self-knowledge and are guided by justice, courage, and wisdom. Perhaps the best exemplar of these traits is Harry himself.

Harry's Cloak, the Ring of Gyges, and the Temptations of Power

As it turns out, Harry can be trusted with power. How can we be sure? Recall Plato's Ring of Gyges.[19] It measures our probity, or incorruptibility, by asking what we would do if we were invisible. Rowling resurrects Plato's character-o-meter with Harry's Invisibility Cloak. Throughout the series Harry has countless opportunities to abuse his unique power. He never once, aside from breaking some minor rules (such as staying out late), used it to his own advantage at the expense of others. Unlike Gyges, Harry certainly did not kill and seize political control. He instead sought to use his power for the greater good—the *real* greater good, that is. In the face of an opportunity for advancement, Scrimgeour's offer of Harry's dream job, Harry seeks not his own interests but those of the entire wizarding community. As Harry learns of Horcruxes, the most dangerous idea in all of dark magic, he is not tempted to seek eternal life through murder as was Voldemort. Rather,

Harry relentlessly searches to destroy the Horcruxes, employing his cloak for the purpose. As early as *Sorcerer's Stone*, Harry displays this admirable quality. As he faces Voldemort for the first time, at age eleven, Harry looks into the Mirror of Erised and finds the Sorcerer's Stone in his pocket. Dumbledore's enchantment, allowing the stone to be found only by someone who had no intention of using it, reveals Harry's lack of selfish desire.

Harry's indifference to the lure of power, it turns out, is the very quality that both Plato and Dumbledore celebrate as conducive to wise and just statecraft. Harry certainly possesses the other necessary virtues to rule, such as courage, justice, and self-restraint. But so do many others. Therefore, it really is this piece of Platonic wisdom, revived and put at the fore of Rowling's world, that ought to guide our search for those fit to rule. Although Harry is ordinary and easy for readers to relate to, there really is something magical about his immunity to the lust for power.

NOTES

1. Both Plato and Alcibiades were students of the great Athenian philosopher Socrates.

2. Plato, "Seventh Letter," 324b–324c.

3. Ibid., 324d.

4. Ibid., 325a.

5. This term is often rendered "philosopher-king," but we find this misleading because Plato—ahead of his time here, as often elsewhere—believed that women were perfectly capable of fulfilling the duties of this highest political office.

6. Plato, *The Republic*, 494b–494d.

7. Ibid., 521a.

8. Ibid., 520d.

9. Ibid., 360b–360c. One finds the same theme in the relatively recent film *Hollow Man*, where a decent research scientist played by Kevin Bacon becomes invisible and goes on a rampage worthy of Gyges himself.

10. Plato himself is deeply suspicious of the unnecessary multiplication of rules and regulations, which only serves to cheapen their value. See *Republic*, 425e–426e.

11. *Order of the Phoenix*, p. 266.

12. *Half-Blood Prince*, p. 276.

13. Ibid., p. 361.

14. Ibid., p. 361.

15. Interestingly, plenty of defenders of a more enlightened egoism would suggest that Voldemort's egocentrism was self-defeating because it contained the seeds of his destruction. Had he truly loved himself more, he would have realized that the best way to promote his own interests was not to be so transparently egoistic.

16. *Deathly Hallows*, p. 717.

17. Ibid., pp. 717–718.

18. For more on this theme, see Gregory Bassham's chapter on Dumbledore in this volume, "Choices vs. Abilities: Dumbledore on Self-Understanding."

19. This parallel is noted in David Baggett and Shawn E. Klein's "The Magic of Philosophy," in *Harry Potter and Philosophy: If Aristotle Ran Hogwarts* (Chicago: Open Court, 2004), p. 3. Notably, another philosopher, Jean-Jacques Rousseau (1712–1778), asked himself the same question that faces Gyges and Harry: "I have often asked myself what use I would have made of this ring?" His answer turns out to parallel Harry's actions—namely, that he would use his power to promote the public good. Jean-Jacques Rousseau, *Reveries of the Solitary Walker*, translated by Charles Butterworth (Indianapolis: Hackett, 1992), p. 82.

PART FOUR

THE ROOM OF REQUIREMENT: A POTTER POTPOURRI

IS DUMBLEDORE GAY?
WHO'S TO SAY?

Tamar Szabó Gendler

On October 19, 2007, before a packed audience at Carnegie Hall in New York City, J. K. Rowling made a remarkable announcement. In response to a question about whether Albus Dumbledore had ever been in love, Rowling announced that she had "always thought of Dumbledore as gay."

Reaction was immediate and emphatic. Within two days, close to 3,000 comments had been posted at the Leaky Cauldron message board, with another 2,500 at MuggleNet. There were articles in *Time* and *Newsweek*, reports on CNN and NBC, and even an op-ed piece in the *New York Times*.

Responses fell into three categories. Some readers were delighted by the news. As one Leaky Cauldron poster wrote, "You go Jo! Finally a strong, wise, non-stereotypical portrayal of a gay man!"[1] A second group was dismayed. "I am extremely disappointed at Jo for her comments on Dumbledore. It was not necessary for her to promote such a perverse lifestyle in connection to a series of books that millions of children will take interest in now and in the future," wrote another.[2]

But the most interesting type of response was the third. These readers responded to the declaration by challenging Rowling's authorial authority. "Unless she decides to write Book Eight, Ms. Rowling has missed her chance to impart any new information about any of the Harry Potter characters. If the series is truly at an end, then the author no longer possesses the authority to create new thoughts, feelings, and realities for those characters," wrote one reader.[3] "To insist on ownership (as she has done) and the right to define or re-define those characters as she sees fit after the fact, is to insist on an absolute control over the literary experience of her readers she cannot possibly have," wrote another.[4]

On its surface, this third response is perplexing. After all, at the Carnegie Hall interview, Rowling revealed all sorts of things that are not explicitly part of the Harry Potter stories. She told the audience about things that happened after the Potter books end, about things that happened before the books begin, and about things that happen during the books. But no one wrote in to comment that Neville Longbottom *didn't* go on to marry Hannah Abbott or that Remus Lupin, prior to Dumbledore taking him in, *didn't* lead "a really impoverished life because no one wanted to employ a werewolf" or that Petunia Dursley *didn't* "almost wish Harry luck when she said good-bye to him" at the beginning of *Deathly Hallows*—all of which were things that Rowling revealed only in the course of the interview.

What we face here is a version of what philosophers call the problem of *truth in fiction*.[5] Are there facts about what is true in the world of a story, and if so, what determines those facts? Is it simply a matter of the statements that are canonically expressed by the story's author? What role is played by the story's readers (or hearers) or by what the author was thinking? What about conventions governing the genre to which the story belongs? And so on.

Truth in Fiction

Because we're trying to determine whether a particular statement is true in a work of fiction, one obvious strategy would be to think about the problem in analogy with nonfiction. So let's ask: how does a historian or a biographer go about determining whether a particular statement is true? Well, she looks at the way the actual world happens to be, using things such as archival documents and historical records and archaeological evidence. On this basis, she might determine that the statement "George Washington was president of the United States" is true. It's true because (in the actual world) George Washington *was* president of the United States.

How would this go in the fictional case? Can we learn that "George Weasley was a Gryffindor Beater" is true (of the world of Harry Potter) by learning that (in the world of Harry Potter) George *was* a Gryffindor Beater? In the case of George Washington, we looked at the actual world. So, in the case of George Weasley, we simply have to look at the Harry Potter world. The problem is, we don't really know which world that is. After all, presumably there is some *other* imaginary world—call it the world of Harry Schmotter—where George Weasley happens to be Seeker for Slytherin. And another—call it the world of Harry Plotter—where George happens to be Chaser for Hufflepuff. And what about the world of Harry Putter, where they play golf instead of Quidditch? Or the world of Harry Hotter, where they wear bathing suits instead of robes? The problem, as the philosopher David Lewis (1941–2001) pointed out, is that "every way that a world could possibly be is a way that some [imaginary] world is."[6]

So, it's simply not useful to think of the task of the (fictional) storyteller as being like the task of the (real-world) historian or biographer. It's pretty clear that the historian is engaged in an act of *discovery*, and it's pretty clear what kinds of things she's discovering. Only one world is the actual world, and the hard part for the historian or the biographer is figuring out what happened in it. But there are as many imaginary worlds as there are imaginative possibilities, so the hard part for the fictional storyteller is deciding *which* imaginary world to tell us about. And it's far from clear whether to call this an act of discovery or instead to call it an act of *creation*.[7] To put the same point in a slightly different way, the problem with figuring out whether "George Weasley was a Gryffindor Beater" is true (of the world of Harry Potter) is the problem of figuring out *which one* of the infinitely many possible imaginary worlds is the world of Harry Potter. And that leaves us right where we started.

Let's try to approach our problem from a slightly different direction. Let's think about Harry Potter as an act of communication in which a writer, J. K. Rowling, is trying to give her readers access to a particular imaginary world that she envisions. She does this by writing certain words that she expects her readers to understand in certain ways. (Let's assume for the time being that there are no difficulties involved in understanding the literal meanings of the sentences she has written.) By writing those words, she lets the readers know exactly which world she is envisioning—that is, she lets them know which world is the world of Harry Potter.

And let's try again from this perspective to ask, What is true in the world of Harry Potter? We can start with a simple two-part proposal, one that we will end up needing to revise. According to this proposal, what's true in the world of Harry Potter are (a) *all* and (b) *only* those things that appear on 4,100 pages that together compose the seven core Harry Potter volumes (perhaps with the addition of *Quidditch through the Ages, Fantastic Beasts and Where to Find Them*, and *The Tales of Beedle the Bard*).

How does part (a) of this proposal fare? It certainly seems like a good beginning, but there's one minor problem. If we require that the stories be consistent (we can talk in a minute about whether this is a reasonable requirement), then we *can't* take everything that appears on those pages as true in the fiction. For there are trivial inconsistencies across the books. In *Sorcerer's Stone*, for example, Percy Weasley's prefect badge is described as silver, whereas in *Order of the Phoenix*, we are told that prefect badges are scarlet and gold; in *Chamber of Secrets*, we are told that Moaning Myrtle haunts the toilet's S-bend, but in *Goblet of Fire*, she is said to haunt the toilet's U-bend. If we require consistency, we'll need to accept *either* the S-bend claim or the U-bend claim—but not both. (Which one should we choose? Presumably, the one that Rowling tells us she really meant. We'll come back to this issue in a later section.) With this caveat in place, it seems reasonable to say that all of the things that are written down on those 4,100-plus pages are true in the world of Harry Potter. That is, it seems reasonable to say that the world of Harry Potter is one of the worlds in which the things written down on those 4,100-plus pages are true. Let's call these things the world's *primary truths*.

Before we turn to (b), let's return to the claim that the world of Harry Potter is supposed to be internally coherent. What sense of "supposed to be" are we talking about? Well, it seems pretty clear that for the most part, the world described in the Potter books *is* a coherent one—as evidenced by the fact that the inconsistencies are so rare. And Rowling's readers *expect* her to be describing an internally coherent world—as evidenced by the fact that when there are inconsistencies, readers point them out as notable. It's also obvious that Rowling *intends* to be describing a coherent world—as evidenced by the fact that she corrected these inconsistencies in later editions. Moreover, it seems apparent that the Harry Potter books are the kind of books in which internal consistency is prized; they belong to a genre (that is, a category of literary compositions characterized by certain conventions) where internal consistency is a hallmark.

We'll come back to these four criteria—textual evidence, reader response, authorial intent, and genre constraints—in our discussion further on. But to get there, let's consider (b)—the suggestion that the *only* things that are true in the world of Harry Potter are the primary truths. In contrast to (a), (b) seems more problematic. For here are some things that are not primary truths in the world of *Harry Potter*: that Hermione Granger has ten fingers, that Lavender Brown is more than two feet tall, that Helga Hufflepuff was never governor of Missouri, and that Cedric Diggory does not play for the Boston Red Sox. After all, there's no sentence in any of the Potter books that reads: "Hermione had ten fingers" or "Cedric Diggory, though an excellent Quidditch player, was not a member of a major league baseball team." And if it seems reasonable to think that these things *are* true in the world of Harry Potter, along with tons of others that are not explicitly stated in the text, then what makes them true? What principles govern the generation of what we might call *secondary truths*?

One major source of secondary fictional truths are nonfictional truths imported from the actual world. Presumably, most readers think that in the world of Harry Potter, the Earth revolves around the sun, cats have four legs, and January precedes February. Although these things aren't explicitly stated in the books, they are consistent with the story's primary truths, and they help fill out the imaginary world in a way that seems useful and natural. But is it true in the world of Harry Potter that Christopher Columbus set sail in 1492 or that John Lennon sang with the Beatles? Although these things are consistent with the story's primary truths, they don't seem necessary to help fill out the imaginary world. And what about things like Princess Diana and Prince Charles divorcing during Harry's years at Hogwarts or that during those years, iPods became popular? These are not outright inconsistent with the story's primary truths, but they seem somewhat in tension with the imaginary world. And how about the real-world facts about Harry Potter itself: that the movie version of *Goblet of Fire* was directed by Mike Newell or that *Deathly Hallows* sold more than 11 million copies in its first twenty-four hours? Nothing in the stories explicitly rules them out, but, surely, we don't want to say that *these* things are true in the world of Harry Potter.

These examples bring out the problem with accepting what we might call the *maximal inclusiveness* principle: that everything that is true in the actual world is true in the fictional world, unless it is explicitly contradicted by a primary fictional truth. For that principle would make it true *in the world of Harry Potter* that you are reading this chapter right now! Moreover, it's not clear that we even *want* such a precise principle. Do we really think there is a genuine fact of the matter whether it is true in the world of Harry Potter that Isaac Newton and Gottfried Leibniz independently discovered (or invented) calculus? (Thanks, guys!) Would we really want to say that someone who denies that this is true in the world of Harry Potter is wrong or that he doesn't properly understand the story? And wouldn't a similar issue arise, whichever specific principle we chose?

As Aristotle famously said, "Our discussion will be adequate if its clarity fits its subject-matter. . . . The educated person seeks exactness in each area to the extent that the nature of the subject allows. . . . It is just as mistaken to demand demonstrations from the rhetorician as it is to accept merely persuasive arguments from the mathematician."[8] So it looks like when we ask about a story's secondary truths, we should be asking for *rules of thumb* about what allows us to make best sense of—or to best appreciate—the work of fiction. And really, what else could there be? Unless we go back to a picture in which the task of a fiction writer is like that of an actual reporter whose job it is to tell us about a single fully specified imaginary world, it seems odd to require that there must be a definitive fact of the matter about whether every single potential second-ary truth is or is not part of the story world.

So, *Is* Dumbledore Gay?

Let's go back to our central question—is it true in the world of Harry Potter that Dumbledore is gay?—and think about what sorts of considerations we can bring to bear in answering that question. As we noted, there seem to be four places we can look: textual evidence, reader response, authorial intent, and genre constraints.

As far as textual evidence goes, it's clear that "Dumbledore is gay" is not a primary truth in Harry Potter: that sentence appears nowhere in the 4,100-plus canonical pages. So the question is whether it is a secondary truth. Clearly, it's not the sort of secondary truth that can be imported directly from the actual world, because Dumbledore is a fictional character. But is it the kind of implied secondary truth that astute readers can be expected to pick up on—for example, from the way Rowling describes Dumbledore's intense relationship with Gellert Grindelwald in *Deathly Hallows* ("You cannot imagine how his ideas . . . inflamed me"), and the fact that no heterosexual romantic interests of Dumbledore's are ever mentioned.[9] Here it seems fair to say that while it is *compatible* with the story's pri-mary truths (and perhaps even *suggested* by them—we'll come back to this at the end of this section), it is not *strictly implied* by them. And, indeed, this was the response of some of the books' most careful readers: when actress Emma Watson (who plays Hermione) was told that Dumbledore is gay, she responded, "It never really occurred to me before, but now [that] J. K. Rowling's said that he's gay, it sort of makes sense."[10]

Yet why should it matter what Rowling says? As readers have complained, "If the series is truly at an end, then the author no longer possesses the authority to create new thoughts, feelings, and realities for those characters. . . . To insist on ownership . . . after the fact, is to insist on an absolute control over the literary experience of her readers she cannot possibly have."[11] And, indeed, this sort of view of authorial authority is held—in various forms—by leading critics of authorial intent, such as William K. Wimsatt, Monroe C. Beardsley, Hans-Georg Gadamer, Roland Barthes, Michel Foucault, and Jacques Derrida.[12] They point out, for example, that language is a social creation and that authors do not have the power simply to make words mean what they choose. If a professor announces to her class that there will be a test on Thursday, then even if she *intended* to say "Tuesday," she can't simply claim that what her words *meant* was that there will be a test on Tuesday. (Of course, she can claim that she *meant to say* "Tuesday"—but she can't claim that *in saying* "Thursday," she said words that meant Tuesday.) Similarly, if an author has a character recite a piece of poetry that the author *intends* to be a work of great beauty and profundity but that consists of the words: "Hickory dickory dock; Kreacher took my sock," it doesn't follow that "Hickory dickory dock; Kreacher took my sock" is a great poem. By this reasoning, it's not up to *Rowling* to say whether Dumbledore is gay: her texts need to be allowed to speak for themselves, and each of their readers is a qualified listener.

One implication of this view is that there is no single "correct" meaning or interpretation of a given text. Different readers approach the text from different historical and cultural contexts, and their engagement with the text will almost certainly give rise to multiple interpretations. The Harry Potter books might mean one thing to me, another thing to you, and another thing to J. K. Rowling—with no one interpretation privileged over any of the others. According to this sort of view, the whole idea of trying to figure out what is going on in *the* world of Harry Potter is misguided: there isn't a single world that is the "world of Harry Potter"—there are as many Potter worlds as there are readers.[13]

By contrast, "intentionalist" literary theorists such as E. D. Hirsch Jr. argue that authorial intent is what fixes a text's correct interpretation. Without such a constraint, Hirsch contends, one uses the text "merely as grist for one's own mill."[14] And, at least to the extent that readers' primary concern is with understanding what an author meant to communicate, intention *is* obviously central. If I ask you whether you love me, and you respond by reciting a poem, my primary interest will not be in trying to interpret the poem from my unique historico-cultural perspective: my primary interest will be in trying to understand *what you intended to convey* by reciting it. Likewise, if I'm trying to understand a garbled military order; interpreting what I believe to be a divinely authored text; trying, as a judge, to discover a legislature's "original intent"; or offering what I hope will be the definitive interpretation of Plato's *Timaeus*, my primary, if not exclusive, interest will be in reconstructing the relevant authorial intent. And this is also true for many readers of the Harry Potter books.

Why? Because for most Potter fans, Rowling is the patented owner and creator of the Potter universe. She's the master storyteller who has the right—indeed, the unique prerogative—to authoritatively fill out, embellish, and continue her story. Rowling herself seems to endorse this view, claiming that Dumbledore "is my character. He is what he is and I have the right to say what I say about him."[15] And in informing us, extra-canonically, that Dumbledore is gay, Rowling is filling out for us, in a kind of oral appendix to the Potter books, details of the story that she wishes her readers to know. Readers are free, of course, to read the relevant texts differently—it is, as they say, a free country. But most Potter fans are primarily interested in how *Rowling* chooses to fill out her imagined world. And unless we have a specific reason to discount what she says in this case—as we might, for example, if we think she misspoke and said "Dumbledore" when she meant "Madame Hooch"—it's hard to see how we could consistently accept all of the other details and backstories that Rowling has revealed only in the context of her hundreds of interviews and postings.[16]

Closing Speculations: Genre

Although, for many readers, Rowling's declaration settles the matter, it is nonetheless interesting to think about the question from the perspective of our final theme—that of genre. One way that a reader might argue against the suggestion that Dumbledore is gay would be to contend that Harry Potter belongs to a genre of children's stories in which issues of adult sexuality do not arise. According to this sort of account, it simply isn't faithful to the story to say that Dumbledore is gay—not because he's straight or even asexual, but because it doesn't make sense to speak about his sexuality at all.

But while this might be a plausible argument in the case of *Goodnight Moon* or *The Wizard of Oz*, it's hard to see how it could be maintained for Harry Potter, given that Rubeus Hagrid and Madame Maxime have a book-length flirtation, and that Severus Snape's hatred of Harry is partly explained by his unrequited love for Lily Potter. Indeed, one might even counter that facts about genre *help* the case that Dumbledore is gay. For the Harry Potter books *do* belong to a genre of young adult fiction in which adults' personal needs and desires are largely invisible to the youthful protagonists. And this would help explain why no mention of Dumbledore's sexuality is made in the text, despite it being an important fact about the larger imaginary world.

Alternatively, one might argue that Harry Potter belongs to a genre of imaginary stories in which the number of minority identities is limited. While it's true that Cho Chang is Chinese and the Patil sisters are Indian and Lee Jordan is black, it's also true that the decorations at the Yule Ball don't seem to include Hanukkah menorahs, and that we hear nothing about students who are fasting during Ramadan or lighting bonfires for Holi—or making use of a wheelchair or communicating using sign-language or reading in Braille.

Fair enough. But one might counter that Rowling's approach to minority issues is actually rather nuanced. At the level of literal storytelling, tolerance is clearly the norm: interracial dating is such a nonissue as not to warrant explicit mention. But at a metaphoric level, issues of minority identity are raised throughout the novels: think of Tonks's willingness to marry Lupin despite his disability status (werewolf), Hermione's mission to liberate the house-elves, or the recurring talk of Mudbloods and purebloods and wizard supremacy. In this light, the limited literal treatment of issues of minority identity throughout the texts *helps* the case that Dumbledore is gay. For again, it provides some explanation for why no explicit mention is made of this fact in the 4,100-plus canonical pages. By introducing Dumbledore as a character with whom readers come to identify, Rowling catches her readers in an act of unwitting toleration; she brings them to recognize that like interracial dating, sexual orientation is such a nonissue as not to warrant explicit mention.

Finally, one might argue against Dumbledore's being gay on the grounds that it does no work in illuminating the story, which renders Rowling's declaration at best an irrelevant fillip. But it seems clear that Dumbledore's love for Grindelwald does important plot work. As Rowling remarked at Carnegie Hall, "To an extent, do we say it excused Dumbledore a little more because falling in love can blind us to an extent? But he met someone as brilliant as he was, and . . . was very drawn to this brilliant person, and horribly, terribly let down by him."[17] Throughout the Harry Potter series, characters fall in true love with those who are their authentic peers: James Potter and Lily Evans are brave and charming; Molly and Arthur Weasley are decent and loyal; Tonks and Lupin are courageous and unlucky; Bill Weasley and Fleur Delacour are dashing and attractive. Dumbledore's great power is his intellect. Could it be that Dumbledore is gay because Rowling could not conceive of there being a woman who was his intellectual equal?[18]

NOTES

1. "J. K. Rowling at Carnegie Hall Reveals Dumbledore Is Gay; Neville Marries Hannah Abbott, and Much More," www.the-leaky-cauldron.org/2007/10/20/j-k-rowling-at-carnegie-hall-reveals-dumbledore-is-gay-neville-marries-hannah-abbott-and-scores-more/page/8.

2. Ibid., p. 230.

3. Brenda Coulter, "Why J. K. Rowling Is No Authority on Dumbledore's Sexual Orientation," http://brendacoulter.blogspot.com/2007/10/why-jk-rowling-is-no-authority-on.html.

4. Tara Weingarten and Peg Tyre, "Rowling Says Dumbledore Is Gay," www.news week.com/id/50787/output/comments. For a similar response, see Edward Rothstein, "Is Dumbledore Gay? Depends on Definitions of 'Is' and 'Gay,'" *New York Times*, October 29, 2007, p. E1.

5. For some influential recent discussions of this question, see David Lewis, "Truth in Fiction" (1978), reprinted in *Philosophical Papers: Volume I* (New York: Oxford University Press, 1983), pp. 261–280; Gregory Currie, *The Nature of Fiction* (Cambridge, UK: Cambridge University Press, 1990); Kendall Walton, *Mimesis as Make-Believe* (Cambridge, MA: Harvard University Press, 1990).

6. David Lewis, *On the Plurality of Worlds* (Malden, MA: Blackwell Publishers, 2001), p. 2.

7. Indeed, this breakdown between creation and discovery seems to be true for abstract objects in general. Think about what a composer does when she writes down a series of notes: Does she create a new piece of music, or does she specify one of the infinitely many already existing (but previously unnoted) sequences of sounds? Aren't these basically two descriptions of the same thing?

8. Aristotle, *Nicomachean Ethics*, translated by Terence Irwin (Indianapolis: Hackett, 1985), 1.3 (1094b13).

9. *Deathly Hallows*, p. 716.

10. Tim Masters, "Potter Stars React to Gay Twist," http://news.bbc.co.uk/1/hi/entertainment/7085863.stm.

11. Coulter, "Why J. K. Rowling Is No Authority on Dumbledore's Sexual Orientation"; and Weingarten and Tyre, "Rowling Says Dumbledore Is Gay."

12. For an overview of these issues, see Sherri Irvin, "Authors, Intentions and Literary Meaning," *Philosophy Compass*, vol. 1, no. 2 (2006): 114–128 (available online at DOI 10.1111/j.1747–9991.2006.00016.x), and the essays collected in Gary Iseminger, ed., *Intention and Interpretation* (Philadelphia: Temple University Press, 1992).

13. For a general discussion of these issues, see Terry Eagleton, *Literary Theory: An Introduction* (Minneapolis: University of Minnesota Press, 1983), especially chapter 2.

14. E. D. Hirsch Jr., *The Aims of Interpretation* (Chicago: University of Chicago Press, 1976), p. 91.

15. "J. K. Rowling on Dumbledore Revelation: 'He Is My Character,'" www.the-leaky-cauldron.org/2007/10/23/j-k-rowling-on-dumbledore-revelation-i-m-not-kidding.

16. For a large collection, see www.accio-quote.org/.

17. "J. K. Rowling at Carnegie Hall Reveals Dumbledore Is Gay; Neville Marries Hannah Abbott, and Much More."

18. For extremely helpful comments and discussion, I am grateful to Elliot Paul and Mary Beth Willard.

CHOICES VS. ABILITIES
Dumbledore on Self-Understanding

Gregory Bassham

To "know thyself," said Socrates, is the beginning of wisdom. Who am I? What are my deepest desires? What are my talents? How can I live most authentically? Does my life have a purpose? What goals should I pursue? From the beginning of Western philosophy, such questions have been at the heart of the quest for wisdom and perspective.

The search for self-understanding is a central theme of the Harry Potter books. At the beginning of *Sorcerer's Stone*, Harry knows almost nothing about who he is or where he comes from. He thinks he is an ordinary, poor, unknown boy living in a humdrum and nonmysterious world. As the stories unfold, Harry realizes that none of these things are true, and he achieves a progressively deeper understanding of himself, his abilities, and his place in the world. In traditional philosophical language, the Potter books are a tale of personal enlightenment. They describe Harry's long and difficult journey from "appearance" to "reality."

Harry's quest for self-understanding has many twists and turns, and he frequently wrestles with his sense of identity. Remember the end of *Chamber of Secrets*? Harry is alarmed to discover that he shares many qualities with Voldemort, including the rare and somewhat sinister ability to speak Parseltongue. Recalling how the Sorting Hat almost put him in Slytherin, rather than Gryffindor, Harry wonders whether there is a dark side to his character. Professor Dumbledore reassures him, pointing out that his *actions* have been very different from Voldemort's and adding, "It is our choices, Harry, that show us what we truly are, far more than our abilities."[1] The philosopher and Potter scholar Tom Morris has aptly described this as "one of the most important philosophical insights in the Harry Potter books."[2] What does Dumbledore mean? What are choices? How do they differ from abilities? And is it true that our choices tell us more about ourselves than our abilities do?

Choices

"Choice" is a topic philosophers have written a great deal about. One of the earliest philosophers to grapple with the issue was Aristotle (384–322 B.C.E.), who in his *Nicomachean Ethics* carefully distinguished "choice" (*prohairesis*) from related concepts such as wish, appetite, emotion, and voluntary decision. He concluded that choice is a kind of "deliberative desire" for things that are within our power. Aristotle argued that choices are "a better test of character than actions are," and Dumbledore's similar remark may well be an echo of Aristotle's famous discussion.[3]

Philosophers have noted that "choice" is used in various senses. Sometimes it refers to a purely internal mental event, an act of decision that may or may not result in any overt physical act. Someone who says, "Draco Malfoy chose to murder Dumbledore, but in the end he couldn't bring himself to do so," is using "chose" in this purely internal sense.[4] Call this kind of choice "internal-choice."

Sometimes "choice" refers not to any interior mental decision but to an observable physical act performed in a context of presumed alternatives.[5] To say that "Dumbledore made some poor choices in his youth" is to use "choice" in this second sense. Call this kind of choice "act-choice."

There is a third sense of choice that combines both internal and external elements. Consider a well-known example offered by the German philosopher Immanuel Kant (1724–1804). Storekeeper A and Storekeeper B both choose not to cheat their customers. Storekeeper A does this because he's afraid of going to jail. Storekeeper B does it because he's honest and wants to do the right thing. Have Storekeeper A and Storekeeper B made the same choice? No, Kant said: Storekeeper B's choice is a different and morally worthier act than Storekeeper A's.[6] In this scenario, there are three distinguishable aspects of Storekeeper B's choice: an internal act of decision (deciding not to cheat the customer), an observable physical act (dealing with the customer honestly), and an internal motive (treating the customer honestly because it's the right thing to do). In this third sense of "choice," we can't really know what choice a person has made unless we know that person's motive for doing what he or she did. Call this third and most complex sense of choice "motive-choice."

How Revealing Are Our Choices?

Now that we've determined the various meanings of *choice*, we can ask whether Dumbledore is right in claiming that it is our choices, rather than our abilities, that are most revealing of "who we truly are."[7]

Clearly, internal-choices by themselves may tell us very little about our true selves. For example, the mere fact that Dudley Dursley has decided to give up sweets won't give him (or us) much insight into his character unless we know why he gave them up, whether he can stick to his resolution for any length of time, and so forth.

Similarly, act-choices may not reveal a great deal about our inner selves. Character, as Aristotle reminds us, is a matter of settled disposition—of *habit*, not individual actions. Just because Hermione Granger occasionally breaks rules (for example, in helping to organize Dumbledore's Army) doesn't mean that she is a habitual rule-breaker. Moreover, as Kant's example of the two storekeepers makes clear, a person's overt physical actions may tell us little about his or her internal motivations. In the Potter books, this point is brilliantly illustrated in the character of Severus Snape. To outside observers, Snape's actions often appear to be those of a devoted follower of Voldemort. Yet in the end, we realize that Snape's true loyalties were to Dumbledore and the memory of Lily Potter.

The most revealing kinds of choices will generally be motive-choices. Motive-choices convey more information than either internal-choices or act-choices do. They tell us not only what choice we have made (mentally), but also what motivated us to make the choice and whether we had the strength and consistency of character to act on the choice. Dumbledore is probably thinking of choices in this third and most complex sense when he praises Harry at the end of *Chamber of Secrets* and states that choices are more revealing than abilities. The choices Dumbledore is referring to (for example, Harry's decision to risk his life by entering the Chamber of Secrets in order to save Ginny Weasley) are not simply Harry's internal decisions or his bare physical acts. Dumbledore is praising the total package: (a) Harry's *decision* (b) to enter the Chamber of Secrets *in order to save Ginny Weasley*, (c) which he *acted on, despite the obstacles and known dangers*. In this sense, Harry's choice was indeed highly revealing of his character.

Are there cases where our motive-choices won't reveal much about our true characters? Sure. Trivial choices, such as picking Pumpkin Pasties rather than Cauldron Cakes from the cart on the Hogwarts Express won't tell us much about our deeper selves. More significantly, our motive-choices can be uninformative or even downright deceptive if we are mistaken about either our *true motives* in making a particular choice or the *real nature or value* of that choice. With his vast capacity for self-deception, Vernon Dursley may think that his motive for treating Harry so shabbily is to protect him from magical "funny stuff" for his own good. But if his real motive is to punish Harry for possessing special powers or for burdening the Dursleys with his unwanted presence, Uncle Vernon's motive-choice, as he understands it, will conceal his true character, rather than reveal it.[8]

Motive-acts can also deceive those who are unaware of the true nature of their actions. Vernon and Petunia Dursley think they are great parents, who shower their special "Dinky Duddydums" with love and affection. In reality, of course, they are terrible parents who spoil and coddle Dudley shamelessly. Because of their cluelessness in this respect, they mistakenly believe that their parenting choices show their characters in a positive light. Thus, instead of learning from these choices, they are actually misled by them.

In J. K. Rowling's wizarding world, there is a further reason that one's own motive-choices may not contribute to self-understanding. In that world, it may be hard to know whether it was really *you* who made a particular choice.

Think of the scene in *Order of the Phoenix* when Harry thought it was he who attacked Arthur Weasley in the form of a giant snake. Only later does he find out that it was Voldemort who tried to kill Mr. Weasley, and that Harry was sharing the Dark Lord's experiences by means of the fragment of Voldemort's soul that he carries within him.

Or think of the episode in *Half-Blood Prince* when Voldemort steals Morfin Gaunt's wand, uses it to kill his Muggle father and grandparents, and then implants a false memory in

Morfin's mind, making Morfin think that *he* had murdered the Riddles.

Finally, think of the perplexities that can arise due to magical spells such as the Imperius Curse, Polyjuice Potion, and memory modification. Imagine that Fred and George Weasley have bewitched a bottle of Ogden's Old Firewhiskey so that it looks and tastes like butterbeer. You drink it and fall asleep in a stupor. The next morning you're called into Dumbledore's office and accused of transfiguring Filch's cat, Mrs. Norris, into an armadillo. Did you do it? You remember nothing, but three students from Hufflepuff swear they saw you bewitch the cat. Dumbledore performs the Priori Incantatem charm on your wand and determines that it was your wand that cast the spell. Three possibilities occur to you: (1) You performed the spell but can't remember it because of the booze (or perhaps because your memory was modified); (2) you performed the spell, but only because you were under the Imperius Curse, and you have no memory of the act because no one remembers anything they do while under that curse; (3) somebody disguised as you due to Polyjuice Potion performed the spell using your wand. If 1 is true, then it was your choice to transfigure the cat, and you may be at least somewhat responsible for the misuse of magic. If, however, 2 or 3 is true, you didn't (voluntarily) perform the spell, and you're not guilty of misuse of magic. What really happened? There may be no way to know. Consequently, no firm conclusions about your character can be drawn from the episode (except that you were a dimwit to ever trust Fred and George).

As these examples make clear, there are special difficulties in the wizarding world in knowing what choices you have made. The boundaries between self and other are less clear in that world than in ours, and the possibilities of manipulation, control, and illusion are greater. Still, in Rowling's world as in ours, choices do often reveal valuable insights about ourselves. According to Dumbledore, choices are "far more" informative in this way than abilities are. To see whether he is right, we need to understand what abilities are and how they differ from choices.

Abilities

The notion of *ability*, as the psychologist Michael J. A. Howe notes, is a "fuzzy concept."[9] In general, an ability is a power or a capacity to do something. Thus, Voldemort has the rare ability to fly without a broomstick because he possesses the requisite magical skills that allow him to fly in this way. Similarly, Sirius, as an Animagus, has the ability to transform himself into a large black dog because he has the self-taught capability to do so.

This much is clear, but what makes the concept of an ability "fuzzy" is that abilities come in degrees and often vary with circumstances. I speak about seventy words of Mermish (the language of the mer-people); you speak three hundred words. Do I have the ability to speak Mermish? To some extent, but not as well as you. I can conjure a chipmunk Patronus, but only when I'm really mellow and relaxed, which is rare. Do I have the ability to conjure such a Patronus? Sometimes, but not very often. In other words, it's not always clear whether someone "has" a certain ability or not.

This is one way that choices differ from abilities—choices tend to be more clear-cut than abilities are. As we've seen, choices are *acts*, either mental or physical. Normally, there's a definite answer whether someone did or did not make a particular choice.[10] Did Peter Pettigrew choose to betray Harry's parents, rather than be killed by Voldemort? No question. Did Harry choose to break up with Ginny at the end of *Half-Blood Prince* in order to protect her? Absolutely. By contrast, abilities are *powers* or *capacities*, rather than acts.[11] As such, they tend to come in degrees and to be more variable than choices are.

How Revealing Are Our Abilities?

Dumbledore suggests that our choices tend to be more self-revealing than our abilities. Is he right? Well, some kinds of abilities will reveal little or nothing about a person's character or inner self. In general, these include abilities that are:

- Trivial (e.g., the ability to wiggle your ears)
- Very widely shared (e.g., the ability to digest granola)
- Not within one's conscious control (e.g., the ability to breathe while sleeping)
- Innate, rather than acquired (e.g., the ability to cry)[12]
- Unrecognized (e.g., Harry's ability to speak Parseltongue, before he first became aware of the talent in *Sorcerer's Stone*)

More important, many sorts of abilities won't be particularly revealing because they are *morally neutral capacities* that can be used wisely or unwisely, ethically or unethically. This seems to be Dumbledore's point when he remarks that Harry shares "many qualities Salazar Slytherin prized in his hand-picked students. His own very rare gift, Parseltongue—resourcefulness—determination—a certain disregard for rules."[13] Notice that each of the qualities Dumbledore mentions can be used for good *or* evil ends. For instance, both Voldemort and Harry are resourceful. Yet Voldemort uses his resourcefulness to pursue his goals of world domination and personal immortality, whereas Harry uses his to save his friends and fight tyranny. Likewise, both Dumbledore and Voldemort possess exceptional magical abilities. Yet Dumbledore uses his magical talents to do good, whereas Voldemort uses his to do evil. So, simply *having* qualities like resourcefulness or advanced magical abilities won't reveal much about what kind of person you are. It's how you use these abilities that really matters.

Does this mean that abilities *never* reveal much about a person's character? By no means. Abilities that can be acquired only through hard work, self-sacrifice, and determination can tell us a lot about a person. The same is true of ethical abilities, such as a capacity to empathize with others' suffering, to think of other people's needs before your own, to plan prudently for the future, and to remain resilient in the face of disappointment. So, if Dumbledore means that choices are *generally* more self-revealing than abilities, he is no doubt correct. But at the same time, we should also be honest and self-reflective about our abilities, because they, too, can tell us a great deal about ourselves and how we can live most happily and successfully.

Beyond Choices: Toward a Deeper Self-Understanding

Reflecting on your past choices may tell you a lot about yourself, but it may not. Consider Gilderoy Lockhart. Lockhart thinks about himself a lot—all of the time, in fact. But his self-image is completely out of whack. He imagines that he's a great Defense Against the Dark Arts teacher, but he can't even manage a cage full of Cornish pixies. Although he poses as an expert duelist, he is easily blasted off his feet by Snape's Expelliarmus spell. He vainly imagines that everyone is a fan of his, and when he confidently claims to be able to fix Harry's injured arm, he ends up removing all of Harry's arm bones instead. Why the big disconnect? Because Lockhart is blind to his own faults. He looks but doesn't see.

This is the basic problem with seeking self-understanding simply by reflecting on one's own choices. If you're wearing rose-colored glasses—what psychologists call "cognitive blinders"—you're not going to see the real you.

So, what's a better strategy for achieving self-knowledge? If we look at what the great thinkers have said on this topic, we can identify four major strategies:

- Cultivate a habit of self-examination.
- Be alert to your irrational tendencies.

- Get a little help from your friends.
- Challenge yourself.

As we'll see, each of these principles is well-illustrated in the Potter books.

Cultivate a Habit of Self-Examination

Self-knowledge requires time, openness, and humility. What are my deepest values and commitments? What do I like? What do I dislike? What am I most passionate about? What are my greatest strengths and weaknesses? Am I the person I want to be? How can I make the most of my time and talents? What would I like to be remembered for when I'm gone? These are tough questions, and answering them takes time. It also requires openness and humility, because, as Socrates pointed out, most of us find it very difficult to face unpleasant truths about ourselves and to admit our own limitations.

As the philosopher Thomas Pangle remarked, most of the time when we reflect seriously, it's because we're in trouble. Some life crisis happens—we lose a job, get divorced, flunk out of school, get a really bad haircut. Only then, it seems, do we seriously evaluate where we are in our lives and the choices we've made. But life should not be lived on autopilot. Just as we need to develop good habits of diet and exercise, we need to form positive habits of mindfulness and self-examination. Only by knowing yourself can you live honestly and find your own path.

Dumbledore is a model of a reflective, self-aware individual. When he was a young man, he realized that his besetting weakness was a love of power. Realizing this, he never accepted the position of Minister of Magic, although it was offered to him several times. Dumbledore also drew an important lesson from his infatuation with the future dark wizard Gellart Grindelwald. In a 2008 interview, Rowling stated that Dumbledore "lost his moral compass completely" when he fell in love with Grindelwald.[14] As a result, Dumbledore became very distrusting of his judgment in matters of the heart and decided to live a celibate and scholarly life.

In his effort to live what Socrates called "the examined life," Dumbledore regularly uses the Pensieve, a magical stone basin that allows individuals to view either their own or another person's memories from a third-person perspective. Dumbledore tells Harry that whenever he has too many thoughts and memories crammed into his mind, he uses the Pensieve to siphon off some of these excess thoughts. This unclutters the mind, removes painful or obsessive memories, and improves mental focus. The third-person perspective also makes it "easier to spot patterns and links" and to notice things that weren't consciously observed in the original experiences.[15] Clearly, such a device would be a great tool for self-understanding—not to mention as an instant replay device at the Quidditch World Cup!

Be Alert to Your Irrational Tendencies

Aristotle classically defined humans as the "rational animal"—but, obviously, he had never watched an episode of *The Jerry Springer Show*. The fact is that we humans regularly fall prey to irrational biases, prejudices, egocentrism, close-mindedness, wishful thinking, and stereotyping. And as we've seen, your choices may not tell you much about your true self if, like the Dursleys or Lockhart, your self-image is distorted by poor thinking habits.

The solution is to recognize and actively combat one's irrational tendencies. As much as we might like to think of ourselves as unusually self-aware and perceptive individuals, we're all human and thus heir to all of the thinking flaws that humans are so often prone to.

Pretty much the full range of human irrationality is on display in the Potter novels—think of Percy Weasley's rule fetish and love of power, Malfoy's virulent racism and classism, Ron Weasley's irrational jealousy, Rubeus Hagrid's blind affection for dangerous magical creatures, Cornelius Fudge's close-mindedness, or Luna Lovegood's credulity for tales of the uncanny. But Rowling's best example of irrational thinking is wizards' treatment of house-elves.

House-elves are effectively slaves in the wizarding world. They are bound for life to well-to-do wizarding families or to institutions, such as Hogwarts. They perform unpaid menial tasks, are given limited education, wear cast-off items such as old pillowcases as clothing, are forbidden to use wands, and can be beaten, tormented, and even killed by their masters with apparent impunity. Yet very few wizards see this kind of indentured servitude as morally problematic in the least. Why this ethical blindness? Because as Ron and Hagrid note, with the exception of "weirdoes" like Dobby, nearly all house-elves *like* being slaves and even regard freedom, as Winky does, as something depressing and shameful.[16]

As Hermione points out, however, the fact that house-elves have been conditioned to buy into their own oppression does not justify the practice.[17] Although Harry at first shares the conventional prejudices regarding house-elves, in the end he accepts Hermione's view, digging Dobby's grave with his own hands and writing "Here lies Dobby, a Free Elf" on the tombstone.[18] In this process of moral growth, Harry is greatly helped by his friend Hermione, a tireless advocate for elf rights. This leads to our third pointer.

Get a Little Help from Your Friends

Humans aren't like the Borg in *Star Trek*. We don't have a collective consciousness in which we directly experience other people's thoughts and emotions. Instead, we live our lives from the "inside," from the vantage point of our own personal mini-cam on life. This gives us a privileged access to what's going on inside our own heads. But sometimes we can be too close to ourselves to see us as we truly are. We lack perspective, objectivity. That's where friends can help. Friends can tell you when you're being selfish or rude or making a total fool of yourself. Conversely, they can let you know when you're being kind or generous or need to lighten up on yourself.

In the Potter books, friends frequently play a vital role in enhancing one another's self-understanding. For instance, Hermione helps Harry understand why he was being insensitive to Cho Chang on their trip to Hogsmeade; Harry, Ron, and Hermione assist Neville Longbottom in overcoming his painful shyness and lack of self-confidence; and Hagrid helps Ron understand why friendships should not be wrecked by petty jealousies. By the same token, characters who apparently lack close and supportive friendships, such as the Dursleys, Lockhart, and Professor Slughorn, tend not to progress in self-understanding. Honest and caring friends can be a mirror in which we see ourselves as we really are.

Challenge Yourself

In ordinary life, people tend to behave in stereotypical ways. You can't tell much about a person by watching how she brushes her teeth or walks to the bus stop. It's in out-of-the-ordinary situations—especially situations of challenge or adversity—that the most important differences between people shine through. That's why, as the Roman philosopher-poet Lucretius observed, "It is more useful to scrutinize a man in danger or peril, and to discern in adversity what manner of man he is; for only then are the words of truth drawn up from the very heart, the mask is torn off, the reality remains."[19]

In the Potter books, Harry and his friends are repeatedly tested. Over and over, they are placed in situations that test their courage, loyalty, intelligence, and resourcefulness. With a few notable exceptions (such as Ron's temporary abandonment of Harry and Hermione in *Deathly Hallows*), they pass these tests with flying colors and prove their true mettle.

As a result, they grow in self-confidence and self-knowledge and emerge at the end (much like Frodo and his hobbit friends in J. R. R. Tolkien's *Lord of the Rings*) as humble but battle-tested heroes.

The Ultimate Measure of a Person

So, in the final analysis, Dumbledore is right when he says that our choices tend to be more revealing than our abilities. Our abilities show us what we *can* do, but our choices reveal most clearly our qualities of character and what we care about most deeply. In this sense it is true, as the author Tobias Wolff remarks, that "we define ourselves and our deepest values by the choices we make, day by day, hour by hour, over a lifetime."[20] But as we've seen, some choices are more revealing than others. The ultimate measure of a person is where he stands when tested by challenge or adversity. By this measure, Harry and his friends all earn O's, for Outstanding!

NOTES

1. *Chamber of Secrets*, p. 333.

2. Tom Morris, *If Harry Potter Ran General Electric: Leadership Wisdom from the World of the Wizards* (New York: Doubleday, 2006), p. 23.

3. Aristotle, *Nicomachean Ethics*, translated by J. A. K. Thomson (London: Penguin Books, rev. ed., 1976), p. 116 (1111b5).

4. Andrew Oldenquist, "Choosing, Deciding, and Doing," in Paul Edwards, ed., *The Encyclopedia of Philosophy*, vol. 1 (New York: Macmillan, 1967), p. 96.

5. Ibid., p. 97.

6. Immanuel Kant, *Metaphysical Foundations of Morals*, translated by Carl J. Friedrich, in *The Philosophy of Kant*, edited by Carl J. Friedrich (New York: Modern Library, 1949), pp. 144–145. Kant frames his discussion in terms of "acts," rather than "choices," but I think he would agree that the storekeepers have made different choices.

7. The phrase "who we truly are" is ambiguous. It might refer to the metaphysical self (whether the self is a spiritual substance, for example, or is ultimately identical with the Divine). Or it might refer to the psychological self—our character or personality. Because there's no reason to think our choices would reveal our ultimate metaphysical identities, Dumbledore must be speaking of the psychological self.

8. For more on the Dursleys' talent for self-deception, see Diana Mertz Hsieh, "Dursley Duplicity: The Morality and Psychology of Self-Deception," in David Baggett and Shawn E. Klein, eds., *Harry Potter and Philosophy: If Aristotle Ran Hogwarts* (Chicago: Open Court, 2004), pp. 22–37.

9. Michael J. A. Howe, *Principles of Abilities and Human Learning* (London: Psychology Press, 1998), p. 55.

10. Of course, it's sometimes hard to know whether someone has made a particular choice. ("Marietta looks shifty-eyed. Has she decided to betray Dumbledore's Army?")

11. In Aristotle's terms, choices belong to the category of act, whereas abilities belong to the category of potency. See Aristotle, *Metaphysics*, V, 7.

12. As Dumbledore remarks, "It matters not what someone is born, but what they grow to be," *Goblet of Fire*, p. 708.

13. *Chamber of Secrets*, p. 333.

14. Adeel Amini, "Minister of Magic," http://gallery.the-leaky-cauldron.org/picture/207262.

15. *Goblet of Fire*, p. 597.

16. See, for example, *Goblet of Fire*, pp. 224, 265; and *Order of the Phoenix*, p. 385.

17. It's not uncommon for subordinated peoples to internalize their oppressors' values and come to see their own oppression as natural or just. This is a form of what Marxists call "false consciousness."

18. *Deathly Hallows*, p. 481.

19. Lucretius, *De Rerum Natura*, Book 3, lines 55–59.

20. Quoted in "Moments That Define Spirituality," cnn.com/2008/LIVING/way oflife/06/10/o.spirituality.2.u/index.html.

THE MAGIC
OF PERSONAL
TRANSFORMATION

S. Joel Garver

When we first meet Dudley Dursley, he's an utter prat. Dudley despises Harry and treats him like "a dog that had rolled in something smelly."[1] Dudley always wants his own way, and when it comes to his parents, Petunia and Vernon, he knows how to get it. Dudley thinks he's always in the right and can do no wrong. He can't see himself as anything but God's gift to the world—a model of juvenile perfection, entitled to every good thing that comes his way. And Dudley can't recognize Harry as anything but a nuisance—a worthless distraction, a potential threat to ickle Dudders' own comfort and ease.

Yet by the beginning of *Deathly Hallows*, Dudley has changed dramatically. He leaves a cup of tea for Harry outside Harry's room at Number 4 Privet Drive, and he defies his parents to instead do what Harry urges. Dudley ultimately manages to express something like affection and gratitude toward Harry, even in the face of his parents' incomprehension and his own embarrassment. In the end, when Dudley shakes Harry's hand and says good-bye, Harry sees a "different personality."[2]

What happened? How did Dudley come to see Harry in a new way, not as a nuisance, but with a newfound respect? And does this mean that Dudley came to see *himself* differently than before? If so, how did this change occur?

These are questions about how Dudley develops as a person, but they also raise fascinating epistemological issues. "Epistemology" is the part of philosophy that asks and tries to answer questions about how we know stuff. Specifically, let's consider how Dudley and Harry came to know both themselves and others better than they did before. By examining how these two characters grow and develop, we can understand how Rowling presents knowing as a process of personal transformation. As we'll see, when we encounter ourselves and others in significant ways, we grow in mind and heart and become better knowers.[3]

Positioning Our Prejudgments

In order to know and interpret our world, said the German philosopher Hans-Georg Gadamer (1900–2002), we must come to the world with "prejudgments."[4] Every time we try to interpret a situation, a person, or a text, we bring questions, biases, and expectations with us, like bringing a handful of tools from a well-worn toolbox. Without such prejudgments, we wouldn't have any way to "get into" whatever it is we're trying to understand. It would be like a container sealed shut, and we'd be left standing there, helpless and empty-handed.

Our prejudgments shape, in turn, the kinds of information we're able to get out of what we're trying to understand. But if we come at things with the wrong tools, we aren't going to make much headway. What we're trying to interpret and understand will resist our advances. After all, we can't undo screws very easily with pliers, never mind with a hammer.

Gadamer said that there's no use pretending we don't have prejudgments that craft how we think and perceive. The issue is whether our prejudgments will help us understand better or whether they'll get in the way. It's not simply that the wrong sorts of questions or expectations won't get us very far. Whether they help us understand also depends on how loosely we hold these prejudgments and whether we allow the situations we face to challenge and reshape our strategies. When we're face-to-face with a box screwed shut, do we have the sense to set down the hammer and scrounge around for a screwdriver instead?

The Ignorance of Ickle Dudleykins

If Gadamer's insight applies to our world, might it apply in Harry's as well? Dudley sees himself as the center of the universe and interprets his world through his own bloated ego. This is due mainly to the way Petunia and Vernon constantly dote on him. In their eyes, there is "no finer boy anywhere" than their "baby angel."[5] They build up and reinforce Dudley's sense of self at Harry's expense, favoring their son over Harry with gifts, clothes, and special treats. Aunt Marge likewise is eager to visit her "neffy-poo" Dudley and to slip him a twenty-pound note. How could any child treated in this way feel anything but special and privileged?

Furthermore, Dudley's sense of self resists any sort of retooling or change. Any information that can possibly challenge or modify Dudley's prejudgments is quickly papered over or given a new spin by his parents. They are able to "find excuses for his bad marks," insisting that Dudley is a "very gifted boy" but misunderstood by his teachers, and they brush away accusations of bullying with the contention that although Dudley is a "boisterous little boy . . . he wouldn't hurt a fly." Even when Dudley is forced to go on a diet, Aunt Petunia asserts that he is merely "big-boned," a "growing boy" who simply has not yet shed his "puppy fat."[6] This environment of flattery and indulgence sculpts Dudley's own intellectual outlook by which he understands his world, his place in it, and his cousin, Harry. As Mark Twain said, denial ain't just a river in Egypt.

But Dudley's close encounter with the cold terror of the dementors seriously shakes him and forces him to confront himself in a new way, requiring a radical readjustment of his previous sense of himself. As Harry knows, the dementors cause Dudley to relive the worst moments of his life. All of Dudley's intellectual habits that were designed to reconfigure or push away the awful truth are stripped away. For the first time, Dudley sees clearly who he truly is—"spoiled, pampered, bullying"—and begins to interpret his place in the world properly.[7] When Dumbledore later speaks of "the appalling damage" that Petunia and Vernon have "inflicted upon [this] unfortunate boy," perhaps Dudley is finally in a position to hear and accept Dumbledore's diagnosis, even if his parents are not.[8]

Dudley's obstinate prejudgments finally change so that he can receive and understand the truth. This new perspective on reality and his own place within it enables Dudley finally to recognize Harry's courage and capacity to help, and to feel gratitude for Harry's rescuing him and perhaps even a certain admiration, if not affection, for his magical family member.

Betrayed by Biases

Dudley's experience isn't unique but rather reflects the similar experiences of J. K. Rowling's other characters. Harry's temperament, biases, and expectations shape his own intellectual habits. Just consider Harry's ongoing prejudice against Severus Snape, his initial fear that Sirius Black is out to get him, his misplaced trust in the imposter Mad-Eye Moody, his confidence in the veracity of his own dreams, and his trust in the Half-Blood Prince's potions book.

These habits, in turn, blind Harry to the reality of the situations around him. He can't see where the real dangers lie, who truly means him harm, and what's actually going on. He's oblivious to his own liability to deception and the potential harm of the Sectumsempra spell. Harry often comes at his world with the wrong sort of expectations and questions and, as a result, doesn't end up with the right sort of answers. Because it's Harry's perspective we readers experience, we, too, are likely to interpret the unfolding events through the wrong filter.

In similar ways, other characters misjudge the situations and the people around them. Dumbledore's youthful infatuation with Gellert Grindelwald feeds his ill-conceived dreams about wizards ruling the world "for the greater good."[9] Merope Gaunt is attracted to the wealthy Tom Riddle and desires to escape her miserable home life, leading her to think that Riddle might truly fall in love with her, even if she has to assist the process with a potion. In *Deathly Hallows*, Hermione Granger, Harry, and Ron Weasley find their own fears, suspicions, and biases magnified by the locket Horcrux. They end up misreading one another until Ron finally runs off in a fit of paranoia, jealousy, and hurt. Likewise, the Malfoys' lust for pureblood power impels them to underestimate the depths of evil to which Voldemort would sink.

In each case, prejudgments make the characters misread the truth until the pain of banging up against reality forces them to rethink. This is why the truth is something to care about: false beliefs do not accurately depict the world and thus prove to be an unreliable map for navigating through it.

Dangerous Dreams

Let's consider a specific example involving Harry. In *Order of the Phoenix*, Harry is understandably disturbed by his insight into Voldemort's thoughts. Such flashes of vision mostly happen when Harry is asleep and dreaming, when his mind is at its most "relaxed and vulnerable."[10]

Yet Harry remains cocky in his own sense of mission in opposing Voldemort, wrongly believing that he uniquely understands Voldermort's true nature and capacities. So Harry comes to trust the truth of his dreams as a transparent window and privileged perspective into Voldemort's own mind. Dumbledore, however, warns Harry that if he can see into Voldemort's mind, then Voldemort can probably see into Harry's mind as well. And if Voldemort becomes aware of his connection to Harry, he could use his formidable powers of Legilimency to manipulate and deceive Harry.

Harry, confident in his own ideas, discounts Dumbledore's warnings. Even when Dumbledore emphatically warns Harry that he "must study Occlumency," Harry neglects to practice and quickly falls prey to new dreams.[11] Although Dumbledore himself sent Harry to Snape for lessons in Occlumency, Harry's suspicions against Snape lead him to resist the training. Harry suggests instead that the lessons are making things worse. When Hermione urges him to keep practicing Occlumency and to work harder at it, Harry likewise rejects her advice in a fit of frustration. His later conversation with Sirius Black suggests that Harry never really saw why Occlumency was at all important. It's tempting, therefore, to think that Snape's accusation hits a bit too close to the truth: "Perhaps you actually enjoy having these visions and dreams, Potter. Maybe they make you feel special—important?"[12]

The Cost of Overconfidence

In this case, the price of Harry's prejudices is profound: the death of his godfather, Sirius Black. During his History of Magic O.W.L., Harry dozes and sees Sirius being tortured by Voldemort in the Department of Mysteries. His immediate reaction is to begin plotting some way of getting into the Ministry of Magic to rescue Sirius.

Hermione raises a series of reasonable objections.[13] Rather than doubt his own certainty, however, Harry snaps back at Hermione. He even turns Dumbledore's warnings on their heads in order to prop up his own beliefs, interpreting the Occlumency lessons as proof that his dreams must be real. Hermione finally persuades Harry to check first whether Sirius is still at Grimmauld Place before trying a rescue. Using Professor Umbridge's office fireplace to connect to Sirius's home, Harry finds only the lugubrious and unreliable house-elf Kreacher there. Kreacher is only too happy to confirm Harry's belief that Sirius had left for the Department of Mysteries. This is all Harry needs, so he single-mindedly undertakes the "rescue" that will lead to Sirius's death.

What are we to make of this? Was Kreacher's testimony enough of a fact-check to justify Harry's rescue attempt? Or was Harry again led astray by the bent of his own intellect and emotions, now twisted in the hands of Voldemort's craftiness? The danger of not thinking clearly is that Harry begins to see certain "evidence" as reliable that should instead be considered suspicious. Too often, Harry underestimates the many ways he's far less objective in assessing the evidence than he might like to think.

Nothing up to this point in the story would suggest that Kreacher's testimony is worth taking seriously. Kreacher's behavior seems pretty shady as Harry interviews him; he appears "highly delighted about something," with signs of recent injury to his hands, chuckling and cackling at Harry's interrogations.[14] Indeed, as Dumbledore later points out, he had warned Sirius that his lack of concern and coldness toward Kreacher could have dangerous consequences. Harry, moreover, is acting *all by himself* in his trust of Kreacher's testimony because he never bothers to share with his friends that the house-elf was his source.

We shouldn't be too hard on Harry, however. He is still only a fifteen-year-old kid and is acting with noble intentions. The dangers to which he falls prey remind us of times when we ourselves—because of either youth or cockiness, laziness or impetuousness—have seen what we wanted to see, thanks to blinders that blocked or skewed our picture of reality.

Memories Help Make Meaning

Memory plays a crucial role in how our biases and intellectual habits form, develop, and reshape. If we forget the past, individually or as a culture, we lose knowledge that has already been gained, and we lose valuable tools by which our knowledge may grow. Thus, time can be the enemy of understanding, closing us off from the resources of the past that are necessary for knowing the present. What's already happened can disappear and be lost forever, entirely forgotten, unless traces of the past somehow persist into the present. We can speak of these traces of the past as "memories," especially as they register in our experience and consciousness.

In his classic autobiography, the *Confessions*, the philosopher St. Augustine (354–430 A.D.) tried to explain the nature of time and time's connection to memory. He noted that the past no longer exists and the future hasn't yet come into existence. How, then, can the past stay with us? Moreover, the present, as the place where the past and the future meet, has no duration of its own. What, then, is this ghostly, fleeting thing we call "time"?[15] Augustine's answer was that time is only fully known in human experience. Through us, the memory of the past comes together with anticipation of the future in our present awareness. How we experience "now" is a function of how the past brings us to this moment with all of the remembered patterns and habits we possess. These, in turn, help us anticipate and move into the future.

We can connect Augustine's idea with a point from Gadamer. When it comes to knowing and interpreting reality, prejudgments are a kind of memory we can't do without. Through our prejudgments, what has happened in the past affects how we approach the present and how we view the future. When we realize that prejudgments function almost like memory, we can see why Gadamer connects them with "tradition," a word that comes to us in English from a Latin verb that means to "pass down" from the past.[16]

In our prejudgments, memory is first of all personal. Our personal past experiences—how we're raised and educated, what happens to us growing up, which responses seem to work for us—mold who we become. The way Hermione values books and education was no doubt shaped by her well-educated parents. The older Weasley twins' shenanigans, not to mention Mr. Weasley's penchant for tinkering with Muggle artifacts, likely bolster Ron's understanding that rules are easily bent and meant to be broken.

Memory, however, is also thoroughly social in nature. In the broadest sense, memory isn't only the traces of past events and personal experiences that we carry around in our heads. Memory also includes all of the traces of the past handed down to us within our language and culture, our artifacts and institutions.[17] These, too, mold the intellectual habits, assumptions, and expectations we use to interpret our world and move forward in knowledge, often in ways we're not even aware of.[18]

In Rowling's novels, it's the Pensieve that symbolizes the power of memory—both individually and socially—and its much-needed role in communicating and forming knowledge. In fact, when Dumbledore explains the Pensieve, he describes its primary function as epistemological: to preserve and organize knowledge. Dumbledore remarks that he sometimes has "too many thoughts and memories crammed into [his] mind." With the Pensieve, a person simply "siphons the excess thoughts from one's mind, pours them into the basin, and examines them at one's leisure." Not only are the thoughts and the experiences preserved, but it "becomes easier to spot patterns and links . . . when they are in this form."[19] The Pensieve allows its users to step back and look more observantly at themselves in order to gain a fresh perspective.

The Pensieve isn't only for personal use, however. It also makes memory available to others, reminding us that memory is at root a *social* phenomenon. Through the Pensieve's magic, Dumbledore puts Harry in contact with past events he otherwise would never have known about. And these events provide evidence and context that bump up against Harry's assumptions, provide insight into those around him, and help him to better understand the threats and the opportunities he encounters.

Most of Harry's experiences with the Pensieve occur under Dumbledore's direction and provide Harry with information he needs to understand and vanquish Voldemort. Thus, Harry learns of Tom Riddle's childhood as an orphan, his youthful sadism, his promise as a pupil, and his self-loathing that led him to murder his Muggle family and to buy into pureblood ideology. Harry also learns how Riddle sought immortality, even though it required terrible acts of evil to split his soul and preserve its pieces through dark magic.

In addition, the Pensieve presents reconstructed memories, extracted only with difficulty from Hokey and Morfin Gaunt. Hokey was the house-elf who worked for Hepzibah Smith, from whom Voldemort obtained Slytherin's locket and Hufflepuff's cup. Morfin was Merope's brother, the uncle of Voldemort, whom the young Riddle framed for the murder of his Muggle father and grandparents. With each additional memory, Harry gains more insight into Voldemort's history and character, his past and present activities, and, most important, his vulnerabilities. Just as Dudley needed true beliefs to replace his false ones, Harry needed a fuller picture of Riddle and his history, as well as crucial details about Snape's life, to discover how to defeat the Dark Lord.

Moving Past Misdirection

In each book of the series, Rowling allows Harry's prejudgments and those of the other characters to lead them to false interpretations of their world. But when enough tension builds and enough evidence piles up, it alters their prejudgments until they're forced to fit reality. Dumbledore's dreams of wizard supremacy evaporate when his relationship with Grindelwald leads to his sister's death. Merope's desire for Tom Riddle's love dissolves into despair when she stops using the love potion and he abandons her. Ron comes to his senses as soon as he's away from Harry and Hermione and the influence of the Horcrux. Even the Malfoys begin to see Voldemort for what he truly is once Voldemort's own ambitions threaten the life of their son, Draco.

Most of all, Harry transforms. When we first meet him, he's a naive and hesitant kid, just entering the wizarding world, full of curiosity and questions. Although he's open to learning, he's sometimes led astray or beyond his abilities by his loyalty to friends, disregard for rules, and desire for a sense of importance and belonging. Later, Harry grows into an impetuous and headstrong teenager, often cocky in his own insights and quick to dismiss both friends and authorities he should trust. Through mistakes, tragedies, and struggles, Harry eventually matures into a remarkably courageous young man, able to discern what's happening and what must be done.

Right knowledge and good intellectual habits are necessary not only to get the facts straight, but also to exercise virtues such as bravery, loyalty, and generosity. Harry can't be truly brave, after all, unless he understands the nature of the danger confronting him, what sort of confidence he must marshal in the face of it, and whose future depends on his actions. Likewise, true loyalty to Dumbledore isn't a matter of minimizing his real faults or clinging to a false, idealized image of who Dumbledore is. Rather, it is to understand that despite Dumbledore's known faults, his missteps, and his failure to disclose key information, his motives and judgment are worthy of trust. And so, personal transformation of character depends on moving past misjudgments, being open to correction, and cultivating a growing sensitivity to what is right and true. In this way, epistemology is inseparable from ethics.

What Harry and his friends go through as characters, we also experience as readers, because Rowling invites us to see Harry's world largely through his eyes. Although we may sometimes see beyond Harry's limited horizon before Harry himself does, Rowling uses narrative misdirection in ways that reinforce our mistaken assumptions and guide us away from crucial questions. Many of *our* prejudgments remain unchallenged, and we, too, along with Harry, go through a process of discovery and reinterpretation on the way to knowledge. And, returning to where we began, if a person such as Dudley Dursley can come to appreciate Harry, there's good hope for even the most resistant and unsympathetic of readers.

The genius of Rowling's work lies not only in its powerful storytelling, but also in its power to change us as readers. If we allow Rowling's magic to work on us, it will engage, challenge, and transform our intellectual habits. As we follow Harry and the other characters, we don't merely become better readers, we become better people.

NOTES

1. *Chamber of Secrets*, p. 5.

2. *Deathly Hallows*, p. 42.

3. Philosophers distinguish several types of knowing. "Personal" knowing is a matter of immediate acquaintance (knowing Luna Lovegood, knowing the Leaky Cauldron). "Propositional" knowing is a matter of knowing that such-and-such is the case, whether or not one is personally acquainted with the relevant object (knowing that Hufflepuff's cup is in Gringotts, knowing that thestrals are visible only to those who have seen death). And "practical" or "procedural" knowing is a matter of how to do something (knowing how to Apparate, knowing how to inflict the Cruciatus Curse). Often, these various kinds of knowing intertwine. Here, we'll focus mostly on acts of self-understanding, which typically involve both personal knowing and knowledge that such-and-such is the case.

4. Hans-Georg Gadamer, *Truth and Method*, 2nd rev. ed., translated by J. Weinsheimer and D. G. Marshall (New York: Crossroad, 1989), especially pp. 265–379.

5. *Sorcerer's Stone*, pp. 1, 21.

6. *Goblet of Fire*, pp. 26–27.

7. *Order of the Phoenix*, p. 30.

8. *Half-Blood Prince*, p. 55.

9. *Deathly Hallows*, p. 357.

10. *Order of the Phoenix*, p. 531.

11. Ibid., pp. 622, 635.

12. Ibid., p. 591.

13. Hermione argues that Harry has never really been to the Department of Mysteries and so can't know for sure what it looks like; that this turn of events is "just so unlikely"; that there is absolutely "no proof" for any of Harry's speculations; that Voldemort might be preying on Harry's well-known (though noble) tendency to save people and act the hero.

14. *Order of the Phoenix*, p. 740.

15. The following points are drawn from or inspired by Augustine, *Confessions*, Book XI.

16. Concerning what Gadamer calls "tradition," see *Truth and Method*, pp. 277–305.

17. We depend on others for what language we speak, on books and teachers for much of what we learn, on parents and grandparents for family history, on mentors for their already acquired wisdom and skill, and on previous discoveries for the technological advances we make.

18. In addition to Augustine and Gadamer, we can also add here Michael Polanyi's work in the epistemology of the sciences, especially his discussions of tradition, apprenticeship, and tacit knowing in *Personal Knowledge* (Chicago: University of Chicago Press, 1974).

19. *Goblet of Fire*, p. 597.

JUST IN YOUR HEAD?

J. K. Rowling on Separating Reality from Illusion

John Granger with Gregory Bassham

There are many ways to unlock the hidden mysteries of the Harry Potter books, but in this chapter we'll consider one key in particular.[1] It comes right near the end of J. K. Rowling's seven-part series, and Rowling herself says that she "waited seventeen years" to use two lines in particular. So, if there is a key to find, this is a good place to look. "Yes, that's right," she said. "All this time I've worked to be able to write those two phrases; writing Harry entering the forest and Harry having that dialog."[2] So, what are those two lines, and what is their philosophical significance?

Tell Me One Last Thing

After Harry sacrifices himself and awakens in the limbo King's Cross, in his last moments of conversation with Albus Dumbledore he asks,

"Tell me one last thing," said Harry. "Is this real? Or has this been happening inside my head?"

Dumbledore beamed at him, and his voice sounded loud and strong in Harry's ears even though the bright mist was descending again, obscuring his figure.

"Of course it is happening inside your head, Harry, but why on earth should that mean that it is not real?"[3]

Rowling's remarkable claim is that she's been writing the 4,100-plus-page series to arrive at just this point, so that Harry could hear these two phrases: "Of course it is happening inside your head," and "why on earth should that mean that it is not real?" These lines are among the most philosophically interesting in the entire series as well, so they provide the ideal chance to explore both their significance to the story and their deeper import.

What Is Real?

Harry's question is a profoundly philosophical one; questions about what is real lie at the heart of the philosophical quest. The branch of philosophy called metaphysics asks just these questions. Do souls exist or God or numbers? These are metaphysical questions, for they deal with the issue of what is ultimately real. The goal of metaphysics is to break free from mere appearances and capture the reality, to replace opinions with knowledge. Metaphysics asks what is real, whereas the branch of philosophy called epistemology is about how we can come to know what is real, so that we're not confusing what is unreal or illusory with what is genuine reality.

It's only natural that Harry should wonder how real his experience was, for we all can be deceived by experiences that seem real but aren't. All of us are vulnerable to wishful thinking, biased perspectives, and other sorts of flawed judgment that can mislead us into mistaking appearance for reality. Perhaps this is why the famous atheist A. J. Ayer, after having a vivid near-death experience near the end of his life, remained unmoved afterward, choosing to chalk it up as a hallucination, rather than as a genuine experience of a transcendent reality. Harry, too, wonders whether his experience is real or simply made up.

Long before Dumbledore and Harry explored a dark and particularly creepy cave together, Plato (428–348 B.C.E.) offered an image of a cave that has stood as an example of what philosophy is all about. Plato asks us to picture men chained inside a cave all of their lives, able to see only flickering images on the wall cast by a fire behind them. Understandably, they take those shadows to be reality, rather than imperfect reflections of real things. But one day a man is released from his chains and makes his way out of the cave. At first, he's blinded by the dazzling light, but eventually he's able to see the world as it really is. He realizes that all of his life, he's been mistaking mere appearances for realities, wavering images on a cave wall for the real world. Wanting to share his wonderful revelation with his fellows, the prisoner returns to the cave but is greeted with hostile skepticism by the captives. Plato was convinced that our entire earthly pilgrimage takes place in a world of appearances and that ultimate reality comes later. The philosopher's job is to raise people's sights to these deeper realities, helping people stop confusing shadows and appearances for authentic reality.

Even before Plato, philosophers grappled with questions of what is real and how we come to know reality. So, Harry's question of what is real is at root a philosophical query, and the distinction he raises between "real" and "in the head" provides a useful starting point for our discussion.

Going Mental

We can easily distinguish things that exist only in our heads from things that exist both in our heads and in the external world. Hermione Granger, for example, as a fictional character exists in our heads but not in reality; likewise Sherlock Holmes, Santa Claus, unicorns, and centaurs. Emma Watson, Oxford, and King's Cross Station, on the other hand, aren't mere ideas in our minds but actual persons, places, and things that exist in reality. Although we might have the idea of Oxford in our minds, Oxford itself has an objective, independent reality that purely fictional ideas do not. So, although the idea of a thing and the thing itself may both exist, to say of something that it exists in the head often means "in the head alone" and so not in external reality. Harry's question isn't straightforwardly silly or stupid, in other words. He was concerned that his dialogue with Dumbledore had merely been a dream or a hallucination, a shadowy image on the cave wall.

Dumbledore's reply, then, is telling. He doesn't deny that Harry's experience has been in his head, but he insists that this doesn't mean that it isn't real. Harry's question, in other words, is based on a false choice: either in the head or real. Harry has taken the two options to be exhaustive and mutually exclusive. The truth of one means the falsehood of the other. But Dumbledore assures him that they aren't inconsistent at all. Mental experiences can also be "real."

A number of philosophers through the centuries have had a similar insight, which is what makes Dumbledore's claim so philosophically fascinating. Let's consider a few of these examples from the history of philosophy. Plato's idea has already been mentioned, so let's start with him. He was a rationalist, who thought all knowledge is rooted in reason, rather than in sense perception. Why? Because reason puts us in touch with what Plato believed is ultimately real: the forms. Consider broomsticks. In Harry's world we see various and sundry broomsticks, but what makes them broomsticks at all, according to what Plato says, is that they resemble, imperfectly, the ideal Platonic form or abstract essence of what a broomstick is. Our senses only put us in touch with imperfect copies, not with the Platonic ideal. Reason is how we get in touch with what's ultimately real. If Plato were to hear a disgruntled philosophy student complaining about having to leave class and go into the "real world," he might suggest that we're never more in touch with the real world than when we're thinking philosophically.

Plato is not the only Western philosopher to claim that true reality can be known only through reason. The great French rationalist philosopher René Descartes (1596–1650) argued that the essences of both material things and minds cannot be known by sense experience but only by rational analysis. The German philosopher Immanuel Kant (1724–1804) argued that physical objects such as rocks, chairs, and trees are mental constructs that result from the interaction of our shaping and categorizing minds with external reality. "Absolute idealists" such as G. W. F. Hegel (1770–1831) and neo-Hegelians such as F. H. Bradley (1846–1924) went even further than Kant in stressing the ultimacy of mind and spiritual values.

Similar views are found in some strands of British empiricism. For empiricists, sense experience, not reason, is the source of all human knowledge. The British empiricist George Berkeley (1685–1753) is famous for his "immaterialist" view that physical objects don't exist at all but are merely ideas in the minds of God and other perceivers. Berkeley believed that for external things like clouds and mountains, "to be is to be perceived." So, all of what we experience as external reality is, in a sense, "in the head" but is no less real as a consequence. Two centuries later, the British empiricist John Stuart Mill (1806–1873) defended a "phenomenalist" account of human knowing, according to which all talk of material reality can be cashed out as talk of actual or possible sensory experiences.

Such views are also found in a variety of Eastern philosophical traditions, including some schools of Hinduism, Buddhism, and Taoism. For example, Yogacara Buddhists believe that everything humans experience as "real" is fabricated by consciousness and thus is *sunya*, empty, and lacking in any definite nature or essence.

Whether the mind creates reality, in whole or in part, or puts us in touch with an already existing reality or corresponds in some sense with an independent reality, philosophers from a broad spectrum of views would agree with Dumbledore's point that what's real and what's in the head aren't necessarily at odds.

Rowling as an Inkling

Now let's explore a suggestive possibility that Rowling may have had in mind when she wrote this exchange between Harry and Dumbledore. It doesn't presuppose that she was staking out well-defined territory among the murky thickets of metaphysics, but it does potentially shed light on questions of what reality is like and how we can come to know it.

This interpretation depends on taking seriously Rowling's claim that she was heavily influenced by C. S. Lewis and his fellow Inklings, such as J. R. R. Tolkien. The Inklings were a group of Oxford dons and their friends who met regularly to discuss one another's writings and other matters, often at the Eagle and Child, an Oxford pub. Among the Inklings were Owen Barfield, Tolkien, Charles Williams, Lewis's brother Warnie, and other well-known Oxford figures.

Rowling has spoken of her debt to Lewis in particular, attributing her decision to write seven books to Lewis's seven-part *Chronicles of Narnia*, which she loved as a child. To be sure, the Potter books are quite different from the *Narnia* books; nowhere is Rowling nearly so obvious in promoting a particular religious message. To the extent that she does, I have argued that it's through symbol and form, implicit more than explicit, and not at all heavy-handed. Still, she has admitted that what helped inspire the stories was her personal struggle to hold onto faith, and she claims to be a Christian whose religious convictions, if known, would have made much of the storyline predictable. So it wouldn't be surprising to find indicators of such influences within the stories.

What could account for the fit between the content of our minds and the real world? Why are our best philosophical insights windows into reality? How is it that reason is so successful in putting us in touch with the truth?

For an intriguing possibility, consider this quote from Lewis, in which he laid out a big lesson he learned from his friend Barfield. Lewis said that Barfield

> convinced me that the [materialistic] positions we had hitherto held left no room for any satisfactory theory of knowledge. We had been, in the technical sense of the term, "realists"; that is, we accepted as rock-bottom reality the universe revealed by the senses. But at the same time we continued to make, for certain phenomena of consciousness, all the claims that really went with a theistic or idealistic view. We maintained that abstract thought (if obedient to logical rules) gave indisputable truth, that our moral judgment was "valid," and our aesthetic experience not merely pleasing but "valuable". . . . Barfield convinced me that it was inconsistent. If thought were a purely subjective event, these claims for it would have to be abandoned. . . . I was therefore compelled to give up realism. . . . I must admit that mind was no late-come epiphenomenon; that the whole universe was, in the last resort, mental; that our logic was participation in a cosmic Logos.[4]

Some readers might recognize here the germ of the argument Lewis would later develop in his 1947 book, *Miracles*, his so-called argument from reason.[5] It was on this very topic that Lewis had his famous debate with the philosopher Elizabeth Anscombe (1919–2001), a debate that required Lewis to amend the chapter.[6] Alvin Plantinga, a leading Christian philosopher,

has recently offered an argument from reason against natural-
ism that owes much to Lewis.[7] The basic idea of the argument
is that for us to retain confidence in the deliverances of reason,
we must be warranted in thinking that rationality is more than
merely subjective. Rather, rationality must somehow be able to
put us in touch with external reality. If the reasons we hold various views are merely because those convictions were formed
through a naturalistic process according to the laws of nature,
there's not necessarily any good basis for taking our conclusions as reliably true.

It's not my aim to assess this argument here but to mention
it as a line of reasoning that might have influenced Rowling. It
might provide some insight into the overlap between reality
and what's in our head. Note the way that Lewis thought of
reality as "mental" and our logic as participation in a larger
structure of rationality within the universe. As a Christian,
he was inclined to cash this out as participation in the divine
logos, by which a Christian means Christ himself. Jesus, as
depicted in John 1:1, is the incarnation of the divine logos, the
word from which we derive our word *logic*.

Some early Greek philosophers conceived of logos as the
impersonal animating principle that upholds reality. Later,
Greek and Roman Stoic philosophers saw logos as the divine
reason that pervades and providentially guides the cosmos.
When John the evangelist came along and announced that
Jesus was the incarnation of the logos, he was espousing something radical. His point, expressed in language that would
have been understood in that context, was that there is indeed
a divine logos, by which reality takes its shape and is held in
existence. But the logos is no mere animating principle or
impersonal force but a person, God the son. According to
this view, human reason and logic, our capacity to engage in
critical reflection and rational thought, are possible and reliable because through the right use of our minds, we are participating in the divine logos. As Rowling has remarked in an

interview, it wasn't a coincidence that Harry's fateful encounter with Dumbledore was at "King's Cross."

Lewis's point about the divine logos raises another suggestive possibility for making sense of Dumbledore's connection between what's real and what's in the head. The suggestion is about both metaphysics and epistemology. How our minds work inexplicably seems intimately related to the way the world is; if we're going to avoid various skeptical hypotheses, something has to account for the conspicuous overlap between external reality and the functioning of human rationality. As so often happens with philosophy, what at first seems an obvious connection yields on reflection a picture that may illustrate some of life's bigger mysteries.

Harry's Near-Death Experience

Dumbledore's remark that things can be real even if they occur only in one's head happens as part of Harry's near-death experience in King's Cross. Nowhere is the difference between "what's real" and "what's in the head" posed more starkly than in near-death experiences. It's worth exploring such experiences as an additional clue to Rowling's meaning.[8]

The current interest in near-death experiences (NDEs) began with the publication, in 1975, of Raymond Moody's best-selling book *Life after Life*.[9] In that book, Moody documented the experiences of more than a hundred people who had been declared clinically dead or had come close to death and had then been revived.

Since Moody's book appeared, an enormous amount of research has been done on NDEs. For the most part, this research has supported Moody's findings. Studies have found that NDEs are relatively common (about 10 to 20 percent of people who survive cardiac arrest report lucid, structured NDEs); that they tend to be basically similar in people of all ages, backgrounds, and cultures; and that they often have many of the characteristic features Moody describes.[10] Based on the studies to date, researchers have identified the following core features of NDEs:

1. Feelings of peace and serenity
2. A buzzing or ringing noise
3. Separation from the body
4. An experience of moving rapidly down a dark tunnel
5. Meeting and being welcomed by others (usually departed friends or family)
6. Encountering a welcoming and loving "being of light"
7. An instantaneous life review
8. A barrier or a border marking a separation of earthly existence from "the other side"
9. Reluctance to come back to one's body

Studies have shown that these elements tend to occur in this order, and that the first few features occur more commonly than the others.[11]

Are near-death experiences "real" in the sense of being genuinely paranormal glimpses of a postmortem world? Skeptics point to two major problems with this interpretation.

First, as the leading NDE researcher Susan Blackmore notes, NDEs are by no means always the same. Some people have terrifying, hell-like experiences.[12] Only a small percentage of NDEers report seeing a light, meeting others, or experiencing a panoramic life review. Some NDEers report having a grayish, transparent "astral" body, while others do not. Children often report being met by living playmates (or even animals), rather than by deceased relatives or a Being of Light. And people of different religious backgrounds often report meeting religious figures or receiving messages that are unique to their own religious traditions.[13]

Second, even if NDEs are often consistent in basic details, this doesn't mean the experiences are genuinely paranormal. As Blackmore argues, it might only mean that we have similar brains that react in similar ways to the physical and psychological stresses of dying. For instance, she notes, lack of oxygen to the brain can produce many of the same effects as NDEs, including loud ringing or buzzing noises, sensations of floating, out-of-body experiences, and bright lights.

Do such objections demonstrate conclusively that NDEs are not "real"? No, as Rowling's tale of Harry's near-death experience in King's Cross shows very well.[14]

Suppose a child has an NDE in which her pet dog, Sparky, greets and welcomes her to "the other side." Sparky is still living, so the child must simply be hallucinating, right? Not necessarily. For the experience might be "real" in the sense of being a genuine divinely created vision of the "other side." The vision could be "true" (real) in the sense of being an authentic supernatural revelation (not unlike Paul's vision on the road to Damascus). In other words, in asking whether an NDE is real, we aren't necessarily asking whether it is a genuine out-of-body experience of another world. An NDE can be real (i.e., genuinely supernatural and revelatory) even if it takes place entirely inside the head of the person having the experience.

It is this ambiguity of the term *real* that Dumbledore is playing on when he tells Harry that an experience isn't necessarily "unreal" just because it's happening inside one's head. Elsewhere, I have defended an iconographic reading of the Potter books that sees Harry as a symbol of the "noetic" or spiritual faculty of the soul.[15] In this reading, the way-station King's Cross is a real "place," namely, logos-land or heaven. (Hence, for example, Harry's ability to create objects there and his apparent semi-omniscience.) Yet in asking whether Harry's experience is real or not, the crucial question isn't *where* Dumbledore and Harry are meeting, but whether it's really *Dumbledore* who is speaking to Harry.[16] After all, in the wizarding world, wizards can "channel" themselves through their portraits, "imprint" their former selves in ghostly form, possess other minds, and probe other wizards' thoughts through Legilimency. So, why shouldn't Dumbledore really be present to Harry's mind even if Harry, felled by Voldemort's killing curse, hasn't left his body but is still lying semiconscious on the forest floor?[17]

The American poet-philosopher Ralph Waldo Emerson once said, "Our faith comes in moments. . . . Yet there is a depth in those moments which constrains us to ascribe more reality to them than to all other experiences."[18] In the same way, perhaps, Rowling is saying, Don't be dismissive of hints and glimpses of the divine just because they occur "in your head." If love really is the most powerful force in the universe, as Rowling thinks, where else would it speak to us, if not in our heads?

NOTES

1. See John Granger's most recent books on Harry: *Harry Potter's Bookshelf: The Great Books behind the Hogwarts Adventure* (New York: Penguin Books, 2009); *How Harry Cast His Spell: The Meaning behind the Mania for J. K. Rowling's Bestselling Books*, 3rd ed. (Carol Stream, IL: Tyndale, 2008); *The Deathly Hallows Lectures: The Hogwarts Professor Explains the Final Harry Potter Adventure* (Allentown, PA: Zossima Press, 2008); and *Unlocking Harry Potter: Five Keys for the Serious Reader* (Wayne, PA: Zossima Press, 2007).

2. J. K. Rowling interview with Pais, February 9, 2008, www.snitchseeker.com/harry -potter-news/entire-spanish-j-k-rowling-interview-54113/.

3. *Deathly Hallows*, p. 723.

4. C. S. Lewis, *Surprised by Joy: The Shape of My Early Life* (New York: Harcourt Brace, 1955), pp. 208–209.

5. C. S. Lewis, *Miracles* (London: Fontana Books, 1960), chap. 3.

6. In recent years, Victor Reppert has argued forcefully for a philosophically sophisticated formulation of Lewis's argument. See his *C. S. Lewis's Dangerous Idea: In Defense of the Argument from Reason* (Downers Grove, IL: InterVarsity Press, 2003).

7. Alvin Plantinga, *Warrant and Proper Function* (Oxford: Oxford University Press, 1993), chap. 12.

8. Some of the language in the following few paragraphs is adapted from Gregory Bassham, William Irwin, Henry Nardone, and James M. Wallace, *Critical Thinking: A Student's Introduction*, 2nd ed. (New York: McGraw-Hill, 2005).

9. Raymond A. Moody, *Life after Life* (New York: Bantam Books, 1975).

10. "Scientists to Study 'White Light' Near-Death Experiences," Fox News, September 15, 2008, www.foxnews.com/story/0,2933,422744,00.html.

11. Susan Blackmore, *Dying to Live: Near-Death Experiences* (Buffalo: NY: Prometheus Press, 1993), pp. 25–26.

12. Ibid., pp. 98–102. An editorial in the British medical journal the *Lancet* reported that "of male survivors of cardiac arrest, 80 percent had dreams of violence, death, and aggression, such as being run over by a wheelchair, violent accidents, and shooting their way out of the hospital only to be killed by a nurse." Quoted in James Rachels and Stuart Rachels, *Problems from Philosophy*, 2nd ed. (New York: McGraw-Hill, 2009), p. 46.

13. Blackmore, *Dying to Live*, pp. 17, 25–27, 126, 181.

14. In describing Harry's encounter with Dumbledore in the way-station King's Cross as a "near-death experience," I don't mean to imply that Harry has died and is experiencing a "life after life." As Dumbledore makes clear, Harry is not dead but could choose to die if he wishes.

15. See *The Deathly Hallows Lectures*, especially chapter 5, "The Seeing Eye," for a fuller explication of my views here. Harry's "traveling" to the Kingdom of Heaven within his head after his sacrificial death explains Dumbledore's parting words. Harry has asked whether what he has experienced is real in strictly empirical terms, that is, "is this place a place of objective measure and quantities or is it a place of only subjective and personal perception not grounded in such quantities?" Dumbledore's response, "Of course it is happening inside your head, Harry, but why on earth should that mean that it is not real?" explodes the false dilemma of empirical epistemology by linking, rather than separating, "the real" and "in your head." This logos creative principle is the "power beyond the reach of any magic" in children's tales about which Dumbledore says, "Voldemort knows and understands nothing. Nothing."

Dumbledore's answer to Harry requires an epistemological and metaphysical conjunction in the divine word or logos. Rowling, as with the other symbolist writers of English tradition, offers this conjunction in story form to give her readers an imaginative experience of this reality that is "bigger inside than outside." The tradition points, too, as Queen Lucy says at the end of Lewis's *The Last Battle*, to the incarnate logos that as a newborn made a stable hold "something inside it that was bigger than the whole world." Separating reality from illusion in a world simultaneously logos-created and logos-known, the "whole universe being mental," is only possible in Christ.

16. In *The Great Divorce*, C. S. Lewis imagines a kind of heavenly ante-chamber that he calls the Valley of the Shadow of Life. Significantly, characters in Lewis's story experience various "places" in the afterlife quite differently, dependent on the state of their souls. Since hell is, as one character in the book remarks, "a state of mind," precisely the same ambiguity of "real" versus "in the head" occurs in Lewis's tale as in *Deathly Hallows*. It's possible that Rowling's King's Cross scene is modeled in part on Lewis's description of the afterlife in *The Great Divorce*.

17. In a recent interview, Rowling notes that "it is Harry's image we see [in the King's Cross scene], not necessarily what is really there." "Webchat with J. K. Rowling," July 30, 2007, available at www.bloomsbury.com/harrypotter/default.aspx?sec=3.

18. Ralph Waldo Emerson, "The Over-Soul," in *The Complete Essays and Other Writings of Ralph Waldo Emerson* (New York: Modern Library, 1950), p. 261.

A PENSIEVE FOR YOUR THOUGHTS?

Harry Potter and the Magic of Memory

Amy Kind

I sometimes find, and I am sure you know the feeling, that I simply have too many thoughts and memories crammed into my mind.

—Albus Dumbledore[1]

Of all of the magical instruments available in the wizarding world, the Pensieve is one of the most intriguing. As important as the Deluminator was for Ron Weasley and the Sword of Gryffindor was for Harry, I'd have been hoping for the Pensieve had Dumbledore singled me out when writing his last will and testament.

Although it's not much to look at—just a shallow basin covered with runes and symbols—the Pensieve allows you to offload your memories from your mind as easily as you offload data from your hard drive. It must be wonderfully liberating to be able to literally get something off your mind, at least for a time—to keep from obsessing over what you should have said or done, to stop endlessly replaying a moment of embarrassment, or simply to gain some distance from a particularly disturbing experience. And it must be wonderfully illuminating to be able to review your own memories from an external perspective at your leisure in the clear light of a new day. As Dumbledore explains to Harry, when you review thoughts and memories in the Pensieve, it becomes easier to spot the patterns and links among them.

Yet it's not only the Pensieve's potential for improving peace and clarity of mind that makes it so special. Even folks like Muggles and Squibs who don't have magical powers can achieve something similar through meditation or medication. Rather, the real intrigue of the Pensieve lies in its philosophical implications for the boundaries of mind, memory, and the self. We typically view an individual's memory as a fundamental part of her own identity, and philosophers have even attempted to understand a person's continuing existence through time in terms of memory and mind. But our understanding of what—and where—the mind is gets called into question if thoughts can be easily extracted from it, tampered with, stored elsewhere, and even discarded. And whose mind is it, once thoughts are shared with someone else?

"A Swirling, Silvery Mass"

The powers of mind and memory are mysterious enough even without the magical possibilities opened up by the wizarding world. While I was watching the movie *In Bruges* recently, it drove me crazy that no matter how hard I tried, I couldn't remember why the actor playing the main character, Ken, looked so familiar to me. Much later, the answer finally popped into my head. It was Brendan Gleeson, the same actor who plays Alastor "Mad-Eye" Moody in the Harry Potter films.

Often it's when we *stop* thinking about something that we finally figure it out. Why can we remember all sorts of useless information, while the things that we want to remember slip through the cracks, no matter how hard we try to recall them? Why does memory work in such quirky ways?

Science has solved many of the mysteries of memory, but it's staggering how much we still don't understand. In fact, we don't really understand the mind itself—either what it is or how it's related to the brain. Severus Snape is right on target when he tells Harry that "the mind is a complex and many-layered thing, Potter . . . or at least, most minds are."[2]

Philosophers who study the mind have long been divided into two camps. The materialists, in the tradition of the British philosopher Thomas Hobbes (1588–1679), believe that everything that exists must be a physical thing, made of matter and existing in space. Certain inhabitants of the wizarding world, such as Nearly Headless Nick and other ghosts, might seem to pose a problem for materialism. But the materialist can accept the existence of ghosts as long as they're made of matter—perhaps not solid matter, but some kind of matter nonetheless.[3] Likewise for the mind. Materialists typically claim that the mind is a material thing and that there is no distinction between the mind and the brain. Some of the descriptions in the Harry Potter books point in the direction of materialism. Consider, for example, the descriptions of thoughts clinging to wands like strands of hair and leaking out of dying wizards like oozing blood.

Dualists, in the tradition of the great French philosopher René Descartes (1596–1650), believe that in addition to material substances, there are also immaterial substances—things that have no spatial extension or location. According to the dualist view, the brain, which is made of matter, falls into the first category, whereas the mind, which isn't made of matter, falls into the second. The common idea that the mind could, theoretically at least, exist without the body, presupposes this dualist view. Harry considers this possibility when he finds himself in what seems like King's Cross Station after Voldemort tries to kill him in the Forbidden Forest. Although he ultimately concludes that he must still have his body "because he was lying, definitely lying, on some surface," he initially thinks that he might exist only as disembodied thought.[4] The dualist recognizes that there are close connections between the brain and the mind; Descartes himself claimed that "I am not merely present in my body as a sailor is present in a ship. . . . I am very closely joined and, as it were, intermingled with it, so that I and the body form a unit."[5] But this intermingling of mind and body doesn't change the fact that for the dualist, they're fundamentally different kinds of things.

Many of us have conflicting intuitions that pull us sometimes toward dualism, sometimes toward materialism. On the one hand, it's hard to understand what it would mean for something to be completely immaterial. On the other hand, thoughts do seem to be more ephemeral and intangible than other material objects such as tables and chairs. J. K. Rowling herself seems caught up in this same tension; her description of Harry's impression of the contents of the Pensieve when he first comes across it in Dumbledore's office provides a beautifully compelling expression of the push and pull between these two views of the mind and the desire to find some middle ground between them: "It was a bright, whitish silver, and it was moving ceaselessly; the surface of it became ruffled like water beneath wind, and then, like clouds, separated and swirled smoothly. It looked like light made liquid—or like wind made solid—Harry couldn't make up his mind."[6]

The Hallows of the Mind

Whether we're dualists or materialists, however, there's a strong inclination to think of a mind as self-contained. Someone might transcribe her innermost secrets in a journal or a blog, but assuming that she's not engaged in dark magic, these transcriptions serve simply as records of her memories. That's what makes Tom Riddle's diary so unusual, even in the wizarding world. As Dumbledore says to Harry,

> "Well, although I did not see the Riddle who came out of the diary, what you described to me was a phenomenon I had never witnessed. A mere memory starting to act and think for itself? A mere memory, sapping the life out of the girl into whose hands it had fallen? No, something much more sinister had lived inside that book . . . a fragment of soul, I was almost sure of it. The diary had been a Horcrux."[7]

We leave Post-it notes scattered around the house to help us remember things, and we key all sorts of important information into our BlackBerrys. But no matter how dependent someone is on a PDA, the device is still a memory *aid*, not a memory *repository*. We don't consider our diaries and iPhone contact lists to be similar to the Pensieve.

Recently, however, some philosophers have questioned this traditional way of looking at the limits of the mind. In their article "The Extended Mind," Andy Clark and David Chalmers reject the claim that the mind is framed by the boundaries of skull and skin.[8] Although their article was written more than a decade ago in the pre-BlackBerry age of the Filofax, even then it was easy to find interesting cases of cognitive reliance on external objects. Most of us can do long division only with the aid of pen and paper, and when playing Scrabble, we do far better at coming up with seven-letter words by physically reshuffling the letter tiles in our trays.[9] Although it's natural to see these external objects as playing the role of "environmental supports," Clark and Chalmers suggest that they often function in more than simply a supporting role. Often, our use of external objects can be seen not only as a kind of action but as a part of *thought*.[10]

Clark and Chalmers propose the radical view that our mental lives need not be solely internal. Rather, the mind extends into the world. We already accept that the body can extend beyond its natural limits. For example, it's not at all farfetched to suppose that a prosthetic leg becomes part of an amputee's body, not merely an artificial accessory to it. More controversially, consider a wizard who has a particularly strong relationship with his wand, as Harry does to his eleven-inch wand made of holly with a phoenix feather core. Harry is so in sync with his wand that he might view it literally as an extension of his own body.[11] We might even see Rita Skeeter's relationship with her Quick-Quotes Quill the same way. And certainly, Moody's magic eye and Peter Pettigrew's silver hand have become parts of their bodies. Similarly, an external object might become a mental prosthesis, extending the mind beyond its natural limits.

Rowling's description of thoughts in the wizarding world makes the idea of an extended mind even more plausible.[12] The gossamer strands of memory belonging to Snape might be inside his skull, leaking out from his body, bottled up in a phial, or stored in the Pensieve. But wherever they are, these memories are Snape's, just as the memories in Riddle's diary are Voldemort's. Their physical location is incidental to their ownership.

But what about in the nonwizarding world? To make their case for the extended mind idea, Clark and Chalmers give the example of Otto, an individual suffering from Alzheimer's. Otto relies on a notebook to help him remember things. He writes down any new information that he learns, and when he needs to recall something, he consults his notebook. This notebook is always at hand, and he's able to retrieve the information inside it immediately and efficiently. According to Clark and Chalmers, Otto's notebook serves the same purpose as a biological memory. We call things up from memory, while Otto calls things up from his notebook; we keep our beliefs in our minds, while Otto keeps his on paper.

Confundus!

At first, the extended-mind theory may sound like something from a *Quibbler* story hatched by Xenophilius Lovegood. (If it were described to Ron, I can easily imagine him saying—no pun intended—"That's mental.") But it begins to make sense when we distinguish between what philosophers call *occurrent* and *nonoccurrent* beliefs. At any given time, the overwhelming majority of a person's beliefs are not consciously available. Ron believes that Ireland won its match against Bulgaria at the 422nd Quidditch World Cup, but, presumably, that belief isn't at the forefront of his mind—it's not occurrent—while he and Hermione are racing to the Chamber of Secrets to retrieve the remaining Basilisk fang during the Battle of Hogwarts. At that point, all of his occurrent beliefs most likely concern the great danger of his present situation: the fastest path to Moaning Myrtle's bathroom and how he's going to manage to say "Open" in Parseltongue, a language he doesn't speak.

Similarly, because the information in Otto's notebook isn't in the forefront of his mind, it doesn't seem at all analogous to our occurrent beliefs. Rather, it functions like our nonoccurrent beliefs. Consider Rita Skeeter's nonoccurrent belief that Bathilda Bagshot lives in Godric's Hollow, which is stored somewhere in her memory, waiting to be accessed. When Rita decides to interview Bathilda in order to gather material for *The Life and Lies of Albus Dumbledore*, she must pause to think for a moment to recall where Bathilda lives. It's only then that the belief becomes occurrent. Likewise, suppose that Otto has his old friend Bathilda's address written in his notebook. When he decides to visit her, he has to take a moment to look up in his notebook where she lives. His belief is stored somewhere inside the notebook, waiting to be accessed. Just as it would be silly to deny that even before she consults her memory, Rita has the belief that Bathilda lives in Godric's Hollow, we should accept that Otto has the same belief even before he consults his notebook.

Clark and Chalmers don't go so far as to claim that every external support we rely on becomes part of the mind; rather, they see something special in Otto's connection to his notebook. It's not the same as Harry's reliance on the marginal notes of the Half-Blood Prince in the Potions textbook he borrows from Horace Slughorn or Neville Longbottom's dependence on a handwritten list to help him remember the frequently changing passwords when Sir Cadogan substitutes for the Fat Lady in guarding the entrance to the Gryffindor common room. Harry's use of the textbook and Neville's use of the list both occur only sporadically, and Neville even ends up losing his list. Otto's connection to his notebook is not even like Hermione Granger's reliance on *Hogwarts, A History*. Although Hermione consults the book regularly and even ends up bringing it along on the search for Voldemort's Horcruxes because she wouldn't feel right if she didn't have it with her, the information in the book seems more like a supplement to the information in her mind, rather than an extension of her mind.[13]

What makes Otto's notebook different from these and other ordinary cases is the way it's integrated into his daily functioning. Even though the information kept in the notebook is external to his body, he always has his notebook with him, and he always consults it when trying to recall information. When using his notebook, he immediately accepts the information within it.[14] There are no deep respects in which the information in the notebook is different from the information in our memories, except for the fact that it's stored outside the boundaries of Otto's skull and skin. According to Clark and Chalmers, that one difference alone isn't enough to keep the information in Otto's notebook from being part of his mind.

Mischief Managed

Suppose, for the sake of argument, that we accept the extended mind idea. Now consider Fred and George Weasley's connection to the Marauder's Map they stole from Argus Filch's office in their first year at Hogwarts. Until they later bequeath it to Harry, they rely on it so heavily in their escapades that it wouldn't be much of a stretch to see their relationship to it as analogous to Otto's relationship to his notebook. The problem, however, is that there are two of them. If the map becomes not only part of Fred's extended mind but also part of George's extended mind, then the twins share even more in common than we'd realized. Their minds actually overlap.

This suggests one of the potentially disturbing ramifications of the extended mind idea.[15] Once we accept that the mind extends beyond the boundaries of skin and skull, we open up the possibility that it extends into someone else's mind. When this overlap occurs, we don't need to be skilled at Legilimency to have the ability to extract thoughts from another person's mind; those thoughts may already be part of our own.

A related worry is the potential threat that an extended mind poses to one's sense of self. Compared to the ordeals that Harry Potter has to endure and the greatness he achieves in spite of them, both the trials and the triumphs experienced by most witches and wizards (and certainly most Muggles and Squibs) seem trivial. But just as Harry's experiences make him the person he is, the personal experiences that each of us undergoes make us who we are. Many philosophers endorse some version of the *memory theory* of personal identity, which dates back at least to the British philosopher John Locke (1632–1704). According to this theory, our continuing identity over time consists in the continuity of memory.[16] It's the chains of memory connecting them that makes the adult Harry who watches his children board the Hogwarts Express the same person as the teenager who faces Voldemort in the Forbidden Forest and the same person as the orphaned infant taken in by the Dursleys. According to the memory theory, our memories are at the very foundations of our identities. If these same memories can be shared with someone else and can even become part of someone else, then how do we know who we really are?

At various times during his Hogwarts career, Harry shares the memories of several other individuals, including three of his professors (Dumbledore, Snape, and Slughorn). And indeed, in almost every instance, he is greatly affected by his forays into the Pensieve. Tortured by the look he got via Snape's memory of his own father's arrogant and unappealing behavior while at Hogwarts, Harry reevaluates not only his sense of his father but also his sense of himself: "For nearly five years the thought of his father had been a source of comfort, of inspiration. Whenever someone had told him he was like James, he had glowed with pride inside. And now . . . now he felt cold and miserable at the thought of him."[17] When he learns, again from Snape's memory, that a part of Voldemort's soul lives within himself, he's forced to reshape his sense of his place in the world: "Finally, the truth . . . Harry understood at last that he was not supposed to survive."[18] In each of these cases, Harry's use of the Pensieve leads to a sort of identity crisis.

But now think about what else can happen in the wizarding world. Physical appearance can be replicated via Polyjuice Potion. Memories can be almost completely erased by a flick of the wand and an incantation of "Obliviate!" False memories can also be implanted. Each of these magical possibilities poses a great threat to the integrity of an individual's identity—much greater, in fact, than the threat of memory-sharing via Pensieve. When Barty Crouch Jr. imprisons Moody in a trunk and uses Polyjuice Potion to impersonate him, he's really engaged in identity theft. Gilderoy Lockhart steals countless identities via memory charms before becoming his own victim through his use of a malfunctioning wand. Hermione has much purer motives when she tampers with her parents' memories, making them believe that they're Wendell and Monica Wilkins, a childless couple fulfilling their lifelong dream of moving to

Australia. But her good intentions don't change the fact that her actions deprive the Grangers of their identities.

Clearly, Harry's experiences with the Pensieve don't fall into this same category. What makes his previous experiences with the Pensieve so difficult is the *content* of the memories he's shared, not the memory sharing itself. Seeing Snape's worst memory is an unpleasant experience for Harry because of the painful facts it reveals, not because it somehow causes his identity to merge with that of the Potions Master. Had Snape been a good storyteller and had Harry been able to trust him, the same awful knowledge that Harry gains from the Pensieve could theoretically have been gained from an oral recounting. Using the Pensieve is more effective, because it allows Harry to see the past events for himself, and is more objective, because Snape's own testimony would probably be tinged with sneering subjectivity. But in principle, any knowledge conveyed via the Pensieve could be conveyed another way.

Lumos!

There are several different sorts of memories. Some are *know-how memories*, memories of skill, as when an aging wizard who hasn't used a broomstick since his Quidditch days remembers how to ride it. Some are *factual memories*, as when Hermione can report the properties of the Mandrake during Herbology. Distinct from both of these are *experiential memories*, memories from the first-person point of view, as when Harry remembers the searing pain caused by Dolores Umbridge's quill as it carved words into his right hand.

The memories that Otto keeps in his notebook are factual memories. When memory theorists invoke memory in explanations of personal identity, however, they're interested in first-person, experiential memories. It is important to note that memories reviewed in a Pensieve are not of this sort. The Pensieve replays memories from the third-person perspective.[19] When Dumbledore thinks about the trial and sentencing of Bellatrix Lestrange, his memory is presumably from the personal perspective that he had on it at the time, from his seat on the highest bench in the gallery of spectators. But when he reviews the memory in the Pensieve, the memory no longer has this—or any—particular point of view. In fact, given what we know about the Pensieve, the memory that Dumbledore shares with Harry should already be shared by all of the spectators at Lestrange's trial.

These facts about the Pensieve are crucial for understanding why its use poses no threat to our individual identities. What's important for personal identity are our first-person memories. Just as using a Time-Turner to revisit past events doesn't jeopardize who you are, neither does sharing memories via a Pensieve.[20] And just as sharing an experience with someone else doesn't threaten your sense of self, sharing one of your memories in a Pensieve with someone else shouldn't either.

This also sheds light, more broadly, on why we needn't be threatened by the thesis of the extended mind. The mind is indeed mysterious, and there's much about it we don't know. But one thing that we can be sure of is that whether your thoughts are kept in a Pensieve, in a mind, or in your notebook, those thoughts are still your own. The Pensieve is a truly magical device, and if I ever see one come up for auction on eBay, I'll bid on it without hesitation or limit. Still, however magical it is, it can't make you someone you're not.

NOTES

1. *Goblet of Fire*, p. 597.

2. *Order of the Phoenix*, p. 530.

3. Since ghosts in Harry's world are described as "pearly-white and slightly transparent," this seems a pretty plausible claim about them; see *Sorcerer's Stone*, p. 115.

4. *Deathly Hallows*, p. 705.

5. René Descartes, *Meditations on First Philosophy with Selections from the Objections and Replies*, translated by John Cottingham (Cambridge, UK: Cambridge University Press, 1986), p. 56.

6. *Goblet of Fire*, p. 583.

7. *Half-Blood Prince*, p. 500.

8. Andy Clark and David Chalmers, "The Extended Mind," *Analysis* 58 (1998): 7–19. Clark's later work, *Natural-Born Cyborgs: Minds, Technologies, and the Future of Human Intelligence* (Oxford: Oxford University Press, 2003), covers many of the same ideas in an especially accessible and engaging way.

9. Clark and Chalmers, "The Extended Mind," p. 8.

10. Ibid., p. 10.

11. Dumbledore supports this way of looking at the relationship between wand and wizard when he explains his theory of what happened the night that Harry and Voldemort fought in the graveyard of Little Hangleton: "I believe that your wand imbibed some of the power and qualities of Voldemort's wand that night, which is to say that it contained a little of Voldemort himself," *Deathly Hallows*, p. 711.

12. Moreover, the creation of Horcruxes would allow not only for an extended mind but also for an extended soul.

13. *Deathly Hallows*, p. 96.

14. Clark and Chalmers, "The Extended Mind," p. 17. See also Clark, *Natural-Born Cyborgs*, pp. 5–6.

15. For other objections to the extended-mind thesis, see, for example, Brie Gertler, "The Overextended Mind," in Brie Gertler and Lawrence Shapiro, eds., *Arguing about the Mind* (New York: Routledge, 2007); also Fred Adams and Kenneth Aizawa, "The Bounds of Cognition," *Philosophical Psychology* 14 (2001): 43–64. Clark surveys many of the most common criticisms and attempts to address them in *Supersizing the Mind: Embodiment, Action, and Cognitive Extension* (New York: Oxford University Press, 2008).

16. For Locke's development of the memory theory, see his *Essay Concerning Human Understanding*, edited by Peter Nidditch (Oxford: Clarendon Press, 1975), Book III, chap. XXVII, sec. 9. A more recent development of the view can be found in Derek Parfit, *Reasons and Persons* (Oxford: Oxford University Press, 1984).

17. *Order of the Phoenix*, pp. 653–654.

18. *Deathly Hallows*, p. 691.

19. This was confirmed by J. K. Rowling in a 2005 interview with the fansites Mugglenet and the Leaky Cauldron (available at www.mugglenet.com/jkrinterview.shtml). When asked whether the memories stored in a Pensieve are truthful reflections of reality or merely interpretations of it from the rememberer's subjective perspective, Rowling was adamant that they're accurate representations from the third-person perspective. According to Rowling, part of the magic of the Pensieve is that you can go back and examine your memories in it and discover all sorts of details that you hadn't noticed at the time:

> Otherwise it really would just be like a diary, wouldn't it? Confined to what you remember. But the Pensieve recreates a moment for you, so you could go into your own memory and relive things that you didn't notice at the time. It's somewhere in your head, which I'm sure it is, in all of our brains. I'm sure if you could access it, things that you don't know you remember are all in there somewhere.

20. I don't mean here to deny that there are all sorts of paradoxes posed by time travel, including paradoxes of identity. But those paradoxes are typically caused by actions a time traveler might take or prevent when he travels to the past—he might kill his own grandfather, for example, preventing himself from being born (or, as Professor McGonagall warns Hermione, he might kill his own past or future self by mistake). Nothing seems paradoxical, in and of itself, about a time-traveler being able to view past events that would otherwise have been inaccessible to him.

A HOGWARTS EDUCATION

The Good, the Bad, and the Ugly

Gregory Bassham

What kid wouldn't love to go to Hogwarts? Boarding school in a really cool castle; tons of adventures; great camaraderie and a sense of belonging; wonderful all-you-can-eat meals ("roast beef, roast chicken, pork chops and lamb chops, sausages, bacon and steak, boiled potatoes, roast potatoes, fries, Yorkshire pudding").[1] And best of all, no boring math, French, or science classes. Pretty much all you learn is—how to do magic! You learn how to fly, to travel instantly from point to point, to conjure things out of thin air, to transfigure objects into whatever you want them to be, to make potions that cure diseases or bring good luck, to defend yourself against dark wizards, creepy dementors, and obnoxious gits like Draco Malfoy. Heck, Hogwarts is like a camp for future superheroes! From a kid's point of view, what could be cooler?

What seems cool to a kid, though, may not seem so swift to an adult—or to a philosopher. What would great educational thinkers—philosophers such as Plato, Aristotle, Kant, and John Dewey—say about teaching and learning at Hogwarts? Is Hogwarts a "model school," as Susan Engel, the director of the Program in Teaching at Williams College, has claimed?[2] Or are there real problems with Hogwarts academics that need to be addressed? Here we'll look at the pros and cons of a Hogwarts education through the lenses of both classic philosophers of education and contemporary educational research.

The Good

The philosopher John Dewey (1859–1952) was the most influential thinker in American education. Early in the twentieth century, Dewey criticized traditional education for its stress on passive listening, rote memorization, undemocratic values, and disconnect with practical, real-life concerns. In opposition to traditional education, Dewey advocated a "progressive" approach to teaching and learning that emphasized three features that have now been widely adopted in American education: hands-on learning, building on the natural interests of children, and connecting schoolwork to everyday life.[3] One of the clear strengths of education at Hogwarts is that it reflects these three progressivist ideals.

Hands-On Learning

As we've seen, kids don't come to Hogwarts to learn calculus or Spanish or world history; they come to learn how to do magic. And by this yardstick, Hogwarts is clearly a successful school; most of its students do learn loads of useful potions and spells, pass their O.W.L.s. and N.E.W.T.s, and graduate as capable magicians. How do the students learn so effectively? Not through listening to Professor Binns's boring lectures on the history of magic or by reading Professor Umbridge's purely theoretical textbook assignments. Instead, they learn to do magic in an apprenticelike way that typically involves (1) demonstration of a magical technique by a skilled teacher, (2) practice of the technique by the students, (3) individualized coaching by the instructor to correct faults, and (4) continued practice by the students until the technique is mastered. Nearly all of the examples of effective pedagogy in the Potter books—for instance, Remus Lupin's teaching Harry how to conjure a Patronus or Harry's teaching of defensive magic to Dumbeldore's Army—involve this kind of hands-on learning by doing. Given that magic is portrayed in the Potter series as a hard-to-acquire skill that can be mastered only through coaching and practice, this kind of teaching makes perfect sense.

Building on the Natural Interests of Children

Dewey believed that children are naturally active and curious, and he urged educators to use kids' natural interests and real-life experiences as hooks to encourage learning. Research has shown that students are more engaged and learn more when they study things they find interesting and relevant.[4]

Hogwarts students are clearly eager to learn magic. They love having magical abilities and enjoy developing those abilities and learning new spells and skills. Moreover, they clearly understand the practical value of what they're learning. When Umbridge won't allow her Defense Against the Dark Arts students to practice defensive magic, the pupils organize their own class to practice on their own. They know that learning to do defensive magic is vital to their success on school exams, in their lives and careers after Hogwarts, and to their efforts as part of Dumbledore's Army to thwart Voldemort's return to power.

Connecting Schoolwork to Everyday Life

Too often, Dewey believed, classwork is seen as a preparation for some remote and speculative future, rather than as part of life itself. Learning the names of Uruguay's three largest rivers might be useful to some pupils (for example, if they plan to open a tugboat business there someday). But for most students, this information will be what the philosopher Alfred North Whitehead (1861–1947) called "inert" knowledge—lumps of undigested, untested, unused information.[5] Dewey believed that education has a practical function and should not be seen as a series of pointless hurdles to jump over before "real life" begins. Education isn't a preamble to life; it's part of life, and it exists to solve practical human problems and meet human needs.

Some of what students learn at Hogwarts is pretty inert. For example, Harry and his friends can't see much point in Rubeus Hagrid's lessons on raising ugly and dangerous Blast-Ended Skrewts or Professor Trelawney's bogus crystal-ball gazing. But, generally, students can recognize right away the practical payoff of what they're learning. They realize that when they leave Hogwarts, they will need to know how to Apparate and Disapparate, to transfigure objects, to defend themselves against dark wizards, and so forth. This makes them eager students and motivates them to learn.

The Bad

What's not to love about Hogwarts? As we've seen, the three real strengths of a Hogwarts education are that it encourages hands-on learning, builds on the natural interests of students, and teaches important, real-life skills. There are other features of Hogwarts academics, however, that are not so attractive. Three major negatives are:

- The school is too dangerous.
- There are too few qualified teachers.
- Students don't get a well-rounded education.

Let's look at these points, one by one.

Too Dangerous

Let's face it, Hogwarts is a pretty hazardous place to go to school. It's located next to a magical forest, where unwary or reckless students may get eaten by giant spiders or set upon by hostile centaurs. There's an ice-cold lake next to the castle full of treacherous water demons (grindylows) and a giant squid. All kinds of lethal creatures (three-headed dogs, trolls, basilisks) may on occasion be found in the school. There's a mischievous resident poltergeist, Peeves, who's constantly trying to trip students up or drop heavy objects onto their heads. Staircases contain vanishing steps that students need to remember to jump over. Unmindful students wandering near the Forbidden Forest may be pounded to a pulp by the Whomping Willow. Students sometimes work with dangerous magical creatures (Professor Kettleburn retires at the end of Harry's second year "in order to spend more time with his remaining limbs").[6] Potions often go awry and injure or disfigure students. The most popular game at Hogwarts, Quidditch, can easily result in serious injuries to players. The Triwizard Tournament involves three high-risk challenges. And even the youngest students carry potentially lethal weapons (wands) that they regularly use to hex and jinx one another.

True, many injuries that students suffer at Hogwarts can be healed quickly by Severus Snape's potions or Madame Pomfrey's skilled nursing care. But not all injuries can be cured (or cured quickly) by magical means, and as Albus Dumbledore says, no magic can reawaken the dead.[7]

Granted, the Potter books are only fiction, and all of this danger and violence makes for exciting stories.[8] But you can bet that if Hogwarts really existed, the WTA (Wizard Teacher Association) would be up in arms!

Unqualified Teachers

Hogwarts teachers are a mixed bag. There are good teachers who are competent, caring, and fair. These include Albus

Dumbledore, Minerva McGonagall, Filius Flitwick, Pomona Sprout, and Remus Lupin.[9] Other teachers are fairly decent but have significant shortcomings. These include Hagrid, who is knowledgeable and engaging but can't resist exposing his students to dangerous creatures; Moody/Crouch, who teaches his students "loads," but, unfortunately (as Dean Thomas notes), turns out to be a disguised homicidal "maniac"; and Snape, who certainly knows his stuff but is bullying, sarcastic, and blatantly biased in favor of Slytherin students.[10]

There are also downright crummy teachers at Hogwarts. The four worst (if you don't count the Death Eaters who briefly join the faculty in *Deathly Hallows*) are Binns, Sybill Trelawney, Gilderoy Lockhart, and Dolores Umbridge. Binns, a ghost who apparently doesn't know that he's dead, regularly puts his History of Magic students to sleep with his droning lectures, doesn't know the names of his pupils, and is barely aware that there are actually any students in his classes. Trelawney is an "old fraud" who teaches a "woolly" subject (Divination) and enjoys predicting her students' early and gruesome deaths.[11] Lockhart is a narcissistic and ineffectual blowhard. And Umbridge, of course, is a twisted, power-hungry racial supremacist who tries to undermine any effective education at the school.

Dumbledore has great difficulties hiring qualified faculty at Hogwarts. Mostly, this isn't his fault. After Professor Quirrell's shocking demise, we're told that no one would take the job of Defense Against the Dark Arts teacher except the hapless Lockhart. Yet the larger problem, as Arthur E. Levine notes, is that the wizarding world has no teacher education programs or certification requirements.[12] Apparently, anybody can teach at Hogwarts, including those with little or no formal magical education, such as Firenze or Hagrid. Without effective teacher training and credentialing procedures, teacher quality at the wizarding school is bound to be sketchy and even pose risks to students.

No Well-Rounded Education

If Harry and his friends were attending a Muggle British boarding school, they would have classes in subjects such as English, history, science, geography, music, mathematics, foreign languages, physical education, citizenship, and religious education. At Hogwarts, the only thing students learn is how to do magic.[13]

Why is this a problem? Because Hogwarts offers a narrow and vocationally oriented education.[14] It provides its students with the tools of power but not the wisdom to use them.

As the noted philosopher of education Mortimer Adler (1902–2001) remarked, a good secondary school should prepare its students to do three things: "to earn a living in an intelligent and responsible fashion, to function as intelligent and responsible citizens, and to make both of these things serve the purpose of leading intelligent and responsible lives—to enjoy as fully as possible all the goods that make a human life as good as it can be."[15] Hogwarts is devoted almost exclusively to the first of these three goals—vocational training. It teaches its students how to make a living in the wizarding world but not how to live.[16]

What is the aim of education? Great educational thinkers have defended various views. For Plato, the first great philosopher of education in Western civilization, the purpose of education is to achieve wisdom, goodness, and a just and well-ordered society.[17] For Plato's pupil Aristotle, education should promote human fulfillment (*eudaimonia*), which he defined as a life filled with intrinsically excellent activities (especially purely intellectual activities).[18] John Locke (1632–1704) claimed that "virtue and wisdom" are "the great business" of education.[19] Jean-Jacques Rousseau (1712–1778) advocated a "natural," child-centered education aimed at producing happy, virtuous citizens uncorrupted by the hypocrisies and false values of civilization.[20] Immanuel Kant believed that character development—becoming a good moral person who wills the right things for the right reasons—is the primary aim of education.[21] Even John Dewey, who, as we've seen, criticized traditional education for its disconnect with real-world concerns, argued that the ultimate aim of education is simply "more education," or "growth" in one's capacity for enriching experiences.[22]

An educated person should be able to write and speak well, think critically, and be well-grounded in the sciences and the humanities that form the foundation of a liberal education. The goal of a liberal education is not to help students "get a good job" but to impart the knowledge, skills, and dispositions needed to fulfill one's human potential; to understand and appreciate the supreme productions of human thought and art; and to live a rich, full, and vibrant life. A good secondary school should lay the foundation for such a liberal education. Above all, as Adler noted, it should seek to impart to its students both "the skills of learning and the wish to learn, so that in adult life they will want to go on learning and will have the skills to use in the process."[23]

Because there are no universities in the wizarding world, it is critical that secondary wizarding schools such as Hogwarts encourage and equip their students to become lifelong learners.[24] Yet Hogwarts clearly fails in this regard. At Hogwarts, Harry and his friends are taught how to perform spells and brew potions. They are not taught to love reading or ideas, to think scientifically, to appreciate art and literature, or to reflect in an informed and disciplined way about the problems of society and the human condition.

Of course, not all education at a residential school like Hogwarts takes place in the classroom, and Harry and his friends learn many important life lessons outside formal class settings. In fact, Harry's most important teacher and role model at Hogwarts is clearly Dumbledore, although he isn't one of Harry's regular instructors. For Harry, Ron Weasley,

Hermione Granger, Neville Longbottom, Ginny Weasley, Luna Lovegood, and their circle, Hogwarts does prove to be a kind of "school of virtue" of the sort that ancient philosophers praised. In assessing the value of a Hogwarts education, it's important to keep in mind what is learned both inside and outside the classroom. My point is simply that Hogwarts' *formal curriculum* is too narrow and vocational. Remember that most Hogwarts students have relatively little contact with Dumbledore during their years at the school. Harry may pick up priceless nuggets of wisdom in Dumbledore's office, but for most Hogwarts students, it's what they learn—or fail to learn—in the classroom that makes the greatest difference in their lives.

Some might argue that people with magical powers don't really need a well-rounded, liberal education—that they can find happiness and achieve their life goals without one. Besides, they might say, any serious misuse of magic will likely be detected and severely punished by the Ministry of Magic.

This misses the point of a liberal education, however. A liberal education is one suited to a free individual. It liberates the mind by enlarging its perspective, refining its sensibilities, and freeing it from ignorance and the limitations of one's time, place, and culture. As Adler said, a proper education cultivates a person's "capacities for mental growth and moral development" and helps her "acquire the intellectual and moral virtues requisite for a good human life."[25]

The Hogwarts curriculum is not well-suited to provide the broad-based knowledge, the intellectual skills, and the solid character virtues that a good school—wizarding or Muggle—should seek to impart. Because of the narrow vocational education they receive, Hogwarts students are ill-equipped to deal with the many problems that confront wizarding society, including (as Hermione says) "this horrible thing wizards have of thinking they're superior to other creatures."[26]

The Ugly

This "horrible thing" is in fact the greatest problem wizards face. The Potter books are a morality tale about a wizard civil war. On one side are Voldemort's racial supremacists, who want wizards to rule over Muggles and pureblooded wizards to rule over those of mixed ancestry. On the other side are Dumbledore and those who reject such radical supremacist views and believe, instead, in the basic equality of all rational (or, at least, all human) creatures on earth.

I say this is the biggest problem wizards face not only because of the repulsiveness of such racial elitism, but because of what is at stake. Totalitarianism, thought control, secret police, mock trials, racial cleansing—all are real possibilities if the supremacists win. And, of course, they nearly *do* win in the Potter books, just as the Nazis nearly won in World War II.

So, what is Dumbledore doing to educate Hogwarts students about the dangers and the irrationality of racial supremacism? Not a heck of a lot. At least, not directly.

True, Hogwarts is open to all students with magical powers, regardless of ancestry, race, or social class. And Dumbledore makes a point of being an equal-opportunity employer, hiring half-bloods such as Snape and members of marginalized groups such as half-giants (Hagrid), centaurs (Firenze), and werewolves (Lupin).

But that's about it. There are, so far as we are told, no class discussions of racism, no workshops, no school assemblies on the topic. Racial slurs are rampant at Hogwarts, but no student is ever disciplined for using one. The fact that Hogwarts houses the largest population of oppressed house-elves in England is nowhere mentioned in the thousand pages of *Hogwarts, A History*, and Hermione's efforts to alleviate the house-elves' plight are given no public support from Dumbledore. Most seriously, Dumbledore does nothing to remedy the great festering source of militant purebloodism at Hogwarts, Slytherin House.

Slytherin is a breeding ground for dark wizards. As Hagrid says, when Voldemort rose to power there wasn't "a single witch or wizard who went bad who wasn't in Slytherin."[27] And this is no accident; students are sorted into Slytherin because they will "use any means to achieve their ends."[28] Because people—especially impressionable children—tend to become like those they associate with, Slytherin is a hothouse of racial intolerance. It is also, inevitably, a source of "fifth columnists" in Hogwarts—students whose ultimate loyalties aren't to Dumbledore or their classmates, but to Voldemort and his warped racist agenda.

This cancer of racial intolerance and elitism is what is "ugly" about education at Hogwarts. The obvious question is why Dumbledore doesn't do more about it.

In one sense, of course, he *does* do something hugely important about it—he works tirelessly and courageously to defeat Voldemort. But Voldemort was powerless for more than a decade after his failed attempt to kill Harry. Why didn't Dumbledore do anything to address the problems with Slytherin then?

Maybe Dumbledore's hands were tied by school by-laws or the tradition-bound Hogwarts Board of Governors. Maybe he would have been fired if he had tried to take decisive action. Maybe, as Travis Prinzi argues, he was a libertarian "gradualist" who believed in changing hearts and minds by personal example and gentle persuasion, rather than by coercive rules or policies.[29] Who knows? There could be lots of reasons he refuses to take stronger action. I, for one, am happy to give him the benefit of the doubt. But it's a fair question, I think, whether Dumbledore shouldn't have done more than he did.

Like Bertie Bott's Every-Flavor Beans, a Mix

Hogwarts, like most schools, has its pros and cons. Its students love the castle, the grounds, the camaraderie, the hands-on focus on practical magic. It's definitely a fun and interesting place to go to school. Yet there are also a few big negatives about a Hogwarts education, including some ineffective teachers, a dangerous environment, a narrow curriculum, and a strong undercurrent of racial intolerance and elitism.

So, would I send my kid to Hogwarts? In the final analysis, yes. It's just too special an opportunity to miss. But I'd also be sure, as I do, to teach my child about the fundamental equality of persons, the vital role of democratic freedoms, and the importance of a well-rounded education. For these are the values that can make our world a truly magical place.[30]

NOTES

1. *Sorcerer's Stone*, p. 123. And for dessert: "Blocks of ice cream in every flavor you could think of, apple pies, treacle tarts, chocolate éclairs and jam doughnuts, trifle, strawberries, Jell-O, rice pudding," ibid., p. 125. You get the point.

2. Susan Engel and Sam Levin, "Harry's Curiosity," in Neil Mulholland, ed., *The Psychology of Harry Potter: An Unauthorized Examination of the Boy Who Lived* (Dallas, TX: BenBella Books, 2006), p. 31.

3. Dewey's major work on education is *Democracy and Education* (New York: Macmillan, 1916). His later book, *Experience and Education* (New York: Collier Books, 1963; originally published in1938), is shorter and more readable.

4. See, for example, Barbara Gross Davis, *Tools for Teaching* (San Francisco: Jossey-Bass, 1993), chap. 23; Ken Bain, *What the Best College Teachers Do* (Cambridge, MA: Harvard University Press, 2004), p. 99.

5. Alfred North Whitehead, *The Aims of Education and Other Essays*, reprinted in Steven M. Cahn, ed., *Classic and Contemporary Readings in the Philosophy of Education* (New York: McGraw-Hill, 1997), p. 262. Of course, students need to learn lots of things they may have little natural interest in studying (irregular verbs and the multiplication tables, for example). For a useful caution about going overboard in catering to student interests, see E. D. Hirsch Jr., *The Schools We Need and Why We Don't Have Them* (New York: Doubleday, 1996), pp. 86–87.

6. *Prisoner of Azkaban*, p. 93.

7. *Goblet of Fire*, p. 697. Moody's disfigured nose and the insanity of Neville's parents are apparently incurable. And as Harry's and Dumbledore's eyeglasses suggest, even bad eyesight apparently can't be fixed by magical means.

8. That the books are *fiction* bears repeating. In pointing out shortcomings with Hogwarts *if it were real*, I am not criticizing either J. K. Rowling or the books. There's no reason to think Rowling means to depict Hogwarts as an ideal institution. She portrays Hogwarts as she does (as dangerous, for example) because that depiction *works as fiction*.

If Rowling herself were headmistress of Hogwarts, no doubt she would recognize and address many of the problems I mention.

9. Lupin might need an asterisk next to his name because of his unfortunate tendency to change into a lethal werewolf once a month. True, Lupin takes Wolfsbane Potion to control his symptoms. But as his dangerous transformation in *Prisoner of Azkaban* makes clear, there is still some risk to students.

10. Professor Quirrell isn't exactly who he seems to be either—he has a bit of a split personality, actually.

11. *Order of the Phoenix*, p. 315.

12. Arthur E. Levine, "No Wizard Left Behind," *Education Week*, November 9, 2005, p. 44. Levine's critique of Hogwarts is tongue-in-cheek.

13. There are exceptions. Hogwarts students learn some social studies in History of Magic and the optional Muggle Studies class. They also study some conventional science in Astronomy.

14. A point also noted by Charles W. Kalish and Emma C. Kalish, "Hogwarts Academy: Common Sense and School Magic," in *Psychology of Harry Potter*, p. 65; and Marc Sidwell, "No Child of Mine Will Go to Hogwarts," ConservativeHome's Platform, http://conservativehome.blogs.com/platform/2007/08/marc-sidwell-no.html.

15. Mortimer J. Adler, *The Paideia Proposal: An Educational Manifesto* (New York: Simon & Schuster, 1998), p. 18.

16. Adapted from Father Richard Connerton, C.S.C., founding president of King's College (Pennsylvania), who stated that King's "teaches students not only how to make a living, but how to live."

17. Plato, *Republic*, translated by Benjamin Jowett (New York: Random House, 1937), especially Books 3 and 7.

18. Aristotle, *Politics*, translated by Benjamin Jowett, in *The Basic Works of Aristotle*, edited by Richard McKeon (New York: Random House, 1941), especially Books 7 and 8.

19. John Locke, *Some Thoughts Concerning Education*, in *John Locke on Politics and Education* (Roslyn, NY: Walter J. Black, 1947), paragraph 200.

20. Jean-Jacques Rousseau, *Emile*, translated by Allan Bloom (New York: Basic Books, 1974).

21. Immanuel Kant, *Thoughts on Education*, translated by Annette Churton, reprinted in Steven M. Cahn, ed., *Classic and Contemporary Readings in the Philosophy of Education* (New York: McGraw-Hill, 1997), p. 216.

22. Dewey, *Experience and Education*, p. 36.

23. Mortimer J. Adler, *Reforming Education: The Opening of the American Mind* (New York: Macmillan, 1988), p. 218.

24. J. K. Rowling, "Scholastic.com Online Chat Interview," February 3, 2000, www.accio-quote.org/articles/2000/0200-scholastic-chat.htm. Nor are there are any primary wizarding schools. Some wizarding children are educated in Muggle primary schools, but most are home-schooled. J. K. Rowling, FAQs, "What education do the children of

wizarding families have before going to Hogwarts?" J. K. Rowling Official Site, www
.jkrowling.com/textonly/en/faq_view.cfm?id=101.

25. Adler, *Reforming Education*, p. 120.

26. *Order of the Phoenix*, p. 171.

27. *Sorcerer's Stone*, p. 80.

28. Ibid., p. 118.

29. Travis Prinzi, "Hog's Head PubCast #54: Revolutionaries and Gradualists," http://thehogshead.org/2008/07/03/hogs-head-pubcast-54-revolutionaries-and-gradualists/. But see Beth Admiraal and Regan Reitsma's critique of this interpretation in this volume, "Dumbledore's Politics."

30. My thanks to John Granger, Bill Irwin, Dave Baggett, and Travis Prinzi for helpful comments on previous drafts. Of course, these friends are partly to blame for any faults in the chapter, for as the Medieval philosopher Thomas Aquinas says (*Summa Contra Gentiles*, Book 3, chap. 135), "He who helps another shares in his work, both in its good and in its evil."

PART FIVE

BEYOND THE VEIL: DEATH, HOPE, AND MEANING

THE REAL SECRET OF THE PHOENIX

Moral Regeneration through Death

Charles Taliaferro

The phoenix is a majestic mythical bird that has the power to ignite in flames and then be reborn from its ashes. This power to be reborn through death might simply be part of the magical background to J. K. Rowling's Harry Potter stories, or it might be something more. As part of that background, Dumbledore's phoenix, Fawkes, plays a brave and noble role in protecting Harry in the Chamber of Secrets and in shielding Dumbledore in the battle at the Ministry of Magic by taking a killing curse. The key opposition to Voldemort is called the Order of the Phoenix, but such references might simply be there to enrich the plot. Yet the magical power of the phoenix may be a clue to a deep theme about the nature of relationships that philosophers have addressed.

Some philosophers propose that something similar to the process of death and rebirth of the phoenix is necessary in mending relationships through a process of remorse, seeking forgiveness, and then developing a new, reformed character. The basic idea is that the person who has committed a serious wrong needs to confess what he has done, express sincere remorse, repudiate any pleasure or gain that he got from the wrongdoing, and form radically new intentions and desires that make any future wrongdoing unthinkable (or at least unlikely). The act of repudiating the past wrong and any illicit pleasure has been understood by some philosophers as a kind of death; one burns up or dies to the self who committed the wrong. The reformed person emerges from this process of repudiation and remorse as an essentially new person. Continuity is maintained; the new person emerges from the one who did the wrong. But there is still a radically new self on the other side of this massive shift from bad to good, from evil desires to new, good intentions and resolutions.

This model faces some objections (we will consider two major ones at the end of the chapter), but it has much intuitive appeal. In a friendship broken by betrayal, it seems that the chief road to reconciliation has to involve remorse (the person has to be genuinely sorry about betraying you). And once there has been evident reform, there has to be a genuine acceptance of the person back again into friendship. Sure, both of you might never forget the fact that a betrayal took place, but don't you both have to put aside any ongoing blame? You can't have a very good renewed friendship if every other day you remind the person that she or he did wrong. In effect, the repaired relationship has to be *reborn*; you have accepted the return of your friend and see her or him in a new light, setting to one side resentment or focus on past injury.

This portrait of moral repair as a kind of death and rebirth is found most famously in some religious traditions, especially in Christianity, where the transition from sin to life in God is described as a dying and rising to new life (Romans 5). The Christian rite of baptism is traditionally seen as a kind of death to sin and rebirth into the household of God, in which the redeemed soul may even take on a new name. Secular, contemporary accounts of moral reform have also taken seriously the way in which repentance requires a clear departure from the self that did the wrong and an identification of the reformed person with a new set of desires and essentially a new identity.[1]

In this chapter, we'll explore the ways in which this model may be seen in the work of J. K. Rowling, with a focus on *The Deathly Hallows*. As we'll see, Rowling actually goes further than most philosophers have in illuminating the process of moving to new life through a kind of death by juxtaposing Harry and Dumbledore, on the one hand, and Lord Voldemort, on the other. Voldemort provides a fascinating inversion or, really, a perversion of the process of moving from death to life. Voldemort spreads death by clinging to life, whereas Dumbledore and Harry move to a deeper life by accepting death.

Remorse and Death

In their final confrontation, Harry gives Voldemort a last chance, a possible reprieve. That reprieve must involve remorse. In Harry's invitation or challenge to feel remorse, Harry does not use the title Voldemort, He-Who-Must-Not-Be-Named, or the Dark Lord, but instead his given name: Tom Riddle. Harry seems to be calling Riddle back from his role as a menacing, almost supernatural Dark Lord to take ownership of himself as Tom Riddle, the confused, angry, but highly promising child. The process that the one who calls himself Voldemort would have to undergo to admit and feel remorse for his sordid, ugly crimes as Tom Riddle is too deflationary for the Dark Lord. In other words, Riddle needs to shed or die to his past evil intentions and acts. Unwilling to undergo such repudiation and humility, Riddle as Voldemort attacks Harry and is undone.

Remorse is a key element in the process of reform and regeneration in the Potter stories—remorse and sorrow, as well as regret. The difference between reform and regret is perhaps most apparent when Voldemort commands his snake to kill Severus Snape. After giving the command "kill" to Nagini, Voldemort has this reaction:

> "I regret it," said Voldemort coldly.
>
> He turned away; there was no sadness in him, no remorse. It was time to leave this shack and take charge, with a wand that would now do his full bidding. He pointed it at the starry cage holding the snake, which drifted upward, off Snape, who fell sideways onto the floor, blood gushing from the wounds in his neck. Voldemort swept from the room without a backward glance, and the great serpent floated after him in its huge protective sphere.[2]

Regret involves sorrow or displeasure that some event has occurred, but remorse adds a crucial ingredient: a feeling of profound sorrow that one has committed the act. Regret need not involve any personal acknowledgment of guilt or personal accountability, but remorse implies grief or sorrow over one's role in some past act or omission.

Perhaps Riddle could not begin to feel remorse because he had become so identified with Voldemort or, rather, Riddle had become Voldemort, the wielder of indomitable power, so that he could not see any new life beyond Voldemort through remorse. If one has committed wrong, and all that one feels is remorse for the deed, one is in an almost intolerable position. Moral reform requires that a person proceed to some positive new identity, passing through remorse to a new life.

Dumbledore comes to realize that he needs to pass through death when he recognizes his disastrous mistake of putting on the ring with the goal of using the Resurrection Stone. His error was not motivated by evil or spite. He even thought that he might in some way bring about new life through the stone. As Dumbledore confesses to Harry,

> "When I discovered it, after all those years, buried in the abandoned home of the Gaunts—the Hallow I had craved most of all, though in my youth I had wanted it for very different reasons—I lost my head, Harry. I quite forgot that it was now a Horcrux, that the ring was sure to carry a curse. I picked it up, and I put it on, and for a second I imagined that I was about to see Ariana, and my mother, and my father, and to tell them how very, very sorry I was. [. . .]
>
> "I was such a fool, Harry. After all those years I had learned nothing. I was unworthy to unite the Deathly Hallows, I had proved it time and again, and here was final proof."[3]

Dumbledore realizes his wrong and is aware that this rash deed has released a poison into his system that will be his complete undoing, despite Snape's best attempts to contain the damage caused by the curse. Dumbledore elects to work through this remorseful recognition of a wrong in order to protect Harry and to provide a path for Voldemort's ultimate defeat. By arranging for Snape to kill him using Avada Kedavra, he sacrifices his life (and indirectly saves Draco Malfoy's), dying (as it were) to his past self.

This moving beyond his past is evident in the dialogue between Harry and Dumbledore after Harry's apparent death. Dumbledore fully discloses his plans and intentions, displaying through tears his position as a vulnerable professor and guardian who has (in his view) failed in his tasks. Dumbledore also painfully confesses his weaknesses as a young man with his parents, sister, and brother:

> "I was gifted, I was brilliant. I wanted to escape. I wanted to shine. I wanted glory."

"Do not misunderstand me," he said, and pain crossed the face so that he looked ancient again. "I loved them. I loved my parents, I loved my brother and my sister, but I was selfish, Harry, more selfish than you, who are a remarkably selfless person, could possibly imagine."[4]

It is partly through this dialogue and through Harry's own passage from death to life that Dumbledore and Harry are reconciled.

In the first few books of the Potter series, Dumbledore is a mentor, a father figure like Merlin or Gandalf; he is a teacher and a professor, a headmaster and a half-guardian to Harry, the embodiment of all that is good and chivalric and noble. By the end of the series, we see another side of Dumbledore. We learn that he is a penitent who feels bound to confess his own shortcomings to Harry in the course of giving him the final, vital instruction that he needs to complete his coming of age. Dumbledore concludes by offering Harry this very Socratic-sounding advice: "You are the true master of death, because the true master does not seek to run away from Death. He accepts that he must die, and understands that there are far, far worse things in the living world than dying."[5]

The completion of Harry's great trial (his education or formation), which culminates in his combat with Voldemort, makes peers of Harry and Dumbledore in the end. The exchange between Harry and his mentor, which occurs through the portrait of Dumbledore, suggests that their relationship has changed; they are no longer mentor and mentee. A kind of equality is achieved in their reconciliation and in Harry's victory and resolutions: after Harry told Dumbledore of his plans for the Elder Wand, "Dumbledore nodded. They smiled at each other."[6]

Harry must undergo a death and a rebirth in order to achieve the full integrity that is necessary for his healing and renewal. When Harry was attacked as a child and the killing curse rebounded, a piece of Voldemort's soul attached itself to Harry, thus allowing Harry insight into Voldemort's mind, giving him the ability to speak Parseltongue, and making the Sorting Hat think he might do well in Slytherin. Voldemort's attack left an indelible mark on Harry's forehead that linked him to Voldemort's mind. At times, this bordered on possession, as in the climactic scene in *Order of the Phoenix* when Voldemort speaks through Harry:

> And then Harry's scar burst open. He knew he was dead: it was pain beyond imagining, pain past endurance—
>
> He was gone from the hall, he was locked in the coils of a creature with red eyes, so tightly bound that Harry did not know where his body ended and the creature's began. They were fused together, bound by pain, and there was no escape—
>
> And when the creature spoke, it used Harry's mouth, so that in his agony he felt his jaw move . . .
>
> "Kill me now, Dumbledore . . ."[7]

To overcome this horrifying link with the Dark Lord, Harry needed the piece of Voldemort's soul that was inside him to die, as occurs near the end of *Deathly Hallows*, when Harry allows Voldemort to perform the killing curse on him. All is explained in the following conversation, as Dumbledore reassures Harry that Harry is not, as he initially believed, dead:

> "I let him kill me," said Harry. "Didn't I?"
>
> "You did," said Dumbledore, nodding. "Go on!"
>
> "So the part of his soul that was in me . . ."
>
> Dumbledore nodded still more enthusiastically, urging Harry onward, a broad smile of encouragement on his face.
>
> ". . . has it gone?"

"Oh yes!" said Dumbledore. "Yes, he destroyed it. Your soul is whole, and completely your own, Harry."[8]

A little later on in the conversation, Dumbledore elaborates,

"You were the seventh Horcrux, Harry, the Horcrux he never meant to make. He had rendered his soul so unstable that it broke apart when he committed those acts of unspeakable evil, the murder of your parents, the attempted killing of a child.

"But what escaped from that room was even less than he knew. He left more than his body behind. He left part of himself latched to you, the would-be victim who had survived."[9]

To become whole once again, Harry must die to release the Voldemort link.

While this dramatic case of dying and rising involves Harry ridding himself of that which is fundamentally foreign to his true identity or core values, there is a sense, in every book, in which Harry undergoes a process of remorse and regenerating with respect to his own feelings and faults. So, for example, in *Order of the Phoenix*, his mistrust of Hermione Granger and Ron Weasley needs to be redressed.

But before he knew it, Harry was shouting.

"SO YOU HAVEN'T BEEN IN THE MEETINGS, BIG DEAL! YOU'VE STILL BEEN HERE, HAVEN'T YOU? YOU'VE STILL BEEN TOGETHER! ME, I'VE BEEN STUCK AT THE DURSLEYS' FOR A MONTH! AND I'VE HANDLED MORE THAN YOU TWO'VE EVER MANAGED AND DUMBLEDORE KNOWS IT— WHO SAVED THE SORCERER'S STONE? WHO GOT RID OF RIDDLE? WHO SAVED BOTH YOUR SKINS FROM THE DEMENTORS?"

Every bitter and resentful thought that Harry had had in the past month was pouring out of him; his frustration at the lack of news, the hurt that they had all been together without him, his fury at being followed and not told about it: All the feelings he was half-ashamed of finally burst their boundaries.[10]

Harry has to renounce his temper and his rash decisions, and there is a recurring sense in which love has a role in solidifying his continuous development, his rebirth, as it were. So, for example, when he and Ginny Weasley kiss after a long separation, this is described in terms of Harry's sense of reality:

"There's the silver lining I've been looking for," she whispered, and then she was kissing him as she had never kissed him before, and Harry was kissing her back, and it was blissful oblivion, better than firewhisky; she was the only real thing in the world, Ginny, the feel of her, one hand at her back and one in her long, sweet-smelling hair.[11]

Harry's love for others and their love for him is the foundation for his maturation and his protection from Voldemort. As Dumbledore observes, "That power [of love] also saved you from possession by Voldemort, because he could not bear to reside in a body so full of the force he detests."[12]

The Inversion of Voldemort

As Voldemort, Tom Riddle displays almost the exact opposite pattern of development as do Harry and Dumbledore. Rather than feeling remorse, repentance, and renewal, with each murder Voldemort more deeply takes ownership of his identity as a murderer and a tyrant, one who sees his life as infinitely more important and interesting than the lives around him. Voldemort's pursuit of eternal life—in a sort of perverse inversion of the Christian ideal of life through dying-to-self—leads him to a form of self-division in which he divides his soul into seven (unwittingly eight) parts.

> "[T]he more I've read [about Horcruxes]," said Hermione, "the more horrible they seem, and the less I can believe that he actually made six. It warns in this book [*Secrets of the Darkest Art*] how unstable you make the rest of your soul by ripping it, and that's just by making one Horcrux!"
> Harry remembered what Dumbledore had said about Voldemort moving beyond "usual evil."
> "Isn't there any way of putting yourself back together?" Ron asked.
> "Yes," said Hermione with a hollow smile, "but it would be excrutiatingly painful."
> "Why? How do you do it?" asked Harry.
> "Remorse," said Hermione. "You've got to really feel what you've done. There's a footnote. Apparently the pain of it can destroy you. I can't see Voldemort attempting it somehow, can you?"[13]

The Horcrux embodiments of Voldemort's soul become the repositories of vile malice. Each must be destroyed to finally defeat the Dark Lord.

Notice the inversion here. Remorse and rebirth serve to foster a deeper, more natural life for Harry and Dumbledore, whereas Voldemort's pursuit of evil makes him increasingly unnatural. For example, friendship between Harry and his mates and his interaction with Dumbledore often involve eating (or, really, feasting), games, and affectionate exchanges of gifts. With Voldemort, there is no feasting but (most perversely) the drinking of blood. Rather than Voldemort's action leading to fullness of life, his evil acts threaten his natural embodiment. When he tried to kill the infant Harry, his evil act seemed to vaporize him, turning him into a mist, a disembodied being.

> He pointed the wand very carefully into the boy's face . . .
> "Avada Kedavra!"
> And then he broke: He was nothing, nothing but pain and terror, and he must hide himself, not here in the rubble of the ruined house, where the child was trapped and screaming, but far away . . . far away.[14]

Until Voldemort can become re-embodied, his "life" is parasitic on the blood and the limbs of others. (He needs Harry's blood and Wormtail's hand to regenerate a full-grown body.) In the final volume, Voldemort's body does not seem to be natural; his face is snakelike, and he is able to fly without the aid of a broomstick or other magical means. The contrast with the world of Dumbledore and Harry and his friends could not be more radical, with its real eating and authentic, affectionate touch. At the end of the book, this culminates for Harry and his immediate friends, Ron, Ginny, and Hermione, in romantic love and child-rearing. There is a stark contrast here between the natural world of remorse and regeneration and Voldemort's efforts to hold on to his life at the cost of others'.

The contrast between Voldemort's hideous seeking of immortality by killing or maiming others and his refusing the natural course of regeneration and integration through remorse is almost the complete opposite of Harry's and Dumbledore's willing acceptance of moral, spiritual, and physical death for the sake of love and goodness. As becomes especially apparent in *Deathly Hallows*, physical death in Rowling's world is not the worst thing for a soul or even the end of the soul. On the grave of Harry's parents, we read that "The last enemy that shall be destroyed is death." At first, Harry is horrified that this is "a Death Eater idea," but Hermione explains that the reference is to living beyond or after death. Death itself might be a passage to something more:

> Seeing that Harry and Ron looked thoroughly confused, Hermione hurried on, "Look, if I picked up a sword right now, Ron, and ran you through with it, I wouldn't damage your soul at all."
>
> "Which would be a real comfort to me, I'm sure," said Ron. Harry laughed.
>
> "It should be, actually! But my point is that whatever happens to your body, your soul will survive, untouched," said Hermione.[15]

The death of Voldemort is desperate, unmourned, and ultimately pathetic ("Tom Riddle hit the floor with a mundane finality"), whereas Dumbledore's death is integral to Voldemort's defeat.[16] Moreover, all of those who bravely died in fighting Voldemort (including Dobby, Fred Weasley, Remus Lupin, Nymphadora Tonks, and Colin Creevey) were duly honored and lovingly grieved.

The Integrity Objection

One of the recurring objections to the idea that moral reform involves a radical regeneration akin to the dying and rising phoenix is that it undermines the integrity of personal identity. If you did some wrong, it is always and forever the case that it was you who did the wrong. No amount of renunciation can alter that fact. To imagine that you are somehow a new person after the grieving and the repentance invites a kind of self-deception. Imagine that I harm you wrongly and claim that this act was done by the "Bad Charles," but I am now the "New Charlie," a fresh new person who has little sympathy with that old form of myself. This "rebirth" seems to threaten any kind of integrity I have with my identity over time.

This critique of the regeneration model was advanced by the Freudian psychoanalyst Melanie Klein (1882–1960).[17] She held that personal maturity and continuity require that one keep a solid commitment to the fact that a reformed person is the self-same person who did the wrong in the past. An alcoholic, for example, usually still thinks of himself as an alcoholic even after he has reformed and been sober for decades. The integrity objection thus strongly opposes the regeneration model.

There is some force to this objection. The regeneration model can be abused. If one assumes that the regeneration can be so radical that *there is no continuity at all* between oneself as reformed and the person who did the wrong, self-deception seems to be at work. A case in which I casually split myself into a good and a bad self would seem more like a joke than genuine reform. Clearly, the regeneration model can be pushed too far. But without a real break from the past, involving a genuine renunciation that comes very close to a kind of dying, one's renewal or reconciliation will be incomplete. It may be that people addicted to alcohol will think of themselves as alcoholics their whole lives, but in renouncing alcohol abuse they thereby no longer see themselves as drinkers or drunks. Think of someone who gives up smoking. Doesn't making a shift away from smoking require that one no longer thinks of oneself as a smoker but as a different sort of person? The price of not undertaking a robust renunciation of wrongdoing or past mistakes can be high. Consider the case of Severus Snape.

As revealed in *Deathly Hallows*, Snape truly loved Harry's mother, Lily Evans. When he was a boy, he was attracted to her from afar. She was the one person at Hogwarts who stood up to James Potter and other bullies when they menaced Snape. Snape, however, made the disastrous mistake of calling her a Mudblood, an insulting name for Muggle-born witches. He later made the even more tragic error of inadvertently giving Voldemort the information he needed to find and kill Harry.

Snape does feel deep remorse for these acts, but he is unable to publicly confess his feelings and thus achieve a full integration through remorse and renewal.

Snape owes a life debt to Harry's father, who saved him from Lupin when Lupin was transformed into a werewolf. Snape can be true to this life debt by protecting Harry (which he does on more than one occasion), but he is unable to openly come clean with Harry about his bond with Lily or his debt to James. He nurses resentment toward Harry and is unable to fully detach himself from his past. His motives are at times completely honorable, or as honorable as one's motives can be when one is a spy for the Order who also has to pretend to be a faithful Death Eater.

Snape is not an integrated person in the spirit of Melanie Klein; he is impaired because he can't bring himself to fully renounce his past wrongs and move beyond them. In an ideal case of reconciliation, there might have to be a miracle: the actual restoration to life of James and Lily. But short of that, the best reconciliation available might have been for Snape's true loyalty to Lily (and Dumbledore) to have been acknowledged and honored during his lifetime. This might also have been impossible, however, because Snape apparently needed to retain his cover as Voldemort's servant as long as possible. Short of that, Snape still receives honor in a way that is deep and enduring: Harry names one of his children after Snape. The name given Harry's son is the last word spoken by Dumbledore before he dies: *Severus*.

The Fantasy Objection

Consider briefly a second objection: Rowling has produced a masterpiece partly because she has invented a possible world quite remote from ours. In our world, spells are not cast, people cannot survive the death of their bodies, portraits of dead headmasters do not talk to students, and so on. If all of that is fantastic (literally, a matter of fantasy), why not think that the regeneration model is a matter of fantasy as well? Real ethics and serious models of moral reform need to be fashioned on the basis of realistic narratives, not of imaginary worlds.

As it happens, I have argued elsewhere against some of the philosophical systems that rule out the possibility of life after death.[18] I have also argued that our world is one in which there can be genuine enchantment, spells of sorts.[19] Contemporary ethicists don't address the practices of blessing and cursing, but this is regrettable, given the many ways people can affect one another on subliminal levels. Yet even if we bracket all of this and assume there is no afterlife and no magic at all in our world, note that *Rowling does not treat ethics as a matter of fantasy*. All of the values we share of loyalty, friendship, romantic love, fairness, our opposition to enslavement (free the house-elves!), and the role of remorse, forgiveness, and reform are very much in play in both Rowling's fiction and our own Muggle world. In the name of realism, the fantasy objection would dismiss Rowling's genuine insights about the perils of cruelty, the wrongful pursuit of purity (purebloods), love, and so on. Such "realism" is more a matter of failing to engage the imagination than of falling into the imaginary.

Fawkes's Secret

As we noted at the outset, the role of the phoenix in the Harry Potter books may simply be part of the magical background to Dumbledore's and Harry's lives. Fawkes, after all, mourns his master with "a stricken lament of terrible beauty" and then leaves Hogwarts for good.[20] But it could be that he leaves Hogwarts after the death of Dumbledore because we now have enough wisdom to grasp the message that the phoenix has left behind: that sometimes spiritual or actual death may have to be endured for there to be a regeneration of life, reconciliation, and a triumph of good over evil. Fawkes, after all, did not save Dumbledore when he was poisoned. Perhaps it was impossible, even though the tears of a phoenix can cure terrible wounds. Fawkes did not shield Dumbledore from the Avada Kedavra curse from Snape, nor did Fawkes intervene to prevent Dumbledore's fall from the roof.

We have reason to believe that Fawkes could know the mind of his master, and that Fawkes was probably well aware of Dumbledore's willful sacrifice of himself. Yes, perhaps Fawkes and the pattern of regeneration were a mere coincidence in Rowling's masterpiece, but maybe Fawkes himself was fully aware of the necessity of dying and rising, remorse and regeneration. Fawkes may have left Hogwarts at the end of *Half-Blood Prince*, but he may also have left behind the most important lesson that any of us can learn. Cases of wrongdoing, betrayal, and vice that lead to the rupture of friendships and community need to be healed by a kind of death and rebirth, in which one emerges from the flames of remorseful confession as a new person with radically new desires and intentions, ready to rejoin relationships and community.[21]

NOTES

1. See, for example, Charles Griswold, *Forgiveness: A Philosophical Exploration* (New York: Cambridge University Press, 2007).

2. *Deathly Hallows*, pp. 656–657.

3. Ibid., pp. 719–720.

4. Ibid., pp. 715–716.

5. Ibid., p. 721. For Socrates' views on the philosopher's cheerful acceptance of death, see Plato's *Phaedo*, 64a–68a.

6. *Deathly Hallows*, p. 749.

7. *Order of the Phoenix*, pp. 815–816.

8. *Deathly Hallows*, p. 708.

9. Ibid., p. 709.

10. *Order of the Phoenix*, pp. 65–66.

11. *Deathly Hallows*, p. 116.

12. *Order of the Phoenix*, p. 844.

13. *Deathly Hallows*, p. 103.

14. Ibid., p. 345.

15. Ibid., p. 104.

16. Ibid., p. 744.

17. See Melanie Klein's books *Love, Guilt and Reparation: And Other Works 1921–1945* (London: Hogarth Press, 1975) and *Envy and Gratitude* (London: Hogarth Press, 1975).

18. Charles Taliaferro, *Consciousness and the Mind of God* (Cambridge, UK: Cambridge University Press, 1994).

19. Charles Taliaferro, *Love, Love, Love* (Cambridge, MA: Cowley Press, 2006). See especially the chapter "A Modest Defense of Magic."

20. *Half-Blood Prince*, pp. 614–615.

21. I am very grateful to Elizabeth Clark for conversations about Harry Potter and remorse and her assistance in preparing this essay. Elsa Marty is also thanked for dialogue about the regeneration model.

BEYOND GODRIC'S HOLLOW

Life after Death and the Search for Meaning

Jonathan L. Walls and Jerry L. Walls

After narrowly escaping death only because of his mother's sacrifice, Harry is an orphan, left on the doorstep of his aunt and uncle. Voldemort, we later discover, wishes above all things to avoid death and has performed the most treacherous actions to ensure it. Almost every book in the series results in the death of a significant character, perhaps none more so than Albus Dumbledore in *Half-Blood Prince*. It's easy to hear the resounding echo of death all through the series, culminating in the near-death of Harry himself.

Death and Philosophy

Legend has it that there was a professional philosopher some years ago who decided to run for governor of his state. On the campaign trail, he was asked what the most important lesson was that we can teach our kids. He responded, "That they're going to die." He didn't win the election.

Philosophers deal in the great questions and ideas. Not surprisingly, therefore, many of them have been and are fascinated by death, the ultimate unknown. Because death is so unpleasant a prospect, however, some people try to avoid it, deny it, put it out of their minds. Young people are particularly prone to feeling invincible, as though death is something that happens only to others. They often lack what the philosopher Martin Heidegger (1889–1976) called *authenticity*, which comes from accepting death and reflecting deeply on our mortality.

Some philosophers, such as the Epicureans in ancient Greece, thought that we should be unconcerned about death, because when we die, we cease to exist. Death doesn't exactly happen *to* us, it's merely the end of us. We're no longer around to experience it; the arrival of death corresponds with our departure, so why sweat it? Heidegger, in contrast, thought that authentic living requires a choice to face boldly what our death implies: that we will no longer be. As an atheist, he thought that at death we cease to exist, and living authentically is to live with a poignant recognition that death is ever close at hand. It's not simply a far-off event; it could happen at any time, without warning or the chance to reflect about it, and its imminence should shape how we live and think right now. Our mortality confronts us with the task of defining ourselves, recognizing both our limitations and our opportunities, and not wasting any of our short time living half-asleep.

More than two thousand years ago, Plato expressed similar thoughts. Indeed, he is famous for teaching that "true philosophers make dying their profession."[1] To pursue wisdom is to live in such a way that one is prepared to face death when it comes.

Harry was confronted with death right from the start, so from an unusually young age he was aware of his mortality.

While Harry leads an authentic life, Lord Voldemort lives a highly inauthentic one. To see why, let's consider Harry's climactic death march and what follows in *Deathly Hallows*.

The Approaching Battle

The matured and battle-hardened Harry somberly marches toward the Forbidden Forest for what he honestly believes will be the last time. He's going there to meet his own doom with open eyes. He has just learned that the only way Voldemort can be finished off is for *Harry* to die, taking a piece of Voldemort's soul down with him. As Harry walks, each step bringing him closer to the end, his thoughts come keenly into focus. In the shadow of his impending death, his senses become sharper. A great appreciation wells up within him for all of the things he has possessed (physical or otherwise) but failed to fully value. Yet he remains resolute in the task before him. Dumbledore knew that if faced with this choice, Harry would follow through, even if it meant his death: "And Dumbledore had known that Harry would not duck out, that he would keep going to the end, even though it was his [Harry's] end, because he had taken trouble to get to know him, hadn't he? Dumbledore knew, as Voldemort knew, that Harry would not let anyone else die for him now that he had discovered it was in his power to stop it."[2]

Harry had faced death before when he lost a number of loved ones. And despite Dumbledore's assurance that death could be the next great adventure and despite Nearly Headless Nick's wisdom on departed souls, Harry retained more than a few doubts about what death would bring. The fact that dead bodies decay and rot in the ground filled him with more than a little existential angst. Recall the scene in *Deathly Hallows* when Harry and Hermione Granger finally reach the grave of Harry's parents in Godric's Hollow, and Harry slowly reads the verse inscribed on the gravestone of his parents: "The last enemy that shall be destroyed is death."[3]

At first, Harry worries that this is a Death Eater idea, more in line with Voldemort's quest to escape death than anything else, and he wonders why such an inscription is there. Hermione assures him, "It doesn't mean defeating death in the way the Death Eaters mean it, Harry. . . . It means . . . you know . . . living beyond death. Living after death." But Harry's parents weren't living, Harry thought. "They were gone. The empty words could not disguise the fact that his parents' moldering remains lay beneath the snow and stone, indifferent, unknowing."[4] If this is what death involves, then talk of death's defeat seems a mockery, and death indeed means just this: moldering remains, decaying flesh, end of story.

This was the fate of Harry's parents, and Harry, in that dark hour, senses it is the fate of everyone. Now, as Harry voluntarily marches to his own death, he realizes something: "And again Harry understood without having to think. It did not matter about bringing them [his departed loved ones] back, for he was about to join them. He was not really fetching them: They were fetching him."[5] He can't bring his parents back, but he can, and will, die and thus join them.

Heidegger didn't advise that we should morbidly reflect about death until we're depressed, but, rather, that we come to terms with death and the limitations it implies, so that we can move into our remaining future, however fleeting, boldly, taking advantage of what opportunities we have. Think not only of Harry in our scenario here, but also of Colin Creevey, the underage wizard who sneaks back into Hogwarts to fight in the battle and loses his life. Harry's and Colin's actions, regardless of their beliefs about life beyond death, are great examples of authentic Heidegerrian living: recognizing limitations, seizing opportunities, and accepting one's own mortality.

King's Cross Station

When Harry receives the apparent death blow from Voldemort, he awakens to find himself possessed of unexpected powers and in a place that resembles King's Cross Station—a sort of ethereal realm, where time and space function differently. This scene is one of the strangest in the Potter books, but J. K. Rowling has made it clear that it is vital.

Waiting for Harry in this mysterious place is none other than Dumbledore. This brings up another connection with Heidegger, who held that we should look into our past to uncover new possibilities for understanding life. One of his most important suggestions is that we need to choose our hero from the past, an exemplar we can use to guide us and help us make sense of our experiences. Heidegger proposes that we have a dialogue with this departed hero, thereby gaining insights that were won from his or her own experiences.

So, who better for Harry to meet at this critical juncture than the beloved Dumbledore, who himself suffered death not long before and who'd devoted so much of his life to the fight against Voldemort? Not to mention that Dumbledore was, as Harry often says, the greatest wizard of all time.

Such a powerful wizard, one would assume, would be like a king in this place, but it is not so. He is simply kind, witty, patient Dumbledore. Dumbledore had once desired power and glory, until he realized, to his chagrin and shame, how dangerous these pursuits are, especially for himself. The Dumbledore we now see is the wise, gentle headmaster whom we all know and love, who, by his own admission, is the better Dumbledore.

This mysterious way-station, King's Cross, evokes the image of Purgatory, the place of postmortem penitence, penal retribution, and spiritual growth in Catholic doctrine. As Dumbledore patiently catches Harry up on everything that was involved in Dumbledore's battle plan against Voldemort, we see more than simply answers to riddles; we see repentance and atonement. "For the first time since Harry had met Dumbledore, he looked less than an old man, much less. He looked fleetingly like a small boy caught in wrongdoing."[6] We also witness a full-fledged apology and confession from Dumbledore, tears and all. It is not that Dumbledore himself was wicked or that he is now being caught in some great lie or misdeed. But Dumbledore had been imperfect, and his mistakes, mainly those of his youth, had caused great harm. Now, in death, Dumbledore has come to terms with his past misdeeds and has grown wiser and merrier as a result.

In stark contrast to Dumbledore in the King's Cross scene is the hideous Voldemort creature. One can only assume that the revolting, deformed atrocity present in the train station is the image of the vanquished bit of Voldemort's soul. It seems that the decisions made by Voldemort have rendered his soul quite beyond repair, as Dumbledore points out in the following exchange.

> Harry glanced over his shoulder to where the small, maimed creature trembled under the chair.
>
> "What is that, Professor?"
>
> "Something that is beyond either of our help," said Dumbledore.[7]

Dumbledore puts it into even plainer words as he and Harry discuss whether Harry will return to the living to finish his work or simply go on to the mysterious beyond. "'I think,' said Dumbledore, 'that if you choose to return, there is a chance that he [Voldemort] may be finished for good. I cannot promise it. But I know this, Harry, that you have a lot less to fear from returning here than he does.'"[8]

Ironically, it is Voldemort's misguided fear of death that has driven him to the unspeakable acts that have obliterated any trace of goodness within him, but it is *because* of these choices that Voldemort now *actually* has reason to fear death.

It's worth noting that J. R. R. Tolkien's *The Lord of the Rings*, which ranks with Potter as one of the most popular fantasy epics of all time, echoes this quest-for-immortality motif. As Tolkien noted in his *Letters*, the real theme of *The Lord of the Rings* is not power or heroic resistance to evil, but "Death and the desire for deathlessness."[9] Sauron, the Dark Lord, pours a good part of his life-force into the One Ring, tying his own incarnate existence irreversibly to the Ring. This ring is the catalyst for much evil and eventually must be destroyed. Let's see what this motif represents and what insight it may have for our own lives.

Reap a Destiny

It's said that the great American psychologist and philosopher William James (1842–1910) once wrote in the margin of a copy of his *Psychology: Briefer Course* the following lines: "Sow a thought, reap an action; sow an action, reap a habit; sow a habit, reap a character; sow a character, reap a destiny." The idea is that it starts small and ends big; our thoughts lead to actions, which upon becoming habit yield a character and ultimately a destiny. Voldemort's destiny, as revealed in the King's Cross scene, is the result of a lifetime of choices that put him on a fatal trajectory to destruction.

This scene raises a possibility that would be quite foreign to Heidegger. After being raised a Catholic and seriously considering the priesthood, Heidegger embraced atheism, abandoning belief in the afterlife. He once described his philosophy as a "waiting for God," a phrase that inspired Samuel Beckett's famous play *Waiting for Godot*. But far from thinking that atheism empties life of meaning or significance, Heidegger thought that our mortality made choosing how we live this life all-important. As he saw it, death represents both the ultimate individuating event and the culmination of the process by which each of us forms our essence through our choices, because each of us must go through death's door alone.

Rowling's view is both similar and different. The Voldemort creature at the station is saddled with an unchanging destiny. It represents the culmination of his development of character, a process that is complete. Voldemort no longer merely did evil; he had become evil. He is, as Dumbledore says, beyond help. He's chosen his fate, and it's ugly. As James would have put it, Voldemort's thoughts led to actions, then habits, then a character, and finally a destiny. Aristotle noted how our actions put us on a trajectory, turning us gradually into particular kinds of people, each choice incrementally shaping our souls. Rowling's portrayal of Voldemort's terrifying fate represents the ultimate culmination of such a process, if, contrary to Heidegger's view, we don't cease to exist at death but instead must continue to live with the consequences of who we have become.

To put it another way, we might say that in death we will *fully* become who we were in the process of becoming, and now we must live with our chosen selves forever. Dumbledore was imperfect, but he showed remorse for his mistakes and was freed from their harmful effects. In a similar way, the ghostly images of Harry's loved ones who walk with him to the Forbidden Forest also reflect the good-natured, loving people they had been in life, something that is apparent in their appearance and conduct. Lily Potter is nurturing; James Potter and Remus Lupin are reassuring; Sirius Black is casual and even a bit flippant, just as we remember him.

Voldemort, by contrast, obstinately refuses to turn from his self-imposed path to perdition, all the way to the very end. And it is not as if Voldemort didn't have his chances. Right down to the waning minutes of his life, Voldemort willfully rejects the one thing that can save him: remorse. Facing a terrible, yet vulnerable, Voldemort, Harry tries to offer a path of redemption still: "But before you try to kill me, I'd advise you to think about what you've done. . . . Think, and try for some remorse, Riddle. . . . It's your one last chance. . . . It's all you've got left . . . *I've seen what you'll be otherwise* . . . Be a man . . . try . . . Try for some remorse.[10]

Of course, remorse is not something Voldemort can muster, and this is his undoing. He may have retained his freedom to show remorse even at that last stage, but, undoubtedly, the pattern of behavior that had recurred so often made it exponentially harder for him to do so. For if Aristotle is right, repeated wrong behavior makes us yet more likely to continue in it and makes it harder for us to resist. Willful choices of evil in the end, then, detract from freedom, if Aristotle's philosophy and Rowling's fiction are right. If such a picture of the human condition and our moral development is accurate, our choices bring certain truths into being and forge our characters. James was a firm believer that we are free, an assumption Heidegger made as well. James stressed that this freedom, this liberation from a deterministic universe, is the most intimate picture each of us has of "truth in the making":

> Our acts, our turning-places, where we seem to ourselves to make ourselves and grow, are the parts of the world to which we are closest, the parts of which our knowledge is the most intimate and complete. Why should we not take them at their face-value? Why may they not be the actual turning-places and growing-places which they seem to be, of the world—why not the workshop of being, where we catch fact in the making?[11]

Such freedom, if it exists, is truly one of life's great mysteries, for it would enable us to make decisions on the basis of reasons that aren't causes; we would be morally and metaphysically free agents whose decisions shape our destinies but whose choices aren't written in stone. Such a view of human freedom need not require a denial that all events are caused, but it demands that some events are caused not by other events, such as the physical processes of our brains, but by us, by persons.

According to this view, our actions don't merely reflect who we are; they shape who we are becoming. To the last, Voldemort retains the capacity, however diminished, to show remorse, but he refuses and thereby seals his fate and grows literally beyond redemption. Plato said that evil is done only out of ignorance. But might some people actually prefer the darkness to light, because they've cultivated appetites that only vice can satisfy? Voldemort's fate raises just such a question.

How we live and what the significance of death is are connected in important ways to questions of whether, as Heidegger believed, death is indeed the end or, as Rowling's fiction depicts, there's life after death. Both Rowling and Heidegger highlight the Jamesian point that our choices here shape our destinies: either our completed human essence at the time of our deaths, in Heidegger's case, or the part of ourselves that we take to the next life if death isn't the end. The philosopher John Locke (1632–1704) suggested that the things that give us our most real identity are our memories and character. Locke's view of personal identity as inextricably connected to our characters, together with the possibility that death may not be our end, ratchets up the importance of developing the right character to literally infinite significance. For this will be a character with which we might be stuck for more than three-score and ten, a character that is the result of our own contingent choices, rather than something inevitable or unavoidable.

In one of his most famous arguments, the German philosopher Immanuel Kant claimed that to ensure the ultimate harmony of virtue and happiness, we have to assume the existence of an afterlife. Before him, the French philosopher Blaise Pascal (1623–1662) was astonished at how many people draw up their ethics and carry on their lives indifferent to the question of whether there's an afterlife:

> The immortality of the soul is something of such vital importance to us, affecting us so deeply, that one must have lost all feeling not to care about knowing the facts

of the matter. All our actions and thoughts must follow such different paths, according to whether there is hope of eternal blessing or not, that the only possible way of acting with sense and judgment is to decide our course in the light of this point, which ought to be our ultimate objective.[12]

Heidegger rightly saw that if death is the end of us forever, this has implications for meaning and morality. The flip side of the same coin is that if death is *not* the end but just the beginning, even bigger implications follow.

In the early volumes of her series, Rowling left it ambiguous whether death is the end or merely the beginning in her fictional world. In *Sorcerer's Stone*, Dumbledore, in a trademark showcase of wisdom and foreknowledge, tells Harry that "to the well-organized mind, death is but the next great adventure."[13] Yet it remained unclear just what the great adventure consisted of and whether it included life beyond the grave. Now, however, the scope of the adventure has been brought more fully to light.

One of the most gripping aspects of Rowling's magical fiction is its compelling character development. Imperfect and morally flawed characters tangling with profound choices between what's good and what's easy provide insight into the "moral fiber" of characters we've come to care about. Adding to the drama and lending more potency to watching these characters progress or digress into what they will ultimately be is Rowling's sober recognition of human mortality. Even beyond that Heidegerrian focus, though, is this: if Rowling's fictional portrayal of the afterlife captures an aspect of reality, the choices we make in this life may be vastly more consequential than we could imagine if death, the last enemy, were never destroyed.

NOTES

1. Plato, *Phaedo*, 67e.
2. *Deathly Hallows*, p. 693.

3. Ibid., p. 328.

4. Ibid.

5. Ibid., p. 698.

6. Ibid., pp. 712–713.

7. Ibid., p. 708.

8. Ibid., p. 722.

9. *The Letters of J. R. R. Tolkien*, edited by Humphrey Carpenter (Boston: Houghton Mifflin, 1980), p. 262. Perhaps the clearest example of the quest for immortality in Tolkien's writings is the invasion of Aman, the Blessed Realm, by Ar-Pharazôn and the men of Númenor in *The Silmarillion* (London: George Allen & Unwin, 1977), p. 279. The Númenoreans sought to wrest immortality from the gods (the Valar) and were destroyed for their impiety. For an insightful discussion of this theme in Tolkien's writings, see Bill Davis, "Choosing to Die: The Gift of Immortality in Middle-earth," in *The Lord of the Rings and Philosophy: One Book to Rule Them All*, edited by Gregory Bassham and Eric Bronson (Chicago: Open Court, 2003), pp. 123–136.

10. *Deathly Hallows*, p. 741 (emphasis added).

11. This is a quote from James's last lecture at Harvard, given on December 6, 1906. Quoted in Robert D. Richardson, *William James in the Maelstrom of American Modernism* (New York: Houghton Mifflin Company, 2007), p. 287.

12. Blaise Pascal, *Pensées*, translated by A. J. Krailsheimer (London: Penguin, 1966), p. 427.

13. *Sorcerer's Stone*, p. 297.

WHY HARRY AND SOCRATES DECIDE TO DIE
Virtue and the Common Good

Michael W. Austin

What do Harry Potter and Socrates (470–399 B.C.E.) have in common? At least one important thing, as it turns out. Harry and Socrates both decide to die for very important reasons.

Fulfillment for Muggles and Wizards

Before we consider the momentous decisions of Harry and Socrates, we need to think a little bit about human fulfillment. Important aspects of human fulfillment fall under ethics, which is the branch of philosophy that focuses on how we ought to live and what kind of people we ought to be. Many philosophers believe that the questions of ethics are intrinsically connected to human nature and that to be truly happy and fulfilled as a human being, one must live a moral life.

Why does Socrates give his life for his convictions, and why is Harry willing to do so in *Deathly Hallows*? More generally, why be moral at all? In the *Republic*, Socrates' student Plato offers an answer to this question. Plato (427–347 B.C.E.) argues that to be fulfilled as human beings, we must be moral. For Plato, being a moral individual is necessary and sufficient for true happiness. This means that in order to be truly happy, we must be moral. It also means that if we are moral, then we will be truly happy. In this, Plato is expressing the same views as his mentor, Socrates. Yet just as Harry has an enemy in Lord Voldemort, Socrates has enemies of his own, philosophical and otherwise.

Voldemort and the Sophists

A crucial part of the drama of the Harry Potter books is the conflict that happens not only between the wands of the wizards—although this is very cool—but between the worldviews of Harry and Voldemort. In this conflict, they respectively represent the views of Socrates and his opponents, the Sophists.[1]

The Sophists were a group of teachers-for-hire who were highly skilled in the art of rhetoric and had very little regard for the truth. If they have contemporary counterparts, the best candidates would be unscrupulous advertisers and political spin doctors. According to the Sophists, the just or moral person always gets less than the unjust person does. Immorality pays, because by being immoral one is better able to secure power, wealth, and pleasure. As the Sophist Thrasymachus puts it in his debate with Socrates in Book I of the *Republic*,

> You must look at it as follows, my most simple Socrates: A just man always gets less than an unjust one. First, in their contracts with one another, you'll never find, when the partnership ends, that a just partner has got more than an unjust one, but less. Second, in matters relating to the city, when taxes are to be paid, a just man pays more on the same property, an unjust one less. . . .

When each of them holds a ruling position in some public office, a just person, even if he isn't penalized in other ways, finds that his private affairs deteriorate because he has to neglect them, that he gains no advantage from the public purse because of his justice, and that he's hated by his relatives and acquaintances when he's unwilling to do them an unjust favor. The opposite is true of an unjust man in every respect.[2]

The unjust man is able to gain more wealth because he takes advantage of others in order to do so. He is not held back from doing this by his moral commitments, as the just person is. This reasoning applies not only to the pursuit of wealth, but also to the pursuit of power and pleasure. If the unjust person can get others to trust him, then they become vulnerable to him. We see Voldemort do this time and again, not only with his enemies, but even with his followers. They trust him enough to put themselves at his mercy, and he generally makes them pay for that trust once he no longer needs them. When trust and vulnerability are present, the unjust person can then manipulate and exploit others for his or her own personal gain of power, pleasure, or wealth.

Plato, through the character of Socrates in this dialogue, mounts a counterargument to the views of the Sophists and those who agree with them. The first prong of the argument explains why living a moral life benefits the morally good person. The second prong has to do with the intrinsic goodness of being an ethical person.

First, Plato argues that there will be justice in the afterlife, because the just and the unjust will receive what they deserve.[3] Socrates, during his trial and prior to his death, warns those who are accusing him that he and they will receive what they deserve in the next life. Socrates holds the view that those who pursue virtue will be rewarded in the afterlife, while those who are concerned only with themselves will not.

This sort of cosmic justice comes into play near the end of *Deathly Hallows*, when Harry is attacked by Voldemort in the Forbidden Forest. After being struck down by the killing curse, Harry regains consciousness in a strange bright mist unlike anything he's ever experienced. He hears a pitiful noise and spots its source. "It had the form of a small, naked child, curled on the ground, its skin raw and rough, flayed-looking, and it lay shuddering under a seat where it had been left, unwanted, stuffed out of sight, struggling for breath." After Harry considers offering it some comfort but not being able to do so, he hears the words "You cannot help."[4] It is the voice of Harry's dead friend and mentor, Albus Dumbledore. As we now know, Harry was the seventh Horcrux. And Voldemort's weakness, which he believed to be his strength, was that he neither valued nor sought to understand friendship, loyalty, innocence, children's tales, or, most important, love. Dumbledore tells Harry that these things have a power greater than Voldemort ever had and constitute a truth he can never grasp.

There is justice in the afterlife. The trembling, moaning, pitiful creature in the mist appears to be Voldemort or at least a picture of Voldemort's fate in the afterlife, unless, in Harry's later words, he "tries for some remorse." But the Dark Lord is only further enraged and tries to kill Harry. Tom Riddle ends up dying, sealing his fate in the next life by his choices in this one. The picture is not one of punishment, as the fire-and-brimstone preacher might proclaim, but rather one in which Voldemort is justly allowed to experience the result of his choices in this life.[5]

People who live justly do not need to wait until the afterlife to receive their reward. According to Plato, justice is intrinsically good because the moral life is also the happy life. Plato, however, doesn't mean *happy* in the sense that we often use the term, such as "I'm happy the Chiefs won," or "I'm happy today is Friday." The type of happiness Plato is referring to is a deep and sustainable inner contentment, moral and intellectual virtue, and well-being. Such a state requires that we be moral, that reason rule the soul. For Plato, reason is the aspect of the human soul that desires knowledge, including knowledge of moral reality. Spirit is the aspect of the soul that desires honor and gets angry, and appetite is the aspect of the soul that desires food, drink, sex, and other bodily pleasures. When reason rules over spirit and appetite, there is an inner harmony that constitutes true happiness. A person with the four "cardinal virtues" of wisdom, moderation, courage, and justice is the truly happy person. The virtuous person is in a state of harmony and spiritual health.

Harry's story illustrates Plato's views. He is by no means perfect, but Harry displays many of Plato's virtues. Harry seeks wisdom through the counsel of Dumbledore, and he often displays extraordinary courage, especially in his willingness to face death in order to save his friends. Harry is devoted to justice for wizards and Muggles and is willing to give his life for the common good if necessary.

For Plato, the immoral soul is the sick, disordered soul. When one's desire for honor, pleasure, or wealth takes over, the ultimate result is inner turmoil. We know from experience that a life of cowardice, intemperance, foolishness, and injustice can also lead to external turmoil. Such vices are very damaging to one's personal relationships, for example. We see an excellent illustration of all of this in the character of Voldemort. His lust for power leads to inner misery, and it isolates him from others. The imagery of the Harry Potter books and movies brings this out. The physical appearance of Voldemort reflects his wretched inner life. Contrast that with the physical appearance of Dumbledore, which reflects the inner peace and harmony that constitute his good (though imperfect) moral character.

For Plato, the choice of the moral life is the *rational* choice.[6] Imagine that you are given a choice, perhaps with the aid of some magic from a wizard, between two lives. In the first life, you will have numerous sicknesses, suffer from chronic pain, and end up dying after a long and drawn-out struggle with some terminal disease. In the second option, you will live a life that is free of any serious illness or injury, and you will die of old age in your sleep. If you choose the first option, it would be fair to assume that you are being irrational. No one in his right mind would choose a life of physical illness over one of physical health. The rational choice is physical health.

Similarly, we are given a real choice, Plato believed, between a life of moral and spiritual health and a life of moral and spiritual sickness. The moral life is the best life, and those who choose the immoral life are making an irrational choice. The rational choice is the just and moral life. We see the reality of these truths of ethics and human nature exemplified in the inspiring story of Harry Potter and his long fight against Voldemort. The rational choice and the right choice are the same choice, as Harry illustrates.

The Common Good versus the Greater Good

In the conversation between Dumbledore and Harry near the close of *Deathly Hallows*, Dumbledore is very honest with Harry about his own mistakes. One of those occurred when he was a young wizard and has to do with his relationship with Gellert Grindelwald. The two young wizards dreamed of a revolution and personal glory. As Dumbledore puts it in recounting these events to Harry,

> "Grindelwald. You cannot imagine how his ideas caught me, Harry, inflamed me. Muggles forced into subservience. We wizards triumphant. Grindelwald and I, the glorious young leaders of the revolution. Oh, I had a few scruples. I assuaged my conscience with empty words. It would all be for the greater good,

and any harm done would be repaid a hundredfold in benefits for wizards."[7]

J. K. Rowling is not alone in being skeptical of high-minded— but, in reality, ethically bankrupt—appeals to "the greater good." Many philosophers are also suspicious of the notion of the greater good and instead endorse an ethic that includes the idea of the common good.

What's the difference between the greater good and the common good? This is a difficult question, as sometimes the phrases are used interchangeably. Dumbledore's "justification" for the harm done by the benefits for wizards exemplifies the notion of the greater good. The harm that is inflicted on inno- cent people is supposed to be justified because of the good of the many that will result. When the greater good is given as a justification, the rights, dignity, and integrity of individuals are up for grabs. That is, these things may be sacrificed for the good of the majority. Some can be made to unjustly suffer in order to benefit others. According to Dumbledore and Grindelwald's plan, Muggles would suffer and be forced into subservience, but this would be outweighed by the benefits to wizards.

This is very different from the common good, in which sacrifices are made for the good of *all*. An example from U.S. history illustrates this idea. Part of the appeal of the civil rights movement was that it was not merely the good of African Americans that was at stake in the struggle, but the good of all members of the American community. The claim that the good of all Americans suffers when the rights of some are violated is an appeal to the common good. Harry's decision to return from the mist to fight Voldemort is a decision based on the common good of Muggles and wizards. Dumbledore tells Harry that there is a chance the Dark Lord may be fin- ished, that Harry may defeat him. Voldemort wants to build a new world, but Harry fights and wins on behalf of those who will suffer under the new order. With Voldemort's defeat, the revolution in the name of the greater good is defeated, but the common good is realized, in which the rights, interests, and dignity of all are respected.

Two Keys to the Good Life

Harry was willing to give his life in *Deathly Hallows* in the struggle against the Dark Lord and his allies. Socrates, Plato's teacher, died for what he believed to be true. Socrates was accused of leading the youths of Athens astray with his philosophy, but he refused to give in, choosing death rather than exile. Dumbledore chose to die for something that Socrates, his student Plato, and Plato's student Aristotle all valued—the common good. Harry, too, is willing to die for the common good, if that's what is necessary to defeat Voldemort.

Some might question whether Socrates really did die for the common good. A case can be made, however, that while neither Harry nor Socrates chose to die solely for the common good, the common good was a significant factor in both of their decisions to die. Socrates died for the sake of virtue and the examined life and was unafraid of death, in part because of his views about the afterlife. A case can also be made that Socrates' martyrlike death could have contributed to the common good via his example of virtue, and that this was in part intentional.[8]

Socrates believed that the life of the philosopher is a superior life, and that the philosopher is not afraid to die. In a sense, his own death was the ultimate display of his conviction that a life in pursuit of wisdom is the best kind of life, and his willingness to die for this conviction is an example that others would be wise to follow. In this way, then, the death of Socrates could have contributed to the good of Athens. His friends and followers, if they followed him in the pursuit of virtue, would also have contributed to the good of Athens, inspired by the life and the death of Socrates. Whether Athens did in fact benefit from Socrates' death and the ensuing lives of his students is a question for historical investigation. But it is clear that there can be no common good without individual goodness, and that Socrates acts as an exemplar for others to imitate in his willingness to die for his convictions.

Similarly, Dumbledore is more concerned with defeating the Dark Lord and his allies than with preserving his own life, because he believes that this is what will be best for all. He, of course, wants to avoid being tortured by his enemies, and he wants to preserve his soul. Yet he is also willing to die in order to prevent Severus Snape's spying from being revealed. It is here that the common good comes into play, as it is clearly beneficial for those opposed to Voldemort to have an ally in his inner circle. So, both Socrates and Dumbledore lay down their lives willingly for virtue and the common good.

There is something very important about the individual's commitment to the common good, rather than to mere self-interest (understood as the pursuit of power, pleasure, comfort, or wealth). Voldemort put self above all else, and his exis-tence is not something that we envy, even if he had defeated Dumbledore and Harry. Harry, however, in his unselfishness, devotion to his friends, and loyalty to the good of all, lives a rationally desirable and morally good existence. The les-son here is that we live best when we live for a cause greater than ourselves. This is something of a paradox. Those who, like Voldemort, put self above all else end up worse off than those who often put the common good above the self. The best life is the moral life.

There is another lesson in all of this for those who pursue this type of fulfillment, and it has to do with Harry's relation-ship with Dumbledore. Readers of the Potter series know that Harry's relationship with Dumbledore is vital to his personal growth and fulfillment. It is also crucial to the fulfillment of his destiny. One thing that is highly conducive to living a good life—even (or perhaps especially) for us Muggles—is the presence of one or more mentors in our lives who provide guidance, instruction, and encouragement along the way. Harry has many mentors at different points in his life, but none more significant than Dumbledore.

Why is Dumbledore such a good mentor for Harry? A good mentor is humble in accurately recognizing and sharing his own faults, as Dumbledore does when confessing his past mistakes. A good mentor is honest with his mentee, as Dumbledore is when he refers to Harry's hotheadedness in his conversation in the mist at King's Cross. A good mentor also praises the virtues of his protégé, as Dumbledore does in the same conversation when he notes Harry's courage, unselfishness, and willingness to face death. Finally, a good mentor is able to encourage his mentee at critical times in his life. We've already seen how Dumbledore plays a crucial role in Harry's fulfilling his destiny during their conversation in the mist. There is, however, another pivotal point, in *Order of the Phoenix*, in which Dumbledore's presence and words make all the difference for Harry.

After Sirius Black's death and a confrontation with Voldemort, Harry and Dumbledore take a Portkey back to Dumbledore's office, where they have one of their most significant conversations. Harry is angry, and a part of him feels like giving up the struggle against evil. After Dumbledore explains why he has been keeping his distance from Harry, he offers the words that Harry needs to hear in order to fulfill his destiny. Dumbledore recounts all that has happened in the five years since Harry's arrival at Hogwarts and expresses his pride in all that Harry has done. He in essence tells Harry that he has what it takes to fulfill his destiny, because he has the character to do so. Dumbledore then explains the lost prophecy to Harry, which singles him out as the only person able to defeat Voldemort. Dumbledore's faith in Harry's ability to defeat Voldemort ultimately enables Harry to do so. And it is Voldemort's inability to understand the power of self-sacrificing love that ultimately proves his undoing. This sort of love encompasses virtue and the common good, and it is the reason that Harry and Socrates opt for death.

Returning from the realm of Hogwarts to our own Muggle lives, we can draw two practical lessons related to human fulfillment. First, if we are to live good lives, we must be devoted to something larger than ourselves. Lily Potter, Dumbledore, and Harry decided to die because they believed life was about more than themselves, and that the greatest life one can live is one devoted to the common good of all of humanity. Fortunately, this type of love is not just the stuff of fantasy literature and imaginary heroes like Harry Potter, but of real-life heroes such as Martin Luther King Jr., Gandhi, Jesus, and Socrates. Second, if we want a good life, we need a mentor, too. We need someone who can provide us with and lead us into insight and wisdom about life's big questions and the small daily choices that make up the substance of our answers and our lives. These choices also make up the substance of each individual's character.

The mentor may be a parent, a coach, or a community leader of some sort. Readers have the advantage of not being limited to the present. They can be mentored by some of the greatest minds in history, such as Aristotle, Confucius, and Jesus, to name just a few. A close reading of Aristotle's *Nicomachean Ethics*, the book of Matthew in the New Testament, or King's "Letter from Birmingham Jail" enables us to bridge the gaps of time and space to learn from some of the wisest persons ever to walk the earth. Ideally, our mentors will be able to go through life with us, as Dumbledore does with Harry. And ultimately, if we're committed to the common good, we'll also be mentors to others, whether that occurs in the context of our homes, our workplaces, or religious or community organizations.

The End of the Story

At the end of the day, philosophical reflection on ethics should have an impact on our daily lives. Given this, consider the following question: Who would you rather be, Harry or Voldemort? For any true lover of virtue and the common good, the answer is clear. What might be less clear to some, but is no less true, is that your answer should remain the same even if Voldemort had won. The value of love, in its best form, is not lessened when love is apparently defeated. To underscore this point, I close with the wise words of Albus Dumbledore to Harry Potter, the boy who lived and ultimately won: "You are the true master of death, because the true master does not seek to run away from Death. He accepts that he must die, and understands that there are far, far worse things in the living world than dying."[9]

NOTES

1. Kelly James Clark and Anne Poortenga, *The Story of Ethics: Fulfilling Our Human Nature* (Upper Saddle River, NJ: Prentice Hall, 2003), pp. 7–23. This short and well-written book traces the theme of the relationship between ethics and human fulfillment from ancient times to our era and is worth reading for those interested in pursuing this subject further. Much of what follows is drawn from this work. See also Plato's *Republic*.

2. Plato, *Republic*, translated by G. M. A. Grube, revised by C. D. C. Reeve (Indianapolis: Hackett, 1992), pp. 19–20.

3. See Book X of the *Republic*, 621a–621d.

4. *Deathly Hallows*, pp. 706–707.

5. For more on this theme, see chapter 17 in this volume, "Beyond Godric's Hollow: Life after Death and the Search for Meaning" by Jonathan and Jerry Walls.

6. See Clark and Poortenga, *The Story of Ethics*, p. 21.

7. *Deathly Hallows*, p. 716. The passage is strongly reminiscent of Saruman's attempt to justify to Gandalf his treacherous alliance with Sauron in J. R. R. Tolkien's *The Fellowship of the Ring* (Book 2, chap. 2): "We can bide our time, we can keep our thoughts in our hearts, deploring maybe evil done by the way, but approving the high and ultimate purpose: Knowledge, Rule, Order."

8. For an account of the trial and the death of Socrates, see Plato, *Five Dialogues: Euthyphro, Apology, Crito, Meno, Phaedo*, translated by G. M. A. Grube (Indianapolis: Hackett, 1981). There are several points raised in the dialogues that lend support to the claim that the common good was one of Socrates' motivations regarding his decision to die. In the *Apology* 29d–30c, Socrates expresses his refusal to cease philosophizing in Athens as a refusal to stop calling its citizens to value truth, wisdom, and the state of their souls more than they value wealth and reputation. There is an important connection between the character of the citizens and the character of the

city, and Socrates would rather die than refrain from contributing to the common good through his philosophizing on the streets of Athens. He would rather provide an example to those who continue living of the importance of a life devoted to virtue and the common good. As he says at the end of this passage, "Wealth does not bring about excellence, but excellence makes wealth and everything else good for men, both individually and collectively." Other reasons for Socrates' decision to die that are related to the common good include his belief that the god has given him this mission (*Apology* 30e), his concern for the reputation of Athens (*Apology* 34e), and his belief that he should die rather than flee Athens, because he owes a debt of gratitude to the city (*Crito* 50a–52e).

9. *Deathly Hallows*, pp. 720–721.

CONTRIBUTORS

The Hogwarts
(for Muggles) Faculty

Beth Admiraal, associate professor of political science at King's College in Pennsylvania, is a carbon copy of Lily Potter, except she doesn't have red hair or green eyes, has never conjured a spell, at no point called her future husband an "arrogant toerag," and rarely sees the value in a person before that person sees this value in himself. She does, however, see the value in studying international relations.

Michael W. Austin teaches philosophy at Eastern Kentucky University, with a focus on ethics and philosophy of religion. He has published journal articles on ethics, philosophy of sport, and philosophy of religion. His published books include *Conceptions of Parenthood: Ethics and the Family* (Ashgate, 2007), *Running and Philosophy: A Marathon for the Mind* (Blackwell, 2007), and *Football and Philosophy: Going Deep* (University Press of Kentucky, 2008). He'd love to try Quidditch but can't find a Firebolt anywhere.

Gregory Bassham teaches at King's College in Pennsylvania, where he specializes in philosophy of law and critical thinking.

He wrote *Original Intent and the Constitution: A Philosophical Study* (Rowman & Littlefield, 1992), coauthored *Critical Thinking: A Student's Introduction* (McGraw-Hill, 4th ed., 2011), and coedited *The Lord of the Rings and Philosophy: One Book to Rule Them All* (Open Court, 2003); *The Chronicles of Narnia and Philosophy: The Lion, the Witch, and the Worldview* (Open Court, 2005); *Basketball and Philosophy: Thinking Outside the Paint* (University Press of Kentucky, 2007); and *The Hobbit and Philosophy* (forthcoming, Wiley). Greg hopes to retire early to spend more time with his remaining hair.

Catherine Jack Deavel is associate professor of philosophy at the University of St. Thomas in St. Paul, Minnesota, and also associate editor of *American Catholic Philosophical Quarterly*. She serves on the executive council of the American Catholic Philosophical Association.

David Paul Deavel is associate editor of *Logos: A Journal of Catholic Thought and Culture* and contributing editor for *Gilbert* magazine. The Deavels' collaborative work has included articles in *Logos*, *New Blackfriars*, and *St. Austin Review*, as well as two chapters on philosophy and popular culture. It also includes four children—and they aim to have more than the Weasleys do, although red hair isn't in the genes.

S. Joel Garver teaches philosophy at La Salle University, focusing on freshman teaching, interdisciplinary courses, epistemology, and philosophical theology. He recently presented on Bonaventure and Aquinas on prophecy, *South Park* and ontologies of violence, and the phenomenon of divine revelation. After Olivander disappeared, Joel ended up crafting his own wand, although he wonders whether his cat's whisker is really a proper core.

Tamar Szabó Gendler is professor of philosophy and chair of the cognitive science program at Yale University. Her research focuses primarily on issues in epistemology, philosophical psychology, metaphysics, and aesthetics. She is the author of *Thought Experiments: On the Powers and Limits of Imaginary Cases* (Routledge, 2000) and an editor of *Conceivability and Possibility* (Oxford, 2002), *Perceptual Experience* (Oxford, 2006), and *The Elements of Philosophy: Readings from Past and Present* (Oxford, 2008). She has been unsuccessful in her efforts to allow students to substitute N.E.W.T.s for SATs in applying to Ivy League schools.

John Granger writes and speaks on the intersection of literature, philosophy, faith, and culture. He has published articles in *Touchstone*, has been a keynote speaker at numerous academic and fan conferences and at major universities from Princeton to Pepperdine, and is the author of several books on Harry Potter, including *How Harry Cast His Spell* (Tyndale, 2008), *The Deathly Hallows Lectures* (Zossima, 2008), and *Harry Potter's Bookshelf* (Penguin, 2009). John was also a finalist in the 2006 Witch Weekly "Most Winning Smile" house-elf division. He lives with his wife, Mary, and their seven Harry-loving dwarves in Pennsylvania.

Alan J. Kellner is a graduate student in philosophy at the University of Chicago in the master of arts program in the humanities (MAPH). His main interest in philosophy is the intersection of metaphysics, ethics, and politics in the history of philosophy. Despite the fact that he goes to school in Chicago, Alan lives in Milwaukee, Wisconsin. He has, in fact, discovered a Floo Network going between the two, which is how he commutes each day. When he's not reading or writing, he's petting his cat, Plato.

Amy Kind, whose specialty is philosophy of mind, teaches at Claremont McKenna College. Her research has appeared in journals such as *Philosophy and Phenomenological Research*, *Philosophical Studies*, and *The Philosophical Quarterly*, and she has

CONTRIBUTORS

also previously written on philosophy and pop culture topics such as *Battlestar Galactica, Star Trek, The Hobbit*, and *Angel*. When she recently took an online Harry Potter identity quiz, she was terribly dismayed to discover she matched up best with Percy Weasley.

Andrew P. Mills is the chair of the department of religion and philosophy at Otterbein College, where he has taught just about every philosophy course there is. He's interested in metaphysics, metaphilosophy, and the pedagogy of philosophy, having published articles in the *Canadian Journal of Philosophy, Philosophical Papers*, and *Teaching Philosophy*. His essay "What's So Good about a College Education?" has been used at schools all around the country to explain to students the nature and value of a liberal arts education. At present, he's working to perfect the "aybeeceedee" spell, which will get his papers graded in a flash.

Tom Morris, after teaching philosophy at Notre Dame for fifteen years, became a public philosopher and has since reached millions of Muggles worldwide through the magic of television, radio, and the Internet and in talks on topics ranging from business ethics and excellence to Dumbledore's favorite reading list. He's the author of around twenty books, including *If Harry Potter Ran General Electric* (Doubleday, 2006), *Philosophy for Dummies* (IDG Books Worldwide, 1999), *True Success* (Berkley Books, 1994), *The Art of Achievement* (MJF Books, 2003), *If Aristotle Ran General Motors* (Henry Holt and Co., 1997), *Making Sense of It All* (W.B. Eerdmans, 1992), and *The Stoic Art of Living* (Open Court, 2004). He may well Apparate to a city near you if you contact him on Twitter, where he is holding court daily as TomVMorris; at the *Huffington Post*, where he blogs weekly; or via his magical Web site: www .MorrisInstitute.com.

Jeremy Pierce is a PhD student at Syracuse University in New York, who works on metaphysics, philosophy of race, and philosophy of religion. He is also an adjunct instructor at Le Moyne College, where he teaches ordinary philosophy, and at Hogwarts School of Witchcraft and Wizardry, where he teaches the many means of discovering the future through magic and the many ways of not changing the past with Time-Turners. It wasn't until he had children that he realized that sleep is too important to use Time-Turners to get more accomplished during the day.

Regan Lance Reitsma, assistant professor of philosophy at King's College, works in ethics, especially in the area of moral normativity, when he's not battling Voldemort (nobody has the heart to tell him he's not real). He received a "T" on his grad school comps and invented a howler e-mail. If no response is received within three days, the recipient's computer begins belting out "Muskrat Love."

Eric Saidel teaches philosophy at George Washington University. His interests have to do with the relationship between the mind and the body. If he were an Animagus, he'd like to think that the form he'd take would be a hippogriff. He's sure that he would be too dignified to chase his own tail (but we have our doubts).

Scott Sehon teaches philosophy at Bowdoin College, including courses on topics such as mind, language, religion, law, and logic. His research focuses on philosophy of mind, an area in which he has published a number of articles and a book titled *Teleological Realism: Mind, Agency, and Explanation* (MIT Press, 2005). He hopes to start a philosophical counseling practice, in which he will treat abnormal dementors who suffer from chronic happiness.

Anne Collins Smith teaches philosophy and classical studies at Stephen F. Austin State University. She has taught, published, and given presentations on philosophy in popular culture, as well as Medieval philosophy. In teaching a college course on the philosophy of Harry Potter, she was delighted to find that students who read 700-plus page books for fun are also willing to read great whacking chunks of Aristotle and other philosophers. She enjoys tantalizing her Intermediate Latin students with selections from Peter Needham's *Harrius Potter et Philosophi Lapis*, in which Snape gives an especially impressive demonstration of the use of the subjunctive in indirect questions. It is her opinion that the students at Hogwarts should be learning Latin as well, but so far she has received no response to her application.

Charles Taliaferro is a professor of philosophy at St. Olaf College. He has written or edited eleven books, including *Evidence and Faith* (Cambridge University Press, 2005) and a collection of essays on love called *Love, Love, Love* (Cowley Press, 2006), which contains "A Modest Defense of Magic." In most of his courses that are held in Holland Hall at St. Olaf (which resembles Hogwarts), Taliaferro includes a section on Defense Against the Dark Arts.

Jerry L. Walls is currently senior research fellow in the Center for Philosophy of Religion at the University of Notre Dame and is the author of several books, including *Heaven: The Logic of Eternal Joy* (Oxford University Press, 2002) and *The Chronicles of Narnia and Philosophy* (Open Court, 2005; coedited with Gregory Bassham). He has also authored several articles on pop culture and philosophy. Somebody evidently put a Muggle Repelling Charm on his lawnmower. Every time he comes near it, he suddenly remembers an urgent appointment and has to dash off.

Jonathan L. Walls, Jerry's son, is a former musician and an aspiring filmmaker who switched to his current career path after repeated rejections from the Weird Sisters. He will be finishing film school soon, and he is also somewhat of a Potter proselytizer, having led many people to the joys of Rowling's series.

David Lay Williams is associate professor of philosophy and political science at the University of Wisconsin–Stevens Point. He has published articles in *History of Political Thought*, *The Journal of the History of Ideas*, *Polity*, *Telos*, and *Critical Review* and is the author of the book *Rousseau's Platonic Enlightenment* (Penn State University Press, 2007). Any resemblance of David to Harry Potter is purely coincidental.

THE MARAUDER'S INDEX